52 VOICES
365 AHA! MOMENTS

# WIDE AWAKE.
# EVERY WEEK.

BOOK TWO IN THE WIDE AWAKE SERIES

# WIDE AWAKE. EVERY WEEK.

52 Voices ~ 365 Aha! Moments

To contact the editors: outwriteliving.com and littlebigbay.com

Compiled and edited by Roslyn A. Nelson and Starla J. King
Cover photo: Starla J. King
Book and cover design: Roslyn A. Nelson

ISBN: 978-0-9892822-9-1
Library of Congress Control Number: 2015944673

Publisher: Little Big Bay LLC
littlebigbay.com

52 VOICES
365 AHA! MOMENTS

# WIDE AWAKE.
# EVERY WEEK.

COMPILED BY

## STARLA J. KING

*&*

## ROSLYN A. NELSON

*"I wish I could show you, when you are lonely or in darkness,*
*the astonishing light of your own being."*

HAFIZ

BOOK TWO IN THE WIDE AWAKE SERIES

# WIDE AWAKE AUTHORS

# WIDE AWAKE AUTHORS

# INTRODUCTION

This book was an experiment — to see what might happen when 52 people from various walks of life are given wide creative freedom in which to write about what we call the *"Aha! Moments"* in life.

The idea germinated with the success of our first book in the Wide Awake series: *Wide Awake. Every Day. Daily Inspiration for Conscious Living,* written by Starla and designed and published by Ros.

*Wide Awake. Every Day.* was the first time we had worked together. We were a natural team and found ourselves itching to continue our collaboration. Given the positive feedback and rewards of creating "book one," written by just one person, what might be possible if we expanded the contributor pool to 52? What would *aha moments* mean to each contributor? How would they each choose to express them? Could 52 points of view make a cohesive book?

Fueled by our relentless curiosity, we began by each inviting 25 people to join the collaboration and write one week's worth of aha experiences. Then we invited ourselves. *Wide Awake. Every Week.* was officially in motion; there was no turning back now.

We gave broad guidelines, asking for "engaging descriptions of real-life moments that caught your attention through a sudden understanding, new way of thinking, or flash of clarity — particularly experiences that seemed ordinary just a blink or two before."

Armed with a private Facebook group for sharing deadline angst and inspiration; encouragement to write in any format that would express their voices "brazenly, cunningly, with humor, or as a mere whisper;" and the constraint of a 280-word limit, contributors began to craft their seven pages.

Contributor Darlene Frank shares, "Excited by the invitation to contribute, I dubbed the assignment 'seven easy pieces.' Reality soon set in. Chiseling each piece to a tight word count is a challenge I love, though it delivered more than seven moments of frustration. Writing about aha moments made me notice my current perspective on those that had happened some time ago. The aha moments I describe were life's gifts to me."

We eagerly gathered the stories together over the next many months, hauling in an incredible variety of topics: student life, nature, self-worth, fishing, relationships, environmental degradation, parenting, poverty, gratitude, hunting, childhood, cancer, geology, climbing mountains, and, of course, the territory of every human heart: death, love, and loss. Told with every nuance from gentle to biting, our authors shared moments that had given them pause, and insight.

Author Maggie Kazel shared this, "I try to honor the moment, the people involved, the sacred transfer of energy, or more simply, the love. Honor the love amid all the violence that is our modern culture. So many violations, it is exquisite and vital to honor the love. It keeps us going, wakes us up to our humanity, saves us. So I shared a few of my own personal saving moments." And, "Thank you to sacred life itself, for the inspiration, all the ahas that give us pause and take our breath away. Here's to hoping we don't miss a single one!"

A delightful showcase of wisdom and entertainment culled from everyday life was emerging. Wildy divergent perceptions came from equally divergent sources, including: doctors, naturalists, managers, parents, activists, writers, entrepreneurs, professors, and coaches. *Wide Awake* contributors are gay, straight, white, black, Native American, atheist, Christian, Buddhist, and in-between. Our emails sprang to life with the contributors' passionate words.

Many authors experienced worry around getting the right ideas, writing, and editing but for everyone, as the process moved forward, anxiety lessened. Miriam Showalter wrote in an email during her editing process, "Gutting it out in the midst of significant life stress was a great lesson and reminder in and of itself. Writing is oxygen, in all times and under all circumstances."

We read, laughed, learned, wondered, and watched the work evolve. Authors and editors logged long hours of discussion and edits, and a year of "aha" took shape. Coincidentally, the book creation process also took a year to conclude. And now we offer it to you: 365 pages generously created by 52 wide awake humans to whom we are forever grateful.

— *Starla J. King and Roslyn A. Nelson*

P.S. Opinions on these pages are not necessarily shared by all the contributors, or the editors. We placed a patchwork of writing together in one book in order to offer a range of viewpoints and beliefs, not to suggest that any path taken is right or wrong.

DEDICATED
TO THE CONTRIBUTORS
WHOSE WORDS
GENEROUSLY MADE
THIS BOOK
POSSIBLE

&

TO YOU
DEAR READER

# JANUARY

*"I ask people why they have deer heads on their walls.*
*They always say because it's such a beautiful animal. There you go.*
*I think my mother is attractive, but I have photographs of her."*

ELLEN DEGENERES

# BEAR POEM

In recent years, the backdrop of my life — literally and otherwise — has been a forest. ✍ During the summer, I sometimes string a clothesline from one tree to another. On one lovely day, a mother black bear and her cubs investigated the hanging laundry and I photographed a cub standing upright and holding, rather tenderly, the sleeve of my sweatshirt with his paw. ✍ I sent the laundry photo to a friend with a four-year-old grandson who asked, "Why does she put clothes in the trees?" ✍ I've met many bears over the past few years and loved all of them. I've dreamt that I was a bear; I *became* bear, for one night. ✍ Humans suffer deprivation from having lost what is wild. So, one day, to reach deeper into their world, I held a special poetry event for a mother and her three cubs. I wrote four lines — one for each bear — on very thin, tiny pieces of paper, put each line inside a ball of suet and offered it to them, asking to be adopted and asking them to bring my desire into the forest. ✍ I wanted to photograph them eating the poem but I was too slow and the bears were very fast. In the moments reaching for my camera, the poem was gone.

Big Bear, be my mother.

Cub, hear my affection.

Cub, bring me to the heart of the forest.

Cub, let me dream with you, under the snow.

ROSLYN ANNE NELSON

*"If you wish to make an apple pie from scratch,
you must first invent the universe."*

CARL SAGAN

# SELLING THE HOUSE

It was full summer when I sold the house. I went there with the intention of digging up lots of perennials. The yard needed tending, but it was green and full of plants and trees and flowers. While there, I pulled armfuls of sweet peas out of the rock garden. Although lovely, they take over. Then I put one shovelful of earth and Japanese Irises into a pail and left. ⤿ I saw that the plants there belonged there. I understood that I was sad to leave this house, even though it was my choice to do so, but ripping out plants to bring to a new home could not transplant the past and it didn't feel good. A door had closed on a life left behind and I had to admit it. ⤿ I wondered — what time of day do dreams slip out of the house, and which door do they use? What day in the past was the present? In which weeks did we live for springing out of bed? ⤿ I've moved since then and live in a forest. I have no need for vases. There is no yard flowering with prized plants, tended for over a century by sentimental women like myself. Now I plant native seedlings in a rain garden each year, hoping that they will attract insects to fortify the web of living things here. I've learned to admire the subtlety of their less showy blooms, especially when the butterflies arrive, but in a little corner of that garden is the exotic, deep blue of those irises who have learned to live with wild companions. It took a while. Sometimes my cats chase each other at night and sound like large dogs. I used to get up to see if bears got in the house. Now I just roll over.

ROSLYN ANNE NELSON

*"Write about winter in the summer."*

ANNIE DILLARD

## SNOWMAN PRAYER

Now and then, bright days interrupt mid winter.
Send our spirits soaring.
Light splinters to gold, hitting newly framed barn ribs.
Fresh lumber you can smell a mile away.
Light that inspires brilliant ravens to swoop
just ahead in the road, showing off
their radiant color, grace and superiority.

Open sky. Blue. Blue between dark cedar branches. Blue that drops you to your knees.

Very late that night, a chimney fire roars fearfully, dies out.
We are safe. Tucked in, while in the yard
snowman's traitorous mouth
mutters prayers for the tooth of winter to bite down, for cold to last forever.

If we have sun again tomorrow, his coal smile and eyes will drop,
burn through the snow to frozen grass.
Learn awareness and humility.
Adaptability. Learn how to pray for spring.

ROSLYN ANNE NELSON

# JANUARY 4

*"Where there is love there is life."*

MAHATMA GANDHI

# JOB FOR THE LIVING

In a dream last night, a dead woman spoke from beyond and said,
"I need the people who miss me."
I was so surprised that a dead person still had needs.

ROSLYN ANNE NELSON

# JANUARY 5

*"Men go abroad to wonder at the heights of mountains,*
*at the huge waves of the sea, at the long courses of the rivers,*
*at the vast compass of the ocean, at the circular motions of the stars,*
*and they pass by themselves without wondering."*

SAINT AUGUSTINE

# CALIFORNIA

After the heartbreak of the plains, final sentencing of the mountains, burn of the desert, the country slopes to the Pacific Ocean and unrolls its last revelation in a soft lip of sand bordering on white, and on massive, blue waves. The drama of the westward push becomes succulent, fragrant, and bright. A Lolita girl with come-on eyes drops to her knees, her sunglasses fall to the washed sand. A golden retriever ambles after a yellow tennis ball. A group of mature men play an adolescent game of basketball. A surfer avoids eye contact on his important and proud path to the water.  ⤝  In the coffee shop that morning, a woman in line before me managed to tell everyone her weight — 107 — and in the next few seconds, added the words fat, cellulite, and cholesterol to her request for a muffin. A prayer for forgiveness.  ⤝  Welcome to California.

⤝

ROSLYN ANNE NELSON

*"Forget not that the earth delights to feel your bare feet
and the winds long to play with your hair."*

KAHLIL GIBRAN

# BEST GAME EVER

Watching bears is to be completely in the present. Everybody should have bears to watch and on one summer day, my watching turned into something even better. ➤ The big male, Napping Bear, was snoozing about fifteen feet from the house while a half-grown cub repeatedly returned to a young mountain ash I had recently planted. He would stand as if to rub his back on the tree; or reach for a branch; or reach around the small trunk with his arm (what other word could I use?) and begin to pull it down. I wanted that tree to survive, so I kept an eye out and every time he approached the tree, I went outside waving my arms and yelling, "Bad bear, bad bear!" Meanwhile, Napping Bear watched, still lying relaxed on the ground, without much reaction. He clearly knew who was being yelled at and that it was not him — something I also "told" him each time before I started yelling and waving. ➤ When I made all this commotion, the young bear would retreat a short distance and return within minutes. I chased the bear away about six times before it finally dawned on me that we were playing a game. *Wow, I was playing with a bear!* ➤ During that summer, the poor mountain ash was bandaged, propped up, and staked with rope but over time, the bear won, and the tree and I lost. Small price to pay for such a grand, sweet game. ➤ There are people who believe bears to be innately dangerous but I know better. Loving an animal or loving a human; very small differences, same results.

➤

ROSLYN ANNE NELSON

*"With crayons the child draws a rigid house and a winding pathway.*
*Then the child puts in a man with buttons like tears."*

ELIZABETH BISHOP

# MAYBE STONEHENGE WAS A MALL

Driving home from the city on a cold day, I saw a white form lift off and thought, *Bird?* The gesture caught my heart: the curve, the grace, the color. Looking longer, I saw that it was actually a thin plastic bag lofting and sinking in the air, prevented from flight by being snagged on a fence post.   Isn't it interesting that we respond to such abstract beauty? And that our minds think, *Bird?* Wonderful, big, unusual, familiar, once-in-a-lifetime white bird? The bird that we want to see.   Nearing Lake Superior, the setting sun lit up fuzzy clouds with gold. I saw blue sky and gray clouds, and midst it all, a truncated section of vertical rainbow that was going nowhere at all; a rectangular rainbow without a soaring arch or a pot of gold. But then, it was still winter.   Somewhere along that drive home I realized, with a sort of calmness, that it really can be too late for some things. A wise mentor had once told me, "Love comes back but not from where we expect it." We want it the way we want it. But that's not the way we get it.   When I got close to home, the big dipper was low on the horizon. It hovered just over the trees and the buildings of my small home town. Ready to scoop it all up.

ROSLYN ANNE NELSON

*"Grief can be the garden of compassion.*
*If you keep your heart open through everything,*
*your pain can become your greatest ally in your life's search for love and wisdom."*

RUMI

# MOM'S GONE

On a warm Sunday morning in May, my mother told my sister she was going to die that week. And she did.  ✎  Even though she had been ill for some time, her death felt as though it came out of the blue. Dad and my four siblings and I were with her in the final hours as she tossed and turned, comfort eluding her. It wasn't until Dad lay down beside her that she calmed down. Completely. It was the sweetest thing I've ever seen and the greatest act of love that could have been bestowed upon her in that moment.  ✎  An hour later, as we nervously hovered over her, we knew the final goodbye was upon us. Dad, in a fervent, almost yelling voice, urged Mom to "walk through that door!"  ✎  And with that she quietly took her last breath.  ✎  We were stunned and weeping, all quite new to the raw, heart-on-your-sleeve emotions overwhelming us. We shifted into a flurry of action, making up our moves as we went. Dad — Mr. Take Charge — began calling family, friends, the funeral home. My brother suggested that my sister Janet and I dress Mom in her favorite clothes. We did, chuckling a bit and saying things like, "Come on, Mom. Bend your arm."  ✎  We laid our mother on her bed, the bed that had supported her for much of her 82 years. We stared at her beautiful skin and peaceful countenance, and I thought to myself, *So this is what it means to be on your death bed.*  ✎  In that time of sorrow and grief, endings and beginnings, openness and closure, it was so much more beautiful than I ever expected.

LESLIE HAMP

*"I like to believe that I've got a lot of guardian warriors sittin' on my shoulder including my dad."*

PATRICK SWAYZE

## DAD'S GONE TOO

On what I thought was my last visit with Dad, I gave him a beautiful card full of loving sentiments of how much he meant to me, how he had influenced me, the lessons he taught me. We sat quietly, each thinking this would be our last visit. Ever. ☙ What I really wanted was to climb in his lap like a four-year-old and cry on his shoulder and be held in his arms. Yet I held back, thinking it would be too difficult for him. After all, he was saying good-bye to so many of us. And he had taught us to be tough. ☙ Luckily I had a second chance. ☙ The day before he died I called my sister, who was caretaking 24/7, and said, "Tell me when to come. I'll leave on a moment's notice." She said, "Come now." ☙ And I did. ☙ Twelve long hours later, I arrived. Dad had waited, knowing I was driving to him. My brothers and sisters were already surrounding him, and I took my place next to them. Dad looked at his five children, smiled, told us how much he loved us and how proud he was of us, then said, "I'm going to sleep now. This may take awhile." ☙ This time I didn't hold back. I climbed in bed with him, one of five surrounding and honoring him. We played his favorite music, made him comfortable, and waited. It took awhile. ☙ In the moments following his final breath, his spirit filled the room in a way I had never experienced. I couldn't get enough. And then he was gone.

LESLIE HAMP

*"The thankful receiver bears a plentiful harvest."*

WILLIAM BLAKE

# SILVER LINING

After the passing of my parents, I went back to my business, but my mojo was missing. I couldn't climb out of sadness. My inner voice kept saying, "Let go. Now is not the time." So I let go. Of everything. As I adjusted to the new normal, I was diligent in taking time for me. I practiced Pilates, welcoming that deep breathing and workout, and I journaled like there was no tomorrow — about family, health, gratitude, exhaustion, confusion, and overwhelming grief. One afternoon my sister called with so much excitement in her voice that it lifted me out of the doldrums. She had visited an energy worker, who said her energy was moving back and forth, back and forth and that it was Mom rocking her. We squealed with delight. "That is so like Mom!" I was so happy for Janet but longed for my own message. It came a month later in a dream where I was sitting at a table with Mom and Dad and not engaged with the other guests, who were laughing and having fun. Dad turned to me and with that sweet smile of his said softly, "Join them. Go on. It's okay." I can't remember if he said "We're all right" or if I just wanted to hear that. But he was telling me to get on with my life. A month later, my coach, Nancy, asked me for a word to describe the past year of coaching with her. I closed my eyes, took a deep breath and had an overwhelming sense of six arms around me. Teary-eyed, I described to her the feeling of being supported as I navigated the year of loss and grief. As I reflected on all those arms, I realized they were Nancy's plus Mom's and Dad's! What a gift. My parents were showing up in ways I never anticipated, and little by little I was getting back to my life, to my new normal and a very different perspective.

LESLIE HAMP

# JANUARY 11

*"What makes the desert beautiful is that somewhere it hides a well."*

ANTOINE DE SAINT-EXUPÉRY

## THE PHONE CALL

My dad, a lifelong educator, was one serious guy with very high standards. He could also be one serious party guy. After my wedding 40 years ago, he stayed up into the wee hours of the morning. Actually, he never did go to bed. What was the point when there was so much socializing and celebrating at hand? When my new husband and I arrived the next morning, Dad was still in his tux reading the morning newspaper cover-to-cover. ⬦ After his passing in 2011, I began noticing Dad's energy all around me. One evening I was at dinner with friends. When the bill arrived, Mike quickly picked it up to treat all of us. I laughed, saying, "My Dad used to do that." ⬦ Just then my phone rang. Dad's name and number, which had remained in my phone book, were on the screen. I said to Mike and Belinda, "Look! My dad is calling!" We all stared wide-eyed. ⬦ My phone had been sitting in the middle of the table all evening. I had not inadvertently dialed his number. But clearly he was calling me. We were dumbfounded. ⬦ A week later my sister Trish urged me to check my recent calls. Sure enough; there was Dad's call. My two sisters and I got a good chuckle out of that, marveling at this "Dad sighting." ⬦ I recall my dad saying he thought of his parents every single day. I have new empathy and understanding for that statement, and feel their presence daily. They just keep showing up when I least expect it, and for that I am truly grateful.

LESLIE HAMP

*"There is no remedy for love but to love more."*
HENRY DAVID THOREAU

## THE COLOR OF LOVE

I often visualize in pictures and colors. When I close my eyes to meditate or tap into the words of my coaching clients, I often get an intuitive hit along with a color. It happens during massage as well. In that deep relaxed state, I always — and I mean always — see green and purple. My Zen massage therapist tells me purple represents spirit while green represents the heart. And so you can imagine how surprised and delighted I felt when the color pink, along with a mist, came forward while I was savoring a massage from another massage therapist. As she worked her chakra magic above my heart, I began sharing a story about my mother. In that moment Bonnie also saw the pink mist. She was astounded, a little speechless even, noting that she never ever sees color. I remember saying, "That's my Mom." The next morning as I was meditating, I saw the color pink encircling me and felt my parents circling, circling, circling, and sending me their loving energy. It was the same feeling I had experienced when my massage therapist saw the pink mist. Curious, I did a quick search online and found that pink symbolizes love and romance, caring, tenderness, acceptance, and calm. This was a new way for my parents to show up. And such a blessing when I least expected it.

LESLIE HAMP

*"Your pain is the breaking of the shell that encloses your understanding."*

KHALIL GIBRAN

# MEET ME IN MINNEAPOLIS

My car was packed for an adventure in Minneapolis with my sister Janet. Upon leaving, I kissed the photos of Mom and Dad — recently passed — and said, "You can join us too. Show up whenever you want to."   Mom, Janet, and I had a tradition of adventures. It started when they visited me in Oregon years earlier. We did goofy things like swinging our legs like the Rockettes as we hung on to the fireplace mantel.   In Toronto, we laughed gleefully as a rickshaw pedaled us from theater to hotel.   In Vegas, Mom had a magic touch with slot machines. And in her later years, we stayed at Janet's condo and met Dad for dinner — all simple pleasures.   It made sense to "invite" my parents on the Minneapolis adventure and they showed up while we visited an intuitive.   At the end of my reading, Cynthia said, "Your parents' energy has been so strong from the moment you walked in. I wondered if they would share anything. They want you to know they are fine and happy. Your Mom is laughing and enjoying herself, and your Dad is rolling his eyes at her shenanigans. I see him sitting at a waterfall enjoying nature."   Wow. Cynthia said many people come to her seeking connections with loved ones. I had heard of mediums, but that had never crossed my mind. So when my parents spoke through Cynthia, I embraced the gift. 'Tis a gift to be open to Spirit. I was learning that at a deep level. How could I carry sadness, knowing my parents were free and happy? I think of them daily but the hole in my heart has mended.   With that is a new understanding of Spirit and a deeper connection to all that is here and there.

LESLIE HAMP

# JANUARY 14

*"The soul should always stand ajar,
ready to welcome the ecstatic experience."*

EMILY DICKINSON

## HEARTS AND GRATITUDE

Is it possible for your heart to grow bigger? It certainly feels as though that's what has happened to me over the past five years. As I navigated the path of caretaking my parents, of losing them, and of new beginnings, I was diligent in writing in a gratitude journal. I so wanted to be present with my parents and to experience the gifts of the moment. Writing just three to ten gratitudes a day shifted everything and allowed me to focus on the gold.  ≈  I continue that practice today along with a morning ritual that always brings a smile to my face. As my tea is steeping, I close my eyes, inhaling love and exhaling gratitude. After three deep, nourishing breaths, I continue the deep breathing, sending heart energy to my honey, my awesome kids, their life partners, my family, my friends, my clients, my colleagues, my communities. The ball of energy gets so big I can't keep up.  ≈  These days I see hearts everywhere. Perhaps it's another way my parents are showing up. Perhaps it's a reminder to look for the blessings that abound. Either way, the hearts shift me into gratitude.  ≈  Is it possible for one's heart to grow bigger, to love more, to be more accepting, to be more present? I think so and thank my parents for that insight.  ≈  I can't wait to see how they show up next.

≈

LESLIE HAMP

*"Years from now, when all the junk they got is broken and long forgotten,*
*you'll still have your stars."*

JEANNETTE WALLS

## ON KINDNESS: GIFTS

I am no longer accepting formal gifts. ⤺ Instead, please write to say that the essay I wrote about my daughter's first month of kindergarten "opened up a vein." While I recover from an emergency C-section and care for a newborn, leave me a voice mail to tell me I'm a "warrior." ⤺ Buy me a pair of navy blue socks with "be present" in gold letters on the sides and attach a note that says, "Thanks for being a friend." ⤺ Take our girls to the aquarium so I can find the quiet that reminds me who I am. ⤺ Introduce yourself because your friend heard me speak about starting my company and found the courage to do the same. ⤺ Tell me about the forgiveness letter you're writing to the man who 20 years ago was blinded by the sun, ran a red light and killed your daughter. Draw me a picture of you and me holding hands, use Teenage Mutant Ninja Turtle stickers for our bodies and write, "Izzy Mom." ⤺ I will remember these gifts forever.

⤺

BETH ANDRIX MONAGHAN

*"The simplest acts of kindness are by far more powerful
than a thousand heads bowing in prayer."*

MAHATMA GANDHI

# ON KINDNESS: BAD NEWS & GOOD NEWS

Bad news sends us to our mental bunkers where we stare straight into the danger on our TV screens and hope we'll discover that *we* are not *them*. We measure the physical distance between danger and our homes. We count the social and economic factors that set us apart from its victims. We stock up on advice about how to get out alive and when to buy emergency supplies. I know all of this and succumb anyway.  ⇝  During the manhunt that followed the 2013 Boston Marathon bombing, I roiled under the shelter-in-place order, scanning our eerily quiet street for danger. The police chief's robocall told us to lock the doors and open them only to uniformed police officers, so when a scheduled repairman rang our doorbell, I turned him away through the window and hurried back to my newsfeed. My hands shook above my keyboard where I simulcast the TV news with Twitter and BuzzFeed, gulping in updates and rumors.  ⇝  I found heroes that day in the runners who continued beyond the finish line to donate blood, and residents who opened their homes to stranded strangers. I needed them to pour light on my city's darkness.  ⇝  But I often wonder why we need that violent edge between dark and light to see kindness. Everyday kindness isn't newsworthy because we aren't compelled to measure its proximity. The undertow of bad news is stronger, it seems, but there are sparks of kindness flickering everywhere — on the way to work, to lunch, to bed — just beyond the dings of the alerts on our screens. If we'd just look up.

BETH ANDRIX MONAGHAN

# JANUARY 17

*"Make it dark, make it grim, make it tough, but then,*
*for the love of God, tell a joke."*

JOSS WHEDON

## ON KINDNESS: SHOPPING CART RAGE

I hate shopping at Whole Foods. I go for the humane meat, the organic produce, and Apple Pay. I leave with shopping cart rage. It's partly because I go at the worst time: Sunday afternoon, with the rest of my Massachusetts town. We survive grocery shopping by mimicking Boston driving. If you speed along and avoid eye contact, people yield to your flagrant velocity.  Not all people though. There is inevitably that woman, the one wearing enormous black sunglasses (and often a fur coat). She will park her entitled cart perpendicular to the narrow aisle and block your path while she examines the fine print on the rice crackers. She's been at this game much longer than you. She's so good that you'll begin to wonder if perhaps she really doesn't notice you waiting there patiently, weighing your options: wait or move her cart? You'll wait.  At the deli there will be a crowd (why-oh-why won't this store just give out numbered tickets?). On this Sunday, I'd lost track of my place in "line." When the sales person called out "Next!" I hesitated. I told the man standing next to me to go first. He looked at me — pregnant — and said, "Oh no, please go right ahead." While we were distracted being nice, yes, that woman in her blinders squeezed right between us and placed her order. I turned to the man hoping he'd help me right this wrong. Instead, he shrugged and laughed out the words, "We are so weak."  I consigned my rage to the deli counter and laughed all the way home, grateful for the gentle flash of perspective that instantly erased my anger.

BETH ANDRIX MONAGHAN

*"The strongest argument for religion is not that it is in touch with God
but that it puts us in touch with one another."*

ADAM GOPNIK

# ON KINDNESS: THE NEIGHBORHOOD OF ANGELS

I only believe in earthly angels. Once, in grade school, I waited for the heavenly kind after I listened to a Hebrew scholar one Sunday at church predict Jesus' return. I was worried I'd have to leave behind Sniffy, my stuffed rabbit with one floppy ear and green floral overalls, because she wasn't real.  ⟜  It turns out I'd been looking in the wrong place. The day I found the angels was dank, the air an acrid mix of rot and stale ashes. It was three days before Christmas and my family's house was smoldering in front of me, smoke trailing up through the bare tree limbs. Frigid water from the fire hoses had saturated the ground and was seeping into my leather oxfords, creating dark stains at their seams.  ⟜  The only lights piercing that dark December sky came from the roaming beams of looters' flashlights searching through the shell of our home. And from the headlights of our neighbor's truck that bore through the cold rain so we could dig a grave for our black lab, Sasha, who'd lost her battle with the smoke.  ⟜  Angels were present though. They took turns digging Sasha's grave with my father. They pulled trash bags over their feet to help us slug through the remains of our things. They came to the door to offer a dinnerware set earned through months of accumulating points. And they snuck into our neighbor's house where we were staying and surrounded our borrowed Christmas tree with gifts, signing each one, "Your Neighbors."

BETH ANDRIX MONAGHAN

*"Some say that love is the sweetest feeling, the purest form of joy, but that isn't right. It's not love — it's relief."*

KAREN THOMPSON WALKER

## ON KINDNESS: FEARS

**1.** I'm terrified of flying. I have a 1 in 4.7 million chance of dying in a plane crash, but in the clutches of flight this knowledge does nothing to slow my racing heart. ✎ **2.** I don't usually talk to strangers. I'm from New England so I assume that a stranger who approaches me on the street is either insane or a tourist in need of directions. ✎ It was unusual, then, that I started a conversation with the woman sitting next to me on a business trip from Boston to Washington, D.C. Maybe it was the warmth in her eyes. Maybe it was her salt-and -pepper hair that reminded me of my mother. Maybe I was just plain scared. ✎ She turned out to be a neighbor of the Tyco CEO who'd later be convicted of financial crimes. It was 2003, the year he made headlines for spending $2 million on his wife's 40th birthday party, and I was solicitously distracted from the flight. I expected gossip, but she gave me compassion. She focused on his humanity by resisting the bandwagon and talking instead about his generosity. ✎ We talked for the hour-long flight and I was surprised when I looked out the window and saw the runway just below us. However, a moment later everything changed when the plane lurched upward into the air again: an aborted landing. My stomach dropped and I clenched the armrests as I began counting to slow my breath. Then I felt this kind stranger take my hand and my fears healed each other.

✎

BETH ANDRIX MONAGHAN

*"I gave them all of the truth but none of the honesty."*

COLUM MCCANN

## ON KINDNESS: HONEST LIES

I vowed to always tell my children the truth, and when our French bulldog died, I passed my first test. Izzy, then three, kept asking, "Ernie go on train to Boston? Ernie at Gamma's house?" Sob. I told her the truth, "Ernie's body stopped working and he can't be with us anymore." ✎ A few months later she also asked my husband, who told her that we buried Ernie's body. To that Izzy asked, "What about his head?" Phew. That one was easy, but as they grow, my children ask harder questions and the truth is that I tell them honest lies. ✎ *Monsters aren't real.* ✎ *Your dad and I will always keep you safe.* ✎ *If you're kind to others they'll be kind to you.* ✎ *There aren't any "bad guys" in our town.* ✎ *Gray hair is just something that happens.* ✎ *We're lucky to live in a country where everyone gets a fair chance.* ✎ *It didn't hurt when I had you because the doctors gave me medicine.* ✎ *Seat belts will keep us safe in the car.* ✎ *Big girls don't cry.* ✎ *You don't have to worry about a fire in our house.* ✎ *Girls can do anything.* ✎ Motherhood has led me to the gray space between honesty and truth. I stand in its bubble holding an umbrella of security up to life's "what ifs?" while I try to show my girls how to be safe, without teaching them how to fear. I'll tell it all … one day, but the hardest truths can sleep through childhood. For now, I'm grateful that Izzy is only on to the truth about the Easter Bunny because she saw her uncle hiding eggs in the yard. Yes, please, let's start there.

✎

BETH ANDRIX MONAGHAN

*"When you help others, your own troubles aren't as heavy.*
*In fact, you can fold them like a handkerchief and place them in your pocket.*
*They're still there, but they're not the only thing you carry."*

ALICE HOFFMAN

# ON KINDNESS: RECOVERY

I know what it's like to contract from the world. ✎ Pregnant with my second daughter, I was not going to have another C-section, but birth plans make better wishes than instructions. My uterus ruptured while I was pushing, and I ended up in emergency surgery, gripping my husband's hand while my OB searched for the source of the bleeding. ✎ My baby Clara and I were lucky. So lucky. Yoga healed my body, and my mind followed as it found gradual distance from my fragile hold on this world. This was my stuff of night sweats. For a year I stumbled along, picking up the lost pieces of myself until one unexpected day when I looked up from a wider viewpoint. ✎ From there, I noticed new friends in front of me, trusted my own voice for my public remarks, joined a task force to help women. I found myself in the company of generous people who needed help and wanted to help, and I was home. Over dinner, I told this to my therapist friend, Michelle, who said, "I know that my patients are on the right path when they begin expanding into their worlds." ✎ I used to think that expansion required reach, an uncomfortable stretch into the unknown. Mine, though, was about a gentle adjustment from within that opened up my aperture. Hardship gives us the common languages of courage and empathy. It peels away our armor and opens us to kindness, the thing that expands us into this world with our arms thrown open.

✎

BETH ANDRIX MONAGHAN

*"When you are sorrowful look again in your heart,
and you shall see that in truth you are weeping for
that which has been your delight."*

KAHLIL GIBRAN

# GETTING ZEN WITH WINTER'S WISDOM

Winter? No thanks. ⤴ For every December gem (my birthday, a holiday), there is the ice-scraping, chapped lips, cracked hands, and uncomfortable bundle of layers. ⤴ I am not wooed by the change of flavors at Starbucks; I cringe at the cacophony of Christmas ads. So this year, I am surprised to have woven into my days a simple gratitude for the wisdom of winter. A solstice poem reminds me to slow, to consider stitching stillness in between errands and appointments, to honor the quiet promise of a buried seed, the permission to savor the retreat into deep, restorative silence. ⤴ Some days it feels like waiting in the darkness backstage of a play: agitated, enthusiastic, impatient. When will the light return? What will the "doing" feel like? What will come next? ⤴ Yet, there is a sacred cue for when to begin. And I am the anxious and eager dancer, relearning the careful balance between rest and restlessness, a solo silhouette sewn against a bleak winter landscape, with only the promise of a steadfast heart flame to illuminate this journey inwards.

⤴

RACHEL MOORE-BEITLER

*"Nature does not hurry, yet everything is accomplished."*

LAO TZU

# SPIRAL LEARNING

Much of life gets laid out for us as kids, chronicled in a linear way: school calendars, tomorrow's plans, graduation, the wedding, the house, the kids — the next level, the next station. So when my Masters of Acupuncture program introduced the idea of "spiral learning," it almost seemed too simplistic. Ah, but it was this simplicity that was so profound for me. We are surrounded by cycles, around us and inside of us: our breath comes in cycles and we live by the cycle of the seasons.  ✎  What if, instead of an endless forward trajectory, we are circling the same path, deepening our experience of what it is to be human each time around? Instead of planning the next benchmark, what if there is no arrival? What of the present do we miss as we look ahead to the next pit stop?  ✎  Perhaps the magic is in the maturation of these ongoing revisions, the evolving experiences of our world, and how we navigate the same blessed roots in our path. Can we gaze gently at these gnarly obstacles? And more importantly, can we love ourselves if and when we trip over them again and again, as we etch our way towards greater awareness, greater depth in the groove of our journey?

RACHEL MOORE-BEITLER

*"Your playing small does not serve the world.*
*As we let our own light shine, we unconsciously give others permission to do the same."*

MARIANNE WILLIAMSON

# ODE TO THE HONEY BADGER

In 6th grade, I was chosen to be the lead in a school musical. This was a big deal, not only because it was an annual springtime ritual for the oldest elementary kids, but because suddenly there was a new pressure on me: not only to memorize the majority of the lines and musical numbers, but also to navigate being visible, literally being in the spotlight in front of my peers. I was shy about celebrating this accomplishment around my friends; I even made my mom wait out the walk to the car after the auditions before I told her. It was a tenuous experience, getting recognition from adults about my talents alongside the simultaneous rocky social scene of jealous friends. Two decades later, I wonder how messages of self-worth and self-consciousness were ingrained from that experience, "Don't shine too brightly." ✑  Which brings me to the honey badger. And my, how I am fascinated by this cunning creature. Determined and quite mischievous, honey badgers scavenge for honey by breaking into bees' nests, regardless of how severely they get stung. They've even been known to scare off much larger predators when protecting their young. Now, when I see someone diving so completely, so unapologetically into their unique experience, I honor their willingness to be seen, to be so bold. Do I dare to let my own inner honey badger shine? You betcha. Well, at least now I do. I'm learning that it's about listening to my intuition, letting go of "perfection," and giving myself permission to take up space in the spotlight long enough to really savor that sweet honey.

RACHEL MOORE-BEITLER

*"A drop of nectar after the scorching sun — ah, such gentleness."*
SWAMI CHIDVILASANANDA

## GO GENTLY

What if I could shift
the quality of the conversation I'm having
with myself —
to tenderly see the "shoulds,"
to acknowledge with a quiet nod
the collection of shadows that have dutifully followed.
And, without forcing release of any fears,
open my heart up to a simple invitation,
an initiation
to take a different sort of step,
with all intentions of a softer landing,
with firm but kind toes curling,
feeling out this new ground.
I would go gently into the center of my pain
and decide that I could trust myself in this renewed moment.
I would notice how refreshing it is to gaze lovingly
at my flaws and imperfections
and know that I am still worthy
of giving and receiving love.

RACHEL MOORE-BEITLER

*"It's also helpful to realize that this very body that we have,*
*that's sitting right here right now ... with its aches and its pleasures ...*
*is exactly what we need to be fully human, fully awake, fully alive."*

PEMA CHÖDRÖN

# BEING IN MY BODY

In college, I used to run on the treadmill three mornings a week. Sure, I was in good shape, but I wasn't "in my body." Rather, I was in my mind, tracking the mileage and the minutes, without stopping to notice how I felt inside my own skin. Learning to listen to the quieter cues of my body didn't really start to happen until I was being asked by my acupuncturist how I was feeling — beyond any physical symptoms — on a regular basis. ⁓ Tending to myself these days is more about assessing my spiritual buoyancy, my resiliency, and my ability to trust myself. It's not always easy, and it's not always pleasant, inhabiting a body with its bumps and bruises and scars and collection of tattoos and fears and insecurities. But it is the vessel for my solo, sacred journey. Now I am tuning in to the subtle differences of my well-being, using guided meditations, walks in nature, attention to breath, and noticing when my mind is a whirlwind and I need to remember my feet on the ground. ⁓ Bodywork is a vast field, and an invitation to shed what no longer serves us; the word *bodywork* is curious, implying an ongoing, evolving, and not necessarily comfortable task. So, I believe that it's worthwhile to find a few key practitioners (massage, body-oriented talk therapy, acupuncture, yoga, meditation) to help me as I learn be gentle with this shell of my singular soul, as I get to know the outer and inner landscape of my being.

⁓

RACHEL MOORE-BEITLER

*"For after all, the best thing one can do when it is raining is let it rain."*

HENRY WADSWORTH LONGFELLOW

# BEFRIENDING THE GAP

The national boards for acupuncture licensure are made up of three 100-question, multiple-choice computerized exams. They're each based on completely different theory than my small acupuncture institution taught, making the preparation a laborious, self-propelled journey into unknown territory.  In my last year of clinic, while juggling clients and clinical assignments, I took on the addition of studying for Exam 1 and missed passing by one point. The computer literally said FAIL (in all caps!) at the end. I was disappointed, and waited until the summer to try for another exam, memorizing the new lingo just to get those blessed 70 points. In the meantime, I graduated, moved to another state to be with my partner, renovated our rental house, and got acclimated to country living.  Then came time to try for Exam 2, which I missed passing by a handful of points. With a track record of honors in high school and college, this was turning out to be a real battle; no longer just an academic obstacle, but clearly one of those "learning opportunities" that made me want to scream and run away to a tropical island.  Thanks to the family and friends in my life who have helped me process this roadblock, I am starting to think that the magic is about befriending the gap between where I am and where I thought I'd be by now. Sure, I get overwhelmed: *How will my practice ever get going? I just want to help people, for goodness sake!* but I am working on loving myself in the meantime, and trusting that the Universe is percolating something unseen, perhaps even spectacular, in my favor.

RACHEL MOORE-BEITLER

*"We are shaped by our thoughts; we become what we think.*
*When the mind is pure, joy follows like a shadow that never leaves."*

BUDDHA

# CAN'T SAVE ALL THE KITTY CATS

We were living in the part of Denver where the blocks are halved by alleyways of long concrete stretches lined with fences, dumpsters, and many stray cats. My animal-loving girlfriend would regularly take an extra can of cat food to our alley, leaving it for a local mama cat and her three kittens.  One day, she dashed inside, breathless with the kind of passion to help that can only come from seeing a kitten in distress. I returned to the alley with her to find the smallest kitten, a scrawny ball of black fur, wearing an ironic Elizabethan collar: a plastic lid from a McDonald's smoothie stuck upside-down around its neck. Naturally, we named it Plastic, and every day we schemed how to catch this feral creature just long enough to remove the hindrance. With much patience, many coos of reassurance, and a small pair of pliers, we were able to coax the kitten to put its head through an opening in a weathered wooden fence. In that instant, I pinched the plastic lid, and in efforts to escape, the kitten wriggled free. My girlfriend and I cheered, we embraced, we felt that anything was possible.  But all those alleyways, all those cats, just in our section of the city? Suddenly, this felt impossible. Could this one tiny victory be enough? Could we find rest in honoring our humble efforts? If you're a heart-on-your-sleeve, sensitive, service-oriented type, it's hard to know when to step back, to replenish your own resources to reset for the next adventure.  You can't save all the kitty cats. Simply to know that you might have saved one, that is the beauty in the precious gesture.

RACHEL MOORE-BEITLER

*"Let your soul stand cool and composed before a million universes."*
WALT WHITMAN

# BEGINNING WITH DEATH

The first time I died, unripe — denying the light to save others pain,
I pushed myself back, back into my meat domain.
Later, the crack in my cranium would leak poetry. My meat would sing.
Rivers sparkled, surged to purge the demons with a salve of rhyme.
Love's rhythmic shivers were painted in pentameter, a tree, alone
in the forest, fell in an etheree, sighs erupted in sonnets, but no haiku for me.

The road was not taken, but trails, streams explored, gardens adored,
monsters, exposed and abhorred. Meek, I would seek the smallest
of libraries, balking at salesmanship, hawking my verbose wares,
daring the spelunker of poetry's caves to find me there like the flowers
of Baudelaire, in the graves of silent words, the sibilant hiss of white noise.

I would use the I, the adjective, the twisted cliché to confound the academic,
flaunt verbal tomfoolery to rough the erect nipple, to dance, scream,
lure the reader into the darkest dream, the resounding *crack* of dawn.
I would use these years and stanzas to paint the wilderness for urban eyes,
the surprise around each bend of each river, to test the bars of conformity's
dank prison, and when my meat is ripe, to live again as a flower
beneath another poet's pen.

ROB GANSON

*"The progress of rivers to the ocean is not so rapid*
*as that of man to error."*

VOLTAIRE

# MOURNING ON THE SIOUX

The sun rose through the cedars.
Beneath the willow, at the head of the pool,
a wand of split bamboo waved gently.

The river slid by with somewhere to go,
flowing like some liquid minstrel, giggling.

A plastic bag rode through the dancing depths,
and I knew why the willow wept.

ROB GANSON

*"I want to do to you what spring does with the cherry trees."*

PABLO NERUDA

## EMERGENCE

In this moist and fecund

thaw, tomorrow's

frogs sing

and the springtime's

favorite loon

Daffodils germinate

in dormant poets

Below the ice

a stream whispers

secrets

In the humid arms

of morning, Buddha

climbs from beneath

the snow

ROB GANSON

# FEBRUARY

*"Never believe that a few caring people can't change the world.*
*For, indeed, that's all who ever have."*

MARGARET MEAD

## TOMORROW'S CHILD

By what regressive protocol
are lakes and oceans polluted,
do many hills and mountains fall,
are life ... profit ... convoluted?

They sell us all this plastic stuff,
killing tomorrow for money,
redefining the word *enough.*
No more trees, bees, no more honey.

Unless we plain folk seize the reins
from greedy kings and potentates,
Earth will die for personal gains.
Men will have killed what god creates.

"Save us a river, save a stream."
Tomorrow's child spoke in a dream.

ROB GANSON

*"I'm thankful to be breathing, on this side of the grass.*
*Whatever comes, comes."*

RON PERLMAN

## THE GREAT ESCAPE

It isn't there, just isn't —
the steel chicanery of economy —
the dread — impossible artificial dread
imposed by lofty titans of excess.

Across the great green breasts
of the Penokees, the dancing crystal veins
diverging along the great divide —
Mother Superior holds up the horizon.

It isn't there, just isn't —
where the soul is cleansed, still —
where elves giggle beneath snowbanks
and stoic bearded men are known to play

like children.

ROB GANSON

*"That it will never come again is what makes life sweet."*

EMILY DICKINSON

## FIRE ISLAND

Every morning, the island
burns ... all the wheels
turn, converge to merge
a turtle's back with fire.

While my waters rise,
the blue moon sinks
into her bed at the head
of the bay.

Magic is clearly in play
at the birth of another
day.

ROB GANSON

*"When I started counting my blessings,*
*my whole life turned around."*

WILLIE NELSON

# TROUT FISHING ON LAKE SUPERIOR

Beyond the smokestack
beyond the superfund fences
far beyond the breakwater
where tenses like past/present
and tomorrow freeze

in the shadow of hallowed hills
and the hunger of thunder
and grinding gears

in the passionate song of wind
a tiny speck of man remembers
that the very best fishing
lies beneath the thinnest ice.

ROB GANSON

*"Forget distinctions. Leap into the boundless and make it your own."*

CHUANG TZU

# DAYBREAK

It was an early pre-dawn morning, late winter 1972. Backpack slung over a shoulder, I was slogging my way to the first class of the day, approaching a footbridge that connected Water Street with the rest of the Main Campus of the University of Wisconsin at Eau Claire. It was then I noticed Leonard Haas, the university president, standing there bundled against the cold. He was in close proximity to construction workers busily revving their machinery and unloading girders needed for the first university building on this side of the river. To him I was just an anonymous student, but he nodded, and dipped his head toward the men scurrying to a wall of partially raised, aurulent brick.  "Beautiful, isn't it?" he observed. I glanced at him and gave a noncommittal smirk. Only a bureaucrat, I thought, could take such joy in the erection of yet another building. The old establishment fogey.  Barely a step later I spied the lavender- and apricot-streaked sky of sunrise peeking over the hill of the upper campus. Lavish with arresting splendor reflected in the Chippewa River, *this*, of course, was the inspiration for his "beautiful" comment.  Did he judge me the boor? I turned and caught him looking at me, the two of us sharing that magnificent daybreak. He saluted me and went back to considering the horizon.

ANNE RUD MILLER

*"If you do not change direction, you may end up where you are heading."*

LAO TZU

## LATE AFTERNOON HIGHWAY

Throw the map in the back seat,

Turn off the air conditioner,

Roll down the car window.

Follow a graying flap of asphalt,

Notice the ripple of road undulating through pasture,

Skirt the scrim of newly plowed field.

Watch the high gap-planked fence

Filter barely a "here now, gone now" sun.

Match the coruscation of its rays.

Hear the syncopation of tire meeting blacktop.

Spot the scarlet dragonfly seeking reed, and gnat and marsh.

Breathe.

ANNE RUD MILLER

*"You left and I cried tears of blood. My sorrow grows. Its not just that You left.*
*But when You left my eyes went with You. Now, how will I cry?"*

RUMI

# STUDENT DEATH: J.R.

I was past 50 and you but 16.

Now, never to debate a moral dilemma or read Thoreau.

Never organize a formal persuasive speech or outline a biography's third chapter.

Never appreciate a double entendre in a Shakespearean play or feel the awe and power
of Harper Lee's prose.

A grateful witness, I recall your classroom joys:

⤙ Treasuring an unexpected fire drill that interrupted a hated test;

⤙ Savoring the unrehearsed joke cleverly delivered by the kid across the aisle;

⤙ Applauding the class goof who one day got the best of the celebrated scholar.

Your shy smile so alluring, your laughter unaffected and uplifting.

Native pride evident, unwavering and constant in your respect for elders.

I was past 50 and you weren't my first young loss.

I pray you'll be my last.

⤙

ANNE RUD MILLER

*"I love you the more in that I believe you had liked me
for my own sake and for nothing else."*

JOHN KEATS

## SPICED DOTAGE

Being in love over 60 is exhilarating.  Made a widow in my forties, I dabbled in dating once my last chick went off to college. The courtship pool was not what I expected. Single men, widowed or divorced, were available. Many were soured on a long-term relationship, or seemed intent on reliving the debauchery of a very distant and squandered youth. Monogamy was a dirty word; commitment a distasteful concept.  Like a treasured credit card, forbearance has its rewards. Roy arrived in my life just as I was ready to close up shop. A passionate spark was there but so was prized and lengthy conversation. So was the pleasure of travel, a regard for the importance of humor, an appreciation of history, a gratitude for the arts, an involvement in politics. Backgrounds to disclose, memories to relate, more chronicles to manufacture and share together.  Roy is a study in kindness and creativity. With him, compromises are inevitable and often rewarding. I am a romantic who relishes a florist's bouquet; he equates cut flowers as wasteful sacrilege. Who can argue with his logic when spring surprises me with 200 blooming daffodils, the bulbs planted surreptitiously the prior autumn?  Roy disregards my foibles and concentrates on my strengths and the attributes that attracted him. After all, past experience has made me resilient. I have clarity. I have patience. I have a pension.

ANNE RUD MILLER

*"In the beginning there was nothing. God said, 'Let there be light!' And there was light.*
*There was still nothing, but you could see it a whole lot better."*

ELLEN DEGENERES

# REJUVENATION

My dearest friend, Francine, suffered and survived a stroke. As she began her slow recovery, her feisty nature and quick wit were sometimes buried in efforts to relearn mundane daily activities: to maneuver through paralysis, to revise her swallowing mechanism, to regain focus. Throughout an extended nursing home stay, husband Dallas encouraged her, cherished her. His goal for his wife of almost 50 years? To secure her return home. Celebrating small victories also meant recognizing limitations. Already a superlative husband who enjoyed spoiling his wife, Dallas morphed into an uber caregiver. He helped Francine dress, served meals, and aided with the toilet. He kept appointments and medications straight, bought fashion accessories, and tolerated television's home decorating channels. With all this manifested love, would she "come back"? I was visiting one day when Francine asked Dallas to scratch her chest. She'd complained of "creepy crawly" tingles on her skin and indeed, her therapists confirmed this sensation as nerves regenerating and rerouting. She moved her permanently clenched left hand aside and plucked at her neckline with her "good" hand. Unruffled, Dallas reached in and mildly scraped her skin until she nodded. Then he rose, kissed her forehead and left to refill our mugs. Francine glanced at his retreating back and looked pointedly at me, a hint of a smile playing across her features. "You know," she said in her new, soft, and carefully enunciated voice, "It didn't really itch."

ANNE RUD MILLER

*"Everything is funny, as long as it's happening to somebody else."*

WILL ROGERS

# NOTE ON A COUNTRY COUNTERTOP

Patsy,

Your window's cracked open.

The fly on your counter,

Fat and healthy,

Seeks the one crumb you missed.

It is iridescent and lively.

So grateful you didn't buy a can

To squeeze out death

And leave for me a casualty —

Withered and brittle.

ANNE RUD MILLER

*"I'm selfish, impatient, and a little insecure. I make mistakes,*
*I'm out of control, and at times hard to handle. But if you can't handle me at my worst,*
*then you sure as hell don't deserve me at my best."*

MARILYN MONROE

# HERITAGE

I talk with my hands. More interested in conversation than perfect table manners, I am often teased for meal remnants exhibited on my garments. Fabric carnage is vast: frills ruined by olive oil trickled while simultaneously brandishing fork and talking politics; cuffs stained with a shadow of red wine, liquid slopped when laughter preceded setting down the goblet. No one need ever ask what I had for supper: daub of chocolate, smudge of French dressing, or blotch of ketchup reveals all. Now blessed with a trio of grandsons, I have tried to set a better example. Though I strive to be careful with tableware, and try to separate repast and response, I sometimes fail. Plan B? Endeavor to discreetly wipe the offending stain and reestablish some semblance of decorum. Recently I realized that my dining habits might well become my legacy. Sharing a restaurant dinner of Italian spaghetti with a daughter and her husband and sons progressed nicely until my son-in-law smiled and glanced at the time. I realized what had occurred; friends and family sometimes place wagers on how long my shirt would remain pristine. Unperturbed, I dipped my napkin in my water glass and prepared to swab my blouse. My efforts were interrupted by my five-year-old grandson. "Don't, Grandma," pronounced Finn. He pointed to the smear of spaghetti sauce decorating his own shirt; his voice filled with empathy and wisdom. "This way people know you belong to me."

ANNE RUD MILLER

*"The biggest adventure you can take is to live the life of your dreams."*

OPRAH WINFREY

## SUMMIT ONE~MT. KILIMANJARO, AFRICA~19,340 FT.

The facts: Mount Kilimanjaro is the highest freestanding mountain in the world. 〜 Later I would realize this mountain was the start of something big in my life ... really big! 〜 Life Lesson 1: *Build memories that will last a lifetime.* 〜 Mt. Kilimanjaro journal entry, 1993: My Father My Friend 〜 "I've been on my around-the-world backpack adventure for about a year now and have seen some incredible sights. Iceland, Scandinavia, Europe, and Russia all are alluring, but none have moved me quite like this continent of Africa. 〜 I'm so lucky to be doing this climb with my dad. It has always been his dream to climb Kilimanjaro and I guess I just love spending time with him. Who knows, I may even get hooked on climbing! Haven't been home from my travels in over a year, so it's wonderful to see him and spend this time together. 〜 We were close, so close, with maybe a hundred feet to go. Dad looked at me and said, 'I don't think I can make it.' I said that I didn't think I could either. We struggled through the ice and snow, hooked arms, and slowly dragged each other to the summit. The sign read: "You Have Reached Uhuru Peak The Highest Point In Africa." We plopped down in the snow in joyful disbelief. It was a triumphant day! Happy 61st birthday, Dad! My hero. I had a tiny birthday cake packed for him. It was frozen solid. Dad was too nauseous to eat it anyway. How lucky I am to have shared this cherished moment with my father. Who knew he would also become my dearest friend?"

LORI SCHNEIDER

# FEBRUARY 13

## SUMMIT TWO~MT. ACONCAGUA, SOUTH AMERICA~22,841 FT.

The facts: Aconcagua ranks as the highest mountain in South America. It is located in the
Andes Mountains of Argentina, with the Pacific Ocean just 90 miles to its west. It is the
highest mountain outside of Asia, and is the highest point in the Western Hemisphere.
⤳ Life Lesson 2: *Find the courage to face your problems.* ⤳ Mt. Aconcagua journal entry,
2000: One Step At A Time ⤳ "It was an emotional day today. A woman climber in the
next tent died last night from altitude sickness. We could hear her crying and coughing
through the nylon walls of our shelter. Many on our team were experiencing dangerous
altitude sickness symptoms also, and had to stay behind. Dad was one of them. I worry
that my 67-year-old father is going down with altitude sickness. Dad worries that his
daughter is going ahead with MS, multiple sclerosis. No one here knows that I have it.
I want to be judged by my personal strength and not by my label of this illness. ⤳ On
the deepest level, this has been a changing day in my life. I learned that my body is strong,
at least for now, and so is my spirit. I am ready to speak of my disease without feeling
shame. The time has come to let go of the pain and start living again. I have learned many
things on this climb, but mostly I learned about courage ... the courage to face my
problems and move forward, one step at a time. I am alive. I am happy. What more could
I want? Not a thing."

LORI SCHNEIDER

*"Do not lose hold of your dreams or aspirations.*
*For if you do, you may still exist but you have ceased to live."*
HENRY DAVID THOREAU

## SUMMIT THREE~MT. ELBRUS, EUROPE~18,510 FT.

The facts: Mount Elbrus is part of the Caucasus Mountain Range in Russia. The range forms both a geological divide and cultural barrier between Europe and Asia. ꜱ Life Lesson 3: *Pain heals pain.* ꜱ Mt. Elbrus journal entry, 2002: Goodbye From On High ꜱ "How do I begin to describe a climb that speaks to me in so many ways? It is another of the Seven Summits, the highest peak in all of Europe. It's that high adventure that sparks life into my soul. On yet another level, it is a challenge to my MS and physical limitations. On the deepest level, it is a time to begin healing from my mother's death, only five devastating weeks ago. ꜱ Last month, the night before I was coming home to visit my family before flying to Russia for another climb, I got the call that every child dreads. Mom had died unexpectedly, so it was time to come home for a different reason. My life crumbled down around me. I canceled my climb and threw my mountaineering bags and two black dresses in the car. It has been a long, sad month, but now I need to move forward. With Dad's encouragement, I joined another climbing team a month later, and here I am. It all feels surreal at times. I get wrapped up in the excitement of the adventure, then I get wrapped up in thoughts of missing my mom and leaving my dad alone. Each grueling step I took today helped numb the mental pain. It is bitter cold, windy, and stings the senses. It's good to at least feel something. So much of me feels numb with sadness."

LORI SCHNEIDER

# FEBRUARY 15

*"Only those who dare to fail greatly can achieve greatly."*

ROBERT F. KENNEDY

## SUMMIT FOUR~MT. MCKINLEY (DENALI)
## NORTH AMERICA~20,320 FT.

The facts: Denali is located in the Alaska Range, just three degrees south of the Arctic Circle. Its latitude and height make it one of the coldest mountains on Earth.  Life Lesson 4: *Climb beyond your perceived limitations.*  Denali journal entry, 2006: No Pain No Gain  "Today was the day from hell. The scenery was the only saving grace, but beyond that I hated it. It was so difficult that I wanted to cry, swear, and quit. I felt defeated, but I made it, carrying a load as heavy as the 11 men on our team carried. I'm the only woman and carry 60 pounds in my pack, pulling another 60 pounds on my sled. Everyone struggled and some of them felt like quitting too. The hike lasted nine hours. Our guide said summit day would be worse.  This entire trip has been the hardest physical thing I've ever done. I've never struggled so much or found such difficulty pulling my mind through the pain. I'll turn 50 next month and I'm in awe of what a body can do when it is challenged. No pain no gain, as they say.  Our guide said today we would suffer and we did. Suffer yes, but my final tears today are not from pain, they are from joy. This climb has tested me physically, and in doing so, emotionally and spiritually as well. You see who you really are when you are pushed beyond your limits. I have proven to myself that I am in control of my physical body and my MS. It does not define me or limit me. Life's possibilities are endless."

LORI SCHNEIDER

*"Life is an adventure, it's not a package tour."*

ECKHART TOLLE

## SUMMIT FIVE~MT. KOSCIUSZKO, AUSTRALIA~7,308 FT.

The facts: Mount Kosciuszko is located in the Snowy Mountain Range of New South Wales. Kosciuszko's exposed location and alpine terrain make this mountain very susceptible to weather extremes. This eight-mile climb is by far the easiest of the Seven Summits. ⮑ Life Lesson 5: *The simplest things in life can often cause the greatest difficulties.* ⮑ Mt. Kosciuszko journal entry, 2008: No Easy Button ⮑ "As we proceed in the total white out, the guide pulls out his compass in hopes of heading us in the correct direction in this sea of white. The GPS proves useless in the storm. We huddle when we need to communicate, because we cannot hear over the voice of the wind. A rock jumps out of the whiteness, and we know there are obstacles to maneuver around. The guide slips down a deep trough next to a protruding rock, and rolls back to his feet. Later he punches through the ice and pulls his foot from a stream. His beard is covered with ice. He jokingly tells me that if he has a heart attack, I should follow the hill's contour to get back down. We trudge forward in the 50 mph winds. I'm grinning from ear to ear. Adventure at its best! We soon realize that there will be no summit today and the compass guides us back down to the shelter. ⮑ Two days later, with an accumulation of two feet of new snow, the monster storm has died down and we gear up to head for the summit. Why is it the things in life that seem so simple on the surface often cause the greatest problems?"

LORI SCHNEIDER

# FEBRUARY 17

*"Life is either a great adventure or nothing."*

HELEN KELLER

## SUMMIT SIX~VINSON MASSIF, ANTARCTICA~16,067 FT.

The facts: Antarctica is the coldest, windiest, driest continent on earth. ⤙ Camping temperatures ranged from -30°F to -60°F. ⤙ Life Lesson 6: *Beauty is not only skin deep.* ⤙ Vinson Massif journal entry, 2008: On Top Of The Bottom Of The World ⤙ "We arrived at High Camp at 1:30 a.m., after six long hours up the fixed lines. We put up our tent in a frantic attempt to provide shelter, as the mercury plummeted to -35° plus the wind chill. Exhausted and frozen, we skipped food and tried to sleep for a few hours. We awoke to howling winds. By noon, the guide felt we were in a threatening environment and needed to get down fast, before the 45 mph gusts got worse. As he informed me, we were now in dangerous life-and-death mode. We made a plan of how we'd quickly proceed, once we stepped outside the tent. Backs to the wind, and protect the fingers at all cost. We packed our gear inside our trembling shelter, then headed out into the relentless wind and yanked down the tent. ⤙ This entire trip has been a drain on my body as well as my mind. My face, hands, and feet are swollen, my eyes are bloodshot and puffy, my hair is greasy after three weeks of wearing a hat 24/7, my skin is red from sunburn, windburn, and frostbite, I have blisters on my toes, my fingertips are cracked and bleeding, my lips and nose have blistered and peeled, and my shins are sore. I want to explain to people that this is *not* my best look! Secretly, inside, I feel really beautiful."

LORI SCHNEIDER

FEBRUARY 18

*"It is not the mountain we conquer, but ourselves."*

SIR EDMUND HILLARY

## SUMMIT SEVEN~MT. EVEREST, ASIA~29,035 FT.

The facts: Mount Everest is the world's highest mountain. 71% of those who attempt Everest fail and of those over the age of 50, 87% fail. Life Lesson 7: *The success is in the journey.* Mt. Everest journal entry, 2009: Why Everest? "For 20 years I taught elementary and special education. My goal as a teacher was to help children believe in themselves and not be afraid to try. Now it is my turn to learn that very lesson. In attempting a goal as lofty as climbing Everest, I give myself permission to try. I have to believe in myself in order to live my dreams. Sure, I may not always succeed at what I attempt, but there is no failure in that. The success is in the journey; it's always in the journey. I am learning to conquer my fear of failure. I have overcome my ideas of what limits me in my life, and have learned that if I believe, I can achieve. There are many things in life that once scared me: being alone, having MS, being broke, or attempting things I was uncertain of. Now at 52, I'm all of those things at once. I'm here on this mountaintop in Nepal with no family to comfort me, $80K in the hole, hanging off the side of a wall made of ice, asking myself, *Am I afraid?* Oddly, the answer is no. I trust that this is where I am meant to be, and I am feeling at peace. I am here to learn about overcoming fear and about trusting my instincts."

LORI SCHNEIDER

*"Pick a flower on Earth and you move the farthest star."*
PAUL DIRAC

# GENERATIONS

If you want to understand me
take yourself out of the equation.
Look beyond base attraction
and see the star-speckled atoms
of all that we are.

I am the adopted lesbian daughter of Mariflo
granddaughter of Eula and Elsie
and on and on
whirling down the invisible ages
past Eleanor, Joan, Mary, Sapho, Lucy, and Aphrodite
all the way back
to the first seed of the universe.

I am quite simply
the generational dust of all the ingenuity, courage, madness,
love, and fear that ever was
and still lands on me
and is inhaled into my soul.

Who are you?

JAN LEE

*"Heaven is not like flying or swimming,*
*but has something to do with blackness and a strong glare."*

ELIZABETH BISHOP

# BREATHE TO SPEAK

Recently, a simple, single sentence jumped off the page and crashed into my soul. "Your silence will not protect you." The writer and poet Audre Lorde wrote that line, and when I read it, a memory deep down inside of me exploded.    I remembered witnessing my beautiful, 50s-era mother respond with silence to my father's alcohol-related abusiveness. Her silence did not protect her, or my brother and me, from the verbal and physical slaps and kicks that came out of the blue. And because children are nothing if not sponges, I absorbed the skill of silence as well.  Lorde wrote on, "Women have been taught to respect fear more than ourselves, we've been taught that silence would save us, but it won't." Another explosion in my soul. I realize now my lips remain, like my mother's, tightly pursed at critical times until it's too late.  Paralyzed when I most need to speak. Terror is not a new weapon; it's age-old.  So for the sake of every woman who has lost her voice to violence and every child who learned silence at her knee, I will do my part to bring this speechless reaction to extinction. Today I imagine a world where every woman and every child is respected and empowered every day. Period. It's not impossible. Start right now. Breathe. Open your mouth. Speak. Repeat.

JAN LEE

*"If you're going through hell, keep going."*
WINSTON CHURCHILL

# NO REGRETS

Regret scares the heck out of me. Always has. So I've run and leapt at every opportunity presented, grasping them with both hands like some kind of "Jan of The Jungle," swinging from tree to tree and yodeling at full voice, "Le-et's go-oo-oo!" However, I've learned that no matter how fast or high I fly, now and then something or someone can come along and cut my vine. And falling hurts. It definitely bruises and sometimes leaves deep scars.  I'm in the second half of my century and yes, with age comes wisdom, and a bit of fear because I realize that usable time is starting to run out. It's disconcerting. I question myself now. *Is this the right thing to do next? Oh my God, what if it doesn't work? What if I fall again? Will I survive?* Then there's that other deep-down messenger. That crazy-ass, niggling voice that fights its way up through my fear and uncertainty, *Hey! You're not dead yet! C'mon! What if ... ?* This mental wrangling wraps me in knots. I'm insecure in a jungle that I have navigated so well in the past. Sure, there's always the chestnut, "Follow your gut" but how do I find my intuition in all this confusion? Here's how. Stop swinging. Sit. Breathe. No talking. Shush ... and in a while ... (wait for it) ... it comes. The answer. Call it a visualization. Call it the voice of God. Call it shutting up. As long as I hear that answer I'm good to grab another vine. Regret only comes from not listening to the answer. And besides, falling doesn't kill you. Dying does.

JAN LEE

*"I celebrate myself, and sing myself."*

WALT WHITMAN

# WHEN I SING

I sing the difference between the cloud and the drop of rain
between the feather and the fragile bone
between the rock and the single flower that grows there.
Between the wave and its muddy edge
between the flame and the oak branch
between life and its last breath.

I sing for all of my mothers
for the safety of my soul
for you — and you — and you
and yes, even you.

I sing the difference between the word and its sound
between atom and antimatter
between the truth and the lie.
Otherwise, I do not sing.

JAN LEE

*"Don't cry because it's over. Smile because it happened."*

DR. SEUSS

# THANK YOU

I never had the honor of witnessing anyone die until my beloved adoptive mother passed away from cancer. She used to say, "Bad news comes in threes" but in my case, fives, since my father, aunt, best friend, and cousin all lost their lives within six months of my losing her. With so many loved ones suddenly missing from my world, I spiraled out into oblivion. I was anywhere but in the aha moment. It was all I could do to figure out which pants to put on each morning, let alone process my grief. For months on end, I ate and drank and keened and wailed like my ancient Scottish relatives — on the moors of my broken heart. After that, my grief subsided to rivulets of tears at the drop of my mother's name or when I least expected it, such as watching an animal cruelty commercial. Recently, while I was once again heaving great sobs into my pillow and screaming to God, "When will this end? Why does it still hurt so bad?" I suddenly got a message back; a quiet voice, but like a bullet. "You only feel this blessing of pain if someone teaches you what love is." ✑ I sat bolt upright. Oh wow ... I had been putting all the emphasis on the grief and not on the gift. My mother, who didn't even give birth to me, had blessed me with the greatest gift of all — unconditional love. I sat there for a few moments, awash in the gratitude of "thank you." Then I got up, dried my eyes and without any effort at all, put on my pants and walked out the door.

JAN LEE

*"The afternoon knows what the morning never suspected."*
SWEDISH PROVERB

# WITNESS

Let us all agree, each of us
with our hearts stretched wide open
that we will never forget one another
And whatever happens, remember how it felt
when we were all here together
united in goodness and decency.

Let us agree, each of us
with our hands ready to hold
and our lungs daring to breathe life
in and out — in and out — in and out
with our heads hung low and our eyes overfull
that love is here in this room
clinging to these sheets.

Let us agree, each of us
with full and fearful knowledge
that death is also here, waiting, watching, witnessing
and making us all better people
than we otherwise would have been.

JAN LEE

# FEBRUARY 25

*"Be humble for you are made of dung.*
*Be noble for you are made of stars"*
SERBIAN PROVERB

## ONE GRAIN, DROP, VOICE

Sometimes, with all the misunderstanding, greed,
poverty, and hatred in the world,
it's hard to imagine that one person
could make a difference.

But one single grain of sand
no matter its color, shape, or size
added to another — and to another — and to another
eventually makes a mighty and rich continent.

One single drop of water, no matter how big or small
added to another — and to another — and to another
eventually makes a mighty and diverse ocean.

One single voice raised
no matter how weak or strong
added to another — and to another — and to another
eventually makes a mighty and righteous choir.

So the question isn't, "Can I make a difference?"
but rather, "How will I make a difference?"

JAN LEE

*"The world is big and I want to have a good look at it before it gets dark."*

JOHN MUIR

## IT BEGINS

ten thousand miles away,
across a turbulence of sea

the whispered words of a prayer,
a breath, a benediction

carried on the shoulders of the waves
beneath the sun's watch and the moon's

carried on the shoulders of the waves,
the waves that taper to a river;
the river tapers to a stream

a stream that tumbles over stones
to reach the nest

the heron's nest, tucked like a secret in the reeds

a breath that sleeps
in the fragile beat in the dark of the egg
till it is lifted on white wings

white wings, reflected in your eyes.

DEBORAH COOPER

*"I came upon no wine as wonderful as thirst."*
EDNA ST. VINCENT MILLAY

# I WANTED TO TELL YOU

I wanted to tell you
the way the white heron, rising,
lifted a part of me away

and the missing
in the part of me that stayed,
what is the name for that?

I want the right phrase
for this last orange ribbon of light,
trembling now upon the lake's pale skin.

What do we call this hue of longing?

I want a way to describe
looking out at the glittered sky
through my mother's eyes,
nine years beyond her death

how it is we know we are inhabited ...
the moon, slowly lowering the veil.

DEBORAH COOPER

*"There are nights when the wolves are silent and only the moon howls."*
GEORGE CARLIN

## BLUE MOON

Though she cannot see it from the bed
the blue moon coaxes her from sleep

the way a mother wakes a child

the slight, warm weight of a hand,
a voice, lilting and falling
in a soft refrain.

She lifts the sheet, eases her way
to the seat beneath the window,
watches the moon's subtle descent,
the movement echoing
inside her

extinguished finally by the windswept sea.

He sighs and breathes, vaguely aware
on the periphery of sleep
the vacant space beside him in the bed

gradually growing cold.

DEBORAH COOPER

# MARCH

*"The heart has its reasons which reason knows nothing of."*

BLAISE PASCAL

# NIGHTLIFE

Awake again at three a.m.
jumble of thoughts, the way
socks tumble in a dryer.
Moving in the dark, window to window,
through these rooms I know by heart.

Ah, there, hung in the branches of the oak tree
that we planted when he died,
the soft, lopsided lantern of the moon.

Across the street
and down the block, across the city,
in a farmhouse miles away,
in other rooms, at other windows,
other women are awake.

Lifted by worry, lifted by
the infant's stirring or the child's urgent cry
lifted by memory, premonition,
or by yearning
by the persuasion of the moon.

DEBORAH COOPER

*"Our love is like the misty rain that falls softly but floods the river."*
AFRICAN PROVERB

# I WANT A LANGUAGE

I want a language for
the murmuring of rain in the night
speaking a promise
of forgiveness

the way we ease into the same dream,
a dream we won't remember
though it is there,
in the hollow of the throat.

I want the word that saves
your heartbeat in my ear
the way, as a child,
I saved the sea in shells.

I want the word that saves
your heartbeat in my ear
long after I raise my head from your chest
and leave you.

DEBORAH COOPER

*"The eyes are the silent tongues of love."*
MIGUEL DE CERVANTES

## PEONIES AND RAIN

She sees the radiant peonies
bow their great heads in prayer,
in praise, in supplication, in the early morning rain.

In the not-quite-light she slips outside
to join their silent congregation.

Sprinkling of holy water
brings her to her knees, in praise, in supplication.
She prays with peonies.

Over toast, he notices her hair is soaked.

He must have slept right through her shower.

But then he notices
her nightdress is drenched too.

And when she goes to fill her teacup,
he can see her knees are caked with mud

which makes him wonder,
though he doesn't ask.

DEBORAH COOPER

*"All, everything that I understand, I understand only because of love."*

LEO TOLSTOY

## IN THE NIGHT

far away
across the hills,
as if a single pulse of light
had graced the dark side of the moon,
a trace of memory unbidden wakes his hidden heart

a trace of memory, then taken by the wind,
the wind that passes like a shiver
through the wilderness of pine

a whisper tossed from crown to crown

and softens finally
with the dawn's light to this breeze,
ruffling the leaves
of the oak tree in the yard,
the yellow nightgown swaying on the line

a trace of memory, released
in the plaintive song of a chickadee,
caught in the intricate curl of your ear.

DEBORAH COOPER

*"I don't believe people are looking for the meaning of life*
*as much as they are looking for*
*the experience of being alive."*

JOSEPH CAMPBELL

## BUSY SIGNAL

So I said to myself, "You're like a cardinal. You wear your heart on your sleeve with a mask over your eyes. You love to sing, but no one ever gets too close." ✑ I can hear the red bird outside my window. He won't come to the feeder. ✑ "Hey, little buddy. Don't be scared. Well, you can be scared. Being scared is healthy. It keeps you on the lookout for predators. And what's a little cortisol between friends?" ✑ He flies to the feeder. Cautious as hell. You know he wants to. ✑ "Having the courage to go forward when scared — that is transcending, sir. That will let you fly above the treetops." ✑ I visit a dark corner or two, then look up. The cardinal is gone. ✑ I cannot hear him singing. He's busy.

✑

PHILIP SORENSEN

# MARCH 6

## TRYING IT ON TIN

*So my fishing buddy got a chance to meet her, have a chat, get to know her, before I got there. He tells her, "He's the most genuine person I know." Me? Seriously? The same on the inside as I am on the outside? Dubious. I wasn't so genuine with her. Well, I was at times. Other times, not so much. It's hard to tell someone you don't love her mind. You're gaga for her body, all the in-bed stuff, but that third bosom, the cockles of her heart, all that soul mate malarkey, that's difficult to tell her when she's fallen so hard so fast. To say so, would be insulting, mean, counterproductive. Let's see … . Looks? Check. Politics? Check. Religion (or lack thereof)? Check. Same recreational pursuits? Check, check, check, and check.* So off you go. And it's not so genuine. Though sometimes souls touch, sometimes they do not. They make corporeal love to each other, thinking they have touched, or they will touch, or one soul believes they have, or both hope they will. Then the mortal coils those souls inhabit carry on as if they had touched. Or may have touched, or very soon one day could touch, so they make love again. The balm's been applied, angst allayed, hope's orange crescent crown peeking from the far horizon. Afterward, craniums tilt in contact. Red horseshoe toy magnet with silver tips passed over a pulled-out drawer of clamps and tacks, pins and paperclips, provisions for picture hanging. Delicate pressure applied on the finger flesh foretells the invisible force field, the mystical delight — until trying it on tin.

PHILIP SORENSEN

*"I am the owner of the sphere, of the seven stars and the solar year."*

RALPH WALDO EMERSON

# YOURS ALONE

The sunrise is proprietary. For regulars and for first-timers. To be there, to witness and experience dawn, is to own it; to claim it as yours and yours alone. ᔐ You can claim the inky blackness or the first hint — the pre-dawn gray which creeps into yellow so faded it barely breathes. Reluctant pinks lend a hand, only to hang on by their fingernails. ᔐ You fall between the extremes that lurk on either side, grasping for purples and roses and peaches to be. ᔐ Yet no orange sphere so far. ᔐ The paint-store whites appear: lunar pearl, Alaskan granite, golden eggshell. A nuance is a nuance even if it remains unseen. ᔐ And you may never behold the fiery ball itself, for cloud cover alone can bring tree bark and ground frost into focus. ᔐ Yet it comes. ᔐ Long ago, my grandmother said, "I just like to sit and watch the sun come up." I thought, *Who's got time for that?* ᔐ But now, when the late risers hear you caught the sunrise, they either say, "Yeah-yeah, you're so special, just because you can't sleep or you have that crappy job to roust you out of bed so damn early." Others nod, wishing they could feel Earth's engine begin to rumble; a twinkling window here and there, a single robin believing it's a good idea to start defending his territory. ᔐ That corner of the world is his. And yours. Not for sale.

PHILIP SORENSEN

*"Perfection is the voice of the oppressor."*
ANNE LAMOTT

# FOUND

So I'm crazy about her and she says she wants to look at my baby pictures. And she handles each page of my baby book with her soft, delicate hands and sighs and says almost to herself, "Oh, Philip ... . " And I'm sitting there with a lump in my throat big as a football. If I try to speak, my voice cracks. I can't breathe. Page after page. Snapshot after snapshot. ✑ Later, after she leaves, I'm like, *What the hell was that?* ✑ Pride? Maybe. But something else rendered me speechless, on the verge of tears, unable to let them fall. ✑ All that pride, all that shielding, all that strength. Layers and layers of conceit and toughness laid over so much innocence. All the imperfections I was told I could conquer, spending a lifetime trying to overcome, but now too proud to admit I ever will. Too scared to look back and acknowledge I never had a chance. ✑ I never knew. I had nothing to do with the pain. ✑ "I raised myself," so I've always said. I've tried to take responsibility for who I am. ✑ Now I understand. I learned to hide my innocence, my helplessness. I was but a cute little bottle baby with a pronated right foot. I was not complicit. I did not cause my pain. All those years I tried to man up, be dependable, self-reliant, strive to be perfect — my arrogance denying I was immature and vulnerable, having little to do with the heaps of shit thrown my way. ✑ So I hid. ✑ And she found me.

PHILIP SORENSEN

*"They all laughed when I said I was going to be a comedian.*
*Well, they're not laughing now."*
BOB MONKHOUSE

## BRAD PITT'S ABS

It's complicated, this Higher Power stuff, but I think I got it, figured it out. It goes some-thing like this: I'll never figure it out. I'll never figure out me, my amygdala, or anyone else's fight or flight, so relax and surrender to The Forces That Put You Here. Always do your best. And be kind. Especially to yourself. But remember your helplessness. Control the things you can control — one day at a time. Let it be. Blah-blah-blah ... . ❧ I had been treating God like a bombastic old potentate, but that's not the Spirit I want to know. I want to hear my heart when it talks to me, but how can I hear God if I don't listen? ❧ My mind is always racing — journaling, worrying, doing sudoku to fall asleep, and when I get up, looking for the next thing. The next email, the next news feed, the next cat video, the next orgasm, the next piece of food on my tongue, the next 10 things I didn't know about Brad Pitt's abs. What's the rush? ❧ Listen. ❧ My god is mine, personal to me. In my heart. For all I know he has been talking to me, but I have not been listening. That's not so complicated. Full of clichés, maybe, but not complicated. Just listen. ❧ Some people have the gift of hearing their own heart. It might take a little more work for me, though, because I have layers. Noisy layers. The noisiest one of all is the self-critic, especially when it's quiet. ❧ So I tell myself to shut the fuck up and listen.

❧

PHILIP SORENSEN

*"I intend to live forever. So far, so good."*
STEVEN WRIGHT

# THE TOAD

Okay, I admit it. I fear death. I know some don't; at least, that's what they say. But given half a chance, I'd beg for my life. I would. Staring down the barrel of a robber's pistol, kneeling in the desert alongside a saboteur's saber, I'd cry like a baby. Or maybe I wouldn't. Maybe I'd choose some form of dignity, even if it was half-assed, like most stuff we do. You know, why-make-a-bad-situation-worse sort of thing. Or maybe I'd go out with a bang and spit in their eye if I knew death was eminent, so long as they didn't torture me for it.

The state of being dead doesn't scare me, though. Missing out scares me. I never went to Tierra del Fuego, I never ate my fill of tempura sushi, I never watched *Gone with the Wind*, never even read it nor *The History of the Decline and Fall of the Roman Empire.* I don't want to bungee jump, but I'd like to experience full flexion in all my joints, practice superlative nutrition and exercise for 21.5 days and then hop like an elf and run like the wind. I'd like to take a vow of silence like Leonard Cohen or listen to every one of his lyrics and totally get it. And who wouldn't want to try all the positions in the *Kama Sutra*, even it were just for kicks and you were giggling the whole time? So what's to stop me from any of it? Which one of my hierarchy of needs do I need to fulfill? What am I waiting for? Abraham Maslow was such a little toad.

PHILIP SORENSEN

# MARCH 11

# THE STATION

"I still have that small bit of hurt and anger," I said. "But now I can put them in a little box, with strings tied around it. Before, the feelings were big, dark, and red. I couldn't squeeze them into a crate without splitting out the sides. So I quit asking why — an insane exercise. Yet I can't help but wonder what the hell you were thinking. I think I simply need to come to terms."  So she says, *"You know what I think? I think you like your little box. You put it in your bag of crap the Universe hands you just so you can carry it around and open it up now and then. You've got to hold on to it because you'd be lost without your hurt. You don't know what pain-free is."*  "But if I put the box down, then the vile thing is no longer vile. It's benign. It wins."  *"No,"* she says, *"it will always be horrid. I don't know why I did what I did. I told you, I was scared. How many times do you want me to say I'm sorry?"*  "I already said you didn't have to. I forgave you."  "Then quit opening the box like you're touching a sore tooth. The more you touch it, the more you're reminded how much it hurts. Ow, that hurts! Ow, that hurts! Ow, that hurts … ."  "Well, I do forgive you."  *"Yeah,"* she says, *"and I forgave you for your intrusions. Now put down the box, and the whole goddamn bag while you're at it. Leave them here at the station. Let's go."*

PHILIP SORENSEN

*"A photograph is a secret about a secret. The more it tells you, the less you know."*

DIANE ARBUS

## THE INFLUENCE OF ANCESTORS

It was not happening — the essay would not take form. ✍ Call it writer's block, or whatever you will, it was terrible in its tenacity. It had been with me a full week when one afternoon the doorbell rang. I was in my rocker, strategically placed before our cast iron stove, its glass window allowing a view of mesmerizing flames. I loved to watch that fire. ✍ My manuscript had lain on my desk for days. By week's end it shouted at me, but I turned a deaf ear as I retreated to my fireside sanctuary. ✍ Then FedEx broke my reverie. A sister had sent a box containing family photographs. Not snapshots, these were from portrait studios, held in cardboard frames with tabs for standing upright, and all were taken decades ago. Some were turn-of-the-century, some were early 1900s and before. ✍ These were my forebearers: mother, father, stepfather, grandparents, uncles, and aunts — all gone now. ✍ The next morning I slowly opened each photo. One by one, ancestors appeared — a resurrection of the dead: my parents' 1933 wedding, both sets of grandparents' weddings — the Millers and the Paaps, from the 1890s. ✍ But there were no smiles on these faces. These were Dutch-German Americans, all hard-working Lutheran folk. There was no nonsense here. They had played to win. ✍ I hadn't written anything for days. My unease grew. Winter was taking its toll. Writing could wait. ✍ But those faces kept looking at me — my ancestral blood kin. Then it hit me. I was kindling the fire, still on my knees, when I turned to face them and knew. It was because of them that I existed, saw each sunrise. They had given me life. I could not wait any longer. ✍ After breakfast I got back to work.

HOWARD PAAP

# MARCH 13

*"But to have been this once, completely,*
*even if only once: to have been at one with the earth,*
*seems beyond undoing."*

RAINER MARIA RILKE

# TOM

When published several decades ago, the Danish postmodern classic *The Imposter*, by Peter Seeberg was a cult novel in its homeland, but was troublesome to many American reviewers. It tells of a contemporary man, simply named Tom, who is quietly disengaged from what goes on around him. He speaks to few, steals from some, and is incomprehensible to most. Just who is Seeberg speaking to here? ☜ Who is this Tom, who does unusual, and finally, immoral things? ☜ Upon finishing the slim little book, it occurred to me that Seeberg was saying that it is the reader who is finally the imposter. It is we, the mass of modern humanity who are the alienated. Tom is us.

☜

HOWARD PAAP

*"Many of our prayers were not answered,*
*and for this we are now grateful."*

WILLIAM FEATHER

# RIDING THE HORSE

Back in the 1970s when I was in a graduate seminar, our professor said that some students' thinking was "like that fellow who jumped on his horse and rode off in all directions." This harsh indictment, even though stated as a method of helping us move to a more focused way of thinking, has stayed with me.    Then, this morning, in a new biography of Arthur Rimbaud, I read that he was "a man who arrived from all time and was on his way everywhere." This remark was offered in an existential sort of praise, a confirmation of the lasting importance of Rimbaud's work, and finally, a confirmation of the significance of the enigma that was his life.    Aren't we all like that fellow jumping on his horse? Aren't we all like Rimbaud? Don't we try to transcend the limits of time as we hurry along to a space that, finally, is everywhere?

HOWARD PAAP

*"I believe a leaf of grass is no less than the journey-work of the stars."*

WALT WHITMAN

## THE LEAF

He bends to pick up the leaf,
the leaf on the forest path.
An ironwood leaf,
its straight veins exquisitely placed,
its midrib and petiole
where they should be.
Its color the greenest of green,
and no flaw, no sign of failure.
Why did it fall?
It is perfect in its making,
yet it let go.
There is nothing else like it,
and in a day it will begin to wither.
Its time is done,
here at the start of summer.
Even the beautiful cannot know
when life will abruptly end.

HOWARD PAAP

*"My dad took me out to see a meteor shower when I was a little kid ...
My heart was beating; I didn't know what he wanted to do. He wouldn't tell me,
and he put me in the car and we went off, and I saw all these people lying on blankets,
looking up at the sky."*

STEVEN SPIELBERG

# THE PENCILED JOURNAL

A few years before his passing, we discovered a small pocket notebook tucked away on an open kitchen shelf. It held penciled entries, their brevity achingly received. ✑ This was a tally of days kept by my father-in-law. It told of the weather, of who came to the house for coffee, of how the kids were doing in their classrooms, and other tidbits of life. ✑ He spoke of the Reservation's baseball team, but little more than who played last Sunday afternoon and the final score. We wanted details, more observations, but found few. The author was a man who wrote, but not at length. ✑ But he did write. And if you knew the community and his times, you knew that little book carried a valuable message. It was a story of how he saw things, how he received his world. Rich in its simplicity while still complex in its knowledge and wisdom, it is a little treasure. ✑ Yes, he walked the walk. He put pencil to paper. He had spent time writing. And when picking the little notebook up yesterday I wondered why I did not. ✑ That sudden insight did it. This morning I was back in my study hard at it while the message of that little notebook burned in my mind.

✑

HOWARD PAAP

*"My little dog — a heartbeat at my feet."*
EDITH WHARTON

# WALKING THE DOG

This morning the temperature was well below zero
when my dogs and I moved along our path
up in the woods here beside Lake Superior.

There were only the sounds we made,
crunching along amidst the silent trees.

It was a world of just us —
the trees, the sky, the snow, the cold.
All else was absent.

Erased.

HOWARD PAAP

*"If you want to build a ship,*
*don't drum up people to collect wood*
*and don't assign them tasks and work,*
*but rather teach them to long*
*for the endless immensity of the sea."*

ANTOINE DE SAINT-EXUPÉRY

## ESSENCE

The most important message of a poem is that which a writer does not put to words, where the words are used only to point to a truth, to raise the unvoiced question. The poet's silence, finally, forms part of the poem's trajectory.  ⬿  After all, this is what kindergarten teachers have been having their young minions do for generations.

⬿

HOWARD PAAP

*"There is a small opening into the new day which closes*
*the moment you begin your plans."*

DAVID WHYTE

# SAVOR THE SMALL OPENING

Slowly I begin to awaken, in this first moment of the day. With a wiggle of my toes, I allow the current to course through my feet, over the anklebones, up my shins, stopping with a tickle at my knees. The journey rolls upward over my crepe paper thighs and into the bowl of my pelvis. My belly rumbles and my arms fan out like a snow angel on the ocean-blue sheets. Over the crown of my head, I lift my hands and tap them together, like a diver positioned on the high platform. With a languorous stretch, my spine lengthens and signals the rest of my body to enter the day. ✍ Stumbling back from the bathroom in bare feet, I crawl into the rumpled bed and assume a lotus position, reach for my iPhone, and set the singing bowl app for twelve minutes. ✍ Once more, my spine straightens and stretches. I dip my chin ever-so-slightly as palms find a resting place on my knees. One deep inhale. Hold. Exhale. A dozen moments and a new day lingers with me here in this one precious opening.

✍

KAYCE STEVENS HUGHLETT

*"The world is full of magic things, patiently waiting*

*for our senses to grow sharper."*

W.B. YEATS

## LEAN INTO MAGIC

When all else fails, lean into the magic. Some days we need every possible ounce of help. For me, this happens when I see my children suffering. Case in point, my young adult daughter: beautiful, smart, talented, and having a really hard time. School seems like a joke. Relationships are hard. Life feels impossible. My own insecurities rise to the surface. I should have been a better parent. I didn't listen well enough. I was too hard on her. I was too easy. This is all my fault.  ᕫ  I want to wipe away her tears. I long to hold her in my arms and cradle her until everything is better. I want to run. I want to stay and tell her what to do. Instead, I nod my head. I listen. I wait. I agree that it's hard. I ask her what I can do. She grumbles. Cries some more. Pushes me away, but she stays too. We are in this together.  ᕫ  "Let's play hooky and go see the baby tigers at the zoo," I say. She giggles. Her eyes brighten. "I can't," she replies, but something has begun to shift. "Why not?" I ask, wishing I were this carefree when she was five. She shakes her head, shrugs on her backpack, and heads out the door. "Have a good day," I call. "I love you." I take a sip of coffee. I dream of tiger cubs. The kitchen door reopens. "Let's go," she says.  ᕫ  It makes no logical sense. I have work. She has school. We both know the world might call us irresponsible, but we don't care. The magic has arrived and it's time to lean in.

KAYCE STEVENS HUGHLETT

*"You are the sky. Everything else — it's just the weather."*
PEMA CHÖDRÖN

# BE THE EAGLE

Walking around our local lake, my friend and I spy an eagle, high on his perch — watching, observing. He has no apparent worries as he sits upright, taking in his surroundings. For him, there are no errands to run or tasks to complete. His only goal in this moment is to soak up the brilliant blue sky. We stop in our midday busyness and stare.  🦅  The scene changes. Out of nowhere, half a dozen crows begin to dive-bomb the eagle — squawking, pestering, pecking at him. Still the eagle exudes calmness and serenity, unlike me who only moments before was annoyed by grumbly store clerks and erratic drivers.  🦅  The eagle doesn't snap or respond with spite. He holds his head high and continues to survey the world around him. "I am the eagle," he seems to say. Soon the crows drift away. They dissipate like scattered clouds or errant thoughts.  🦅  So what if a driver cut me off on the road or I had to wait on the phone for an hour listening to crummy music? Big deal if no one appreciates the work I do. I can be the eagle. I can yield to beauty. I can hold my head high in the midst. My friend and I continue our walk, but now we share a new mantra: be the eagle.

KAYCE STEVENS HUGHLETT

*"My work is loving the world."*

MARY OLIVER

# OF HEARTS AND MOUNTAINS

My work is to open my heart again and again even when my head shouts, *Run! Close up shop. Shutter the windows. Bolt the doors. Don't let anyone in.* ✎ My work is to remember the tickle of kittens' whiskers on my cheek and the smell of puppy breath in my face. My work is to see the light on the mountains and notice the dusting of snow that fell in the night. My work is to move and stretch my body and to feel the inhale and exhale of breath move through my lungs. ✎ My work is to see the connection between my heart and the mountains — to know that dark always turns to light and light reverses back to dark. To know that sometimes strength looks soft and remember the kindest word can melt a frozen heart. ✎ My work is to simply and beautifully *be*. My work is to cross boundaries of fear and choose love. My work is to be both vulnerable and strong. To be flexible enough to fold into a suitcase and strong enough to break myself out of it. ✎ My work is to love the world and to remember that I am a part of that world. My work is to stay steady like the mountain, even when my head and heart say, *Run*.

✎

KAYCE STEVENS HUGHLETT

*"Without leaps of imagination, or dreaming,*
*we lose the excitement of possibilities."*
GLORIA STEINEM

## 13 WAYS TO OBSERVE A SQUIRREL

First, move slowly — no sudden movements allowed.

Maintain eye contact at all times — blinking may prove disappointing.

Imagine you are the squirrel — begin to wiggle your nose.

Inhale deeply with eyes wide open and nose upturned —
follow the scent of the evergreen tree.

Lightly grasp a ripened pinecone, or the shell of a chestnut.

Nibble 'til your heart's content — feel free to drop shells from your perch.

With unburdened abandon, leap!

Fly through the air, sky-walking on twigs no larger than a toothpick.

Hang upside down and defy gravity, until your thinking brain fills with dreams.

Let go, drop to the ground. Scurry on to the next yummy thing.

Watch out for predators — they come in every shape and size.

Store plenty of nuts for the winter. Remember, *Baby, It's Cold Outside.*

Stop, pause, laugh as you observe the transformed creature with unblinking eyes.

KAYCE STEVENS HUGHLETT

*"Taste is an intimate sense.*
*We can't taste things at a distance."*
DIANE ACKERMAN

## FEAST OF LIFE

My life is a breathtaking banquet. Flavors. Colors. Aromas of bounty. Sprinkled with the occasional surprise that makes me cover my mouth and wretch.  ⌘  As moments of life, the appetizers are small, almost like crumbs tossed out for sparrows. But for small birds — like tiny children — size does not matter. The most delicious flavors often arrive without fanfare, like popsicles on a hot summer day.  ⌘  For me, the second course — those middle years — required a palate cleanser. They left a bitter taste.  ⌘  And then, the entrée. The meaty years where life took on its own … well … life. Perspective lost, I chewed and swallowed whatever was placed before me. Taking it all in, but never finding fulfillment or satisfaction. One day I could hold no more. I flung my arm across the carefully set table and shouted, "Enough!"  ⌘  And then life's sweet servant whispered, "Ah, now there is space. What would you like for dessert, my dear?"

⌘

KAYCE STEVENS HUGHLETT

*"Miracles are a retelling in small letters of the very same story*
*which is written across the whole world in letters too large*
*for some of us to see."*

C.S. LEWIS

# A MIRACLE? YES, PLEASE.

I read a story about miracles one day and was so touched that I sat alone in my car and cried. Later when I tried to remember the specifics of the story, my mind went blank — as if the miracle had disappeared.  Maybe that's what miracles are: small unexpected moments that reach out through the ordinary in our day. They grab us and squeeze so tightly that tears stream down our cheeks and we can't say why or how, but we know we've been moved and changed.  The only miracles I heard about while growing up were humongous, heroic gestures like David slaying the giant and Moses parting the Red Sea. Miracles were the unattainable stuff of storybooks. Today, however, I think they might be something different, a quality attainable and available in any given moment.  What if a miracle meant simply changing your attitude about something you thought you'd be stuck with forever? What if it meant opening your eyes to what's right in front of you? What if you saw miracles in tree bark and wrinkles? In squirrels and eagles? In here and now?

KAYCE STEVENS HUGHLETT

*"No army can withstand the strength of an idea*
*whose time has come."*
VICTOR HUGO

# LIGHT BULB

I was on an ordinary walk with my newborn baby, Jacob, in the stroller, enjoying our best part of the day. While I got some much-needed fresh air and exercise, Jacob loved the sights and sounds of the world going by.  ⟡  During that particular walk, I contemplated all of the questions I had about motherhood, from nursing to sleep issues, from cradle cap to "what the heck happened to my career?" I felt alone and needed a village.  ⟡  Then, a light bulb went off: I could apply my career as a fitness professional and help moms get back in shape, and they could help support me in my new role as a mom. Right then and there, I decided to start a moms-with-their-babies fitness class called Stroller Strides. No research. No focus groups. I just did it because it felt so right and I knew I had to do it. Fourteen years later, that class has grown into one of the largest fitness franchises in the nation and we have touched hundreds of thousands of moms. I have my village now, and I feel blessed every single day to love what I do and to do what I love — all because I acted on that light bulb moment.  ⟡  Combine your passion with your purpose and take a leap.

⟡

LISA DRUXMAN

# MARCH 27

*"A friend may be waiting behind a stranger's face."*

MAYA ANGELOU

# HUG DEEP

This is a little story about Starla J. King (you might know her as co-editor of this book). I remember the first time I met Starla. She came up to me and gave me the biggest hug, pulling me in as if I were a longtime friend who she hadn't seen in ages. We had never met before, yet I immediately felt her love and the type of warm person she was just from that hug. It started a friendship that has lasted despite thousands of miles distance between us. ≈ We go so fast in our days and barely give a handshake or a pat on the back. Savoring the moments is good for you. ≈ When you hug, you spark up oxytocin, the cuddle hormone. It makes us feel all warm and lovey inside, promoting feelings of devotion, trust and bonding. Hugs have also been proven to lower blood pressure, strengthen our immune systems, and reduce stress, worry and loneliness. These benefits flow to both people in the hug, so go on and hug it out! Do you need any more reasons?

≈

LISA DRUXMAN

*"Every great dream begins with a dreamer.*
*Always remember, you have within you the strength, the patience,*
*and the passion to reach for the stars to change the world."*

HARRIET TUBMAN

# DAYDREAMER

Almost every report card I ever received said that I was a daydreamer, and it wasn't a compliment. They were right, though. I could rarely focus on the task at hand, as I was always in my own little world.  ⟿  Later in my life, I took those daydreams and made my dreams come true, becoming an author, a speaker, an entrepreneur, a leader. And I am still a daydreamer. The difference now is that I surround myself with a team who compliments me and helps me focus. But the dream part that I kept from childhood is what makes me an innovator today. I have learned that what was once labeled as a weakness is actually my very special gift.  ⟿  Studies show that we are better off developing our strengths than our weaknesses. So where to focus? I'm choosing my strengths!

⟿

LISA DRUXMAN

*"Kid, you'll move mountains."*

DR. SEUSS

# SEE THEIR MAGIC

As a new mom, you can't help but picture what you hope your children will be like. Maybe a scholar, an athlete, or an artist? When they show up as something different, we are inclined to focus on what they didn't accomplish. For instance, if your son comes home with all A's and B's and one D on his report card, what do you focus on? Do you celebrate the A's and B's, or is it all about improving the D? ✎ My 13-year-old son (who is awesome, of course) is not a scholar and not the star athlete. But he found a love for magic that I never expected! So, my husband and I work hard to support that talent. We stop what we are doing each day to watch his latest tricks and to help him work on his craft, and we are taking him to a magic conference. My hope is that when he is a grown man, he will remember his parents supporting his passion, and find confidence and inspiration there. ✎ True unconditional love is felt no matter how you look, who you love, or what you do.

✎

LISA DRUXMAN

*"Fulfillment derives not from lofty achievements,*
*but from ordinary feats. It arrives not once in a lifetime,*
*but every moment of the livelong day."*

KAREN MAEZEN MILLER

## TODAY IS SPECIAL

Today is truly special. It will never happen again and it is passing as we speak. ⤹ How much time do you spend planning big, obviously special days such as weddings or parties or vacations? What can you do today to also make this regular day a lasting memory? You will not remember the dirty dishes or the laundry that needs to be folded. But you will remember an impromptu picnic on the floor, an after-dinner walk to look at Christmas lights, or a belly laugh that made you pee in your pants. ⤹ It doesn't have to cost any money. It doesn't have to have a grand plan. Simply make today special. Make it worth remembering. ⤹ I heard once that life is like a string of pearls, with each pearl representing special moments in your life. The string that connects those pearls is just as important, so make the ordinary days count.

⤹

LISA DRUXMAN

*"Don't let the muggles get you down."*

J.K. ROWLING

# EATING AN ELEPHANT

We have all heard it. "How do you eat an elephant? One bite at a time." This, my friends, is how I live my whole life. 〜 As a child, I was easily overwhelmed. Perhaps it was my ADD or my daydreaming brain. Whatever the reason, I lived in a life of *can't*. I didn't try anything because everything overwhelmed me, and I didn't believe I could do anything successfully. I wasn't good at sports. Or school. I wasn't even good with friends, for that matter. So, I just didn't try. They say that if you don't use it, you lose it; so let's just say that I lost it: I became weaker in all areas simply because I didn't try. 〜 Later in life, I realized my approach needed to change, so I started breaking things down to the smallest achievable bite. If I was assigned a book to read, I broke it down to chapters. Then to paragraphs. Then to sentences. Because that I could do. And I got better. I made small efforts socially, then in sports. And I got better there too. I was never a natural — in anything — but I learned that I can do anything if I take small steps every day. Small steps every day get you anywhere you want to go. 〜 No step is too small. The longest journey begins with just a single step. Go take it!

〜

LISA DRUXMAN

# APRIL

# APRIL 1

*"Upon waking each day my first words to my heart always are,*
*'Tell me all your news of Love.'"*

HAFIZ

# GOD IS LOVE

I am not a religious person. Truth be told, I don't even believe in God. My mom believed in religion, but not God. My dad believed in God, but not religion. Although I now have a respect for religious traditions and am open to a possibility of a higher power, so to speak, I am still more of a realist and lean on science more than higher power. That being said, I do believe in the spirit — the spirit of love. No matter what religion you are, what if we all considered our God to be love? That is the spirit that will give us all strength, comfort, peace. Love is the most powerful force of the universe. If we consider love to be our God, then we will have no war, no fighting, no hate. Remember, we are all truly worshipping love!

LISA DRUXMAN

*"It gets late early here."*
YOGI BERRA

# LATELY

I wait lately
For a solution
For customer service

I wait lately
For the light to return
To order seeds

I wait lately
To soothe the ache
For the kettle to boil

I wait lately
To hear the answer
For the phone to ring

I wait lately
For the hours to pass
For the right time

SALLY KESSLER

# APRIL 3

*"Even if you're on the right track,*
*you'll get run over if you just sit there."*

WILL ROGERS

# MOVING

A life in boxes

Clothes, books, and old magazines

Thoughts I can't contain.

SALLY KESSLER

# APRIL 4

*"And now here is my secret, a very simple secret;*
*it is only with the heart that one can see rightly,*
*what is essential is invisible to the eye."*

ANTOINE DE SAINT-EXUPÉRY

## AGING

I see the reflection

I touch its cheeks. Thank goodness.

The mirror is wrinkled.

SALLY KESSLER

# APRIL 5

## FORECAST

Pretend you don't care

Turn away from the window

Finally it snows.

SALLY KESSLER

*"My grandmother started walking five miles a day when she was 60.*
*She's 97 now, and we don't know*
*where the hell she is."*

ELLEN DEGENERES

## ANTICIPATION

Still, breathless, silent

Alert muscles twitch. Don't move.

It's under the bed.

SALLY KESSLER

# APRIL 7

# RANDOM DEEP THOUGHTS

My new thermos came with warnings.
"Do not drink from the bottle.
Always drink from the cup." And
"Wash before drinking."

Wasn't sure what to do.
So I took a clue from the dog.
Buried it for a while.
I will think of something later.

When it's windy it's impossible
To count the birds at the feeder
And measure the true depth
Of snow in the woods.

Counting to seven
The days are numbered.
Why on earth would I rush
To something called a "deadline"?

**SALLY KESSLER**

*"It is the business of the future to be dangerous."*
ALFRED NORTH WHITEHEAD

# EVERYTHING IS CONNECTED

"Everything Is Connected" should be the title of my car's owner manual. I believe everything *is* connected, at least in the whole, spiritual, Chief Seattle sort of way. I just didn't have proof ... until yesterday. 🦅 My car is equipped with "stability control." On slippery pavement, if the tires aren't gripping, lighted squiggly lines appear, followed by an annoying beep. "Oops! You're sliding a bit. Got it!" But yesterday the light went on and stayed on no matter what I did to reboot the system as the manual suggested. The manual also said: care should be taken; maybe a trip to a professional; maybe don't drive it. How's that supposed to work? I drove anyway. Groceries were needed, the pavement was dry, and I am smarter than my car. 🦅 In the grocery parking lot, I stepped out of the car, slipped and fell. A man helped me up saying, "Must be your stability control." Wait, how did ... ? 🦅 In the produce aisle, I slipped on a wet spot. Keeping my footing this time, I declared to the tomatoes, "Stability control issue." During checkout I sidestepped another wet spot, strode out of the building carrying two environmentally sound bags full of organic stuff, one in each hand perfectly balanced, my footing firm. At the scene of my downfall, I found drier ground, opened the door, took the driver's seat and started the car fully expecting the annoying squiggly light to flash, badgering me about the slippery slope. It did not come on! All I had needed to do was pay attention. My stability control was no longer in question. Everything *is* connected!

SALLY KESSLER

# APRIL 9

*"Image and appearance tell you little.*
*The inside is bigger than the outside when you have the eyes to see."*

WM. PAUL YOUNG

# LICENSE TO WRITE

When I first began to investigate and experiment with the art of writing fiction, my biggest problem was trying to figure out what to write about. One day, I pulled up behind a car at a stoplight. While waiting for the light to change, I watched the young driver of the car in front of me primp and preen in the rear view mirror. He turned his head this way and that, checked his teeth, smoothed his hair and, as the light changed, appeared to blow himself a kiss. As he drove off, I noticed his license plate: DANDY. There are stories all around us if we just take a moment to notice.

TERESA J. WAGNER

*"All hockey players are bilingual. They know English and profanity."*

GORDIE HOWE

## PARLEZ-VOUS FRANÇAIS?

As a high honors graduate in my senior high school class, I was asked to provide a paragraph for the yearbook about where I planned to study next, and what I planned to do with the rest of my life. I wrote that I was going on to the University of Minnesota as a French major, and that someday, I hoped to become the French language announcer for the Montreal Canadiens hockey team. I was only half joking. ⤳ My high school French teacher was a short, stocky, gum-chewing guy with a crewcut. He was a former goalie for the University of Minnesota hockey team and he owned a sheep farm south of the Twin Cities. Every morning, he would dress in his short-sleeved white shirt and tie and make the long drive to the Cities to share with us his deep love of the French language. You couldn't dream up a more atypical French teacher but you couldn't find a better one either. ⤳ Imagine this small powerhouse standing on a chair in front of the class, belting out the theme from *Un Homme et Une Femme*, imploring us all to join in. He had the entire hockey team taking French and loving it. He was the person who helped me realize that it's okay to mess with people's expectations, an aha moment that I've carried with me ever since. All hockey players know English and profanity and some teach French. Vive la différence!

TERESA J. WAGNER

*"While we try to teach our children all about life,*
*our children teach us what life is all about."*
ANGELA SCHWINDT

# THE VIEW FROM KNEE HIGH

One morning, as I was driving to my daughter and son-in-law's home, I saw a colorful, cold-weather, conga line of preschoolers. Bundled in winter gear and following their teachers, they wound their way down the sidewalk in front of the local nursing home. When my four-year-old grandson returned from school that afternoon, I asked him if his class had gone to see the old people at the nursing home that morning. He gave me a puzzled look and then said emphatically, "No. We went to visit our grandfriends." Perspective is everything.

∽

TERESA J. WAGNER

*"There are books of which the backs and covers are by far the best parts."*

CHARLES DICKENS

# YOU CAN'T JUDGE A BOOK ...

For years I believed that if I started a book I had to finish it. I plodded through many bad or at best, mediocre books with which I had nothing in common. The whole exercise was in many ways reminiscent of my dating history. ✑ One day, I finally realized that I didn't have to finish a book just because I had started it. Lightning would not strike, my library card would not be revoked, and Barnes & Noble would not put my photo in a red circle with a slash through it on its doors. ✑ Many avid readers consider it sacrilegious to dismiss a book as not worth reading. The day I first decided to give up on a book was the day my reading adventures began to expand exponentially. Don't like a book? Toss it on the pile and try another. It's easier than it sounds. ✑ Even though I am a fast reader, there are only so many books I am going to be able to read before I make my exit. When that time comes, I hope I'm allowed to pack books for the trip, but so far, I haven't gotten the memo. Until then, when a book doesn't speak to me, I'll put it down and move on to the next. ✑ Funny thing is, books can magically change when left unattended for awhile. Come back to a book years later and you may find it speaks volumes to you, no pun intended. Too bad you can't say that about most former boyfriends.

TERESA J. WAGNER

*"Writing a novel is like driving a car at night.*
*You can only see as far as your headlights,*
*but you can make the whole trip that way."*

E. L. DOCTOROW

# DON'T MAKE ME COME BACK THERE

I always thought that writing a novel was pretty straightforward. Outline the plot, flesh out the characters, get behind the keyboard, and go. But, the more I wrote, the more I discovered I wasn't the only one on the journey without a clear sense of where I was going. Those darn characters I'd invited along seemed to have travel plans of their own. Sometimes they sat in the back seat like petulant children, interrupting at every opportunity and fighting with each other. Or they came down with a sudden case of wanderlust and went off on a tangent. And, at times, they would backseat drive until I just wanted to hand them the keyboard and say, "Write it yourself." On occasion, they did. ➝ Now, when I get behind the keyboard, I embrace the notion that I can only see as far as my headlights or the next turn in the road and that all the characters are going to have a say in where we're going and how we're going to get there. They're a rowdy, questioning, fun-loving, sometimes irritable bunch, but they're all interested in getting to the same place as me. If I don't make it as a writer, I may look into driving a tour bus.

➝

TERESA J. WAGNER

*"It's just life. You can't beat life."*

ALICE MUNRO

# MY LOVE AFFAIR WITH ALICE

When I grow up, I would like to be Alice Munro. I have read every short story she has written many times over and, in my dreams, like to pretend that I can write just as well. Since that's not going to happen, and it's also highly unlikely that she will turn out to be my long-lost sister or cousin, I guess I will just have to settle for being one of her biggest fans. ✑ Alice, as I like to refer to her, writes seemingly ordinary tales about ordinary people, yet does so with extraordinary depth and understanding. Her landscapes of southwestern Ontario call to me and I could swear that I've met many of her characters before. ✑ One day, as I was reading *The Turkey Barn* for the millionth time, I realized that, in essence, Alice is writing the stories of my life. She's writing not only about me, but about my mother and her mother, and my aunts and cousins, and she's even giving me an idea of what it might have been like to have a sister. No matter that they have different names and live in a different country. ✑ Many writers achieve fame and fortune by granting readers access to worlds of super heroes, intrigue, violence, and romance, all in heightened forms. But some writers hone their skill as a tool for unearthing and examining the job we all have of just being a human being. That, to me, is a task worthy of superhero status. I wonder what color Alice would like for her cape.

✑

TERESA J. WAGNER

*"No matter how far a person can go, the horizon is still way beyond you."*

ZORA NEALE HURSTON

# THE WINDOW SEAT

On a flight out of the Minneapolis-St. Paul Airport one night, I peered out the window as the cumbersome capsule full of warm-weather seekers climbed slowly into the night sky. ⮌ I grew up in Minneapolis in the days before the seemingly endless suburbs began their march across the prairie. That night, I marveled at the extensive, intricately woven blanket of lights below that stretched across the earth toward the horizon. In the last glimpse before our plane slipped into the cloud cover, the lights appeared to roll right over the curve of the earth. ⮌ In that moment, I finally began to realize what a small yet important part we all play in this ongoing circus of humanity. All those lights, all those people. Everyone down there on the ground has a story — some happy, some sad, some familiar, some not. ⮌ Now, when I fly, I always choose the window seat because I like to be reminded that I'm part of the ever-unfolding greatest show on earth.

⮌

TERESA J. WAGNER

*"Blessed are the hearts that can bend; they shall never be broken."*

ALBERT CAMUS

# MY MOTHER, THE DRUG ADDICT

Sitting in her doctor's office, waiting in her new wheelchair, my 93-year-old mother looks the picture of antiquity. Her otherwise curious mouth is now a permanent downturn, as if to say a constant "no" to anything placed before her.   Her skin, which has been riddled with age marks for many years, is now brittle and cracking everywhere I can see.   Her normally fierce and attentive eyes scan the room and the faces of my sisters, looking for something lost that she cannot quite remember.   We've assembled here to confront the doctor, who for ten years has been prescribing more and more Oxycodone for my mother's alleged hip pain. After a recent fall, she was not able to regain control of her meds and the Oxycodone misuse came to light. Consequently, withdrawal had set in, the kind of dark and hideous experience reserved for street heroin addicts.   When asked why, the doctor fails miserably to string together a sentence. My mother rises up to defend her, "It's not her fault. I am an addict."   Suddenly my mind clears and what had been my mother is now a person who will do anything to get her fix. While the sound of it rings slightly macabre, the feel of it liberates me from my constant search to find that something that will make her happy again.   Nothing but her drug will do. While it's not the preferred answer, it is the correct one.

BARBARA WITH

*"Patience is bitter, but its fruit is sweet."*
JEAN-JACQUES ROUSSEAU

## AMERIKAN FASCISM

What did the good people of Germany do in the 1930s, when friends and neighbors began to divide into classes and groups and ideologies driven apart by purposeful deviants? What practical steps did those who saw the truth but could not convince others take to stop what they saw was coming down the pike? ☜ After the fact, hindsight was horrifying. During the war, the *New York Times* only mentioned Nazi atrocities a total of six times in seven years. When the Soviets finally stumbled upon Majdanek in Poland in 1944, the scene must have evoked vomiting. Why would no one believe such horrors were possible in Germany? ☜ Today I watch the United States suffer from being so blind, deaf, and dumb. Corporations have reached into every corner of our daily life, stripping us of any awareness of their power over us. And when the enlightened speak, others are blindly confident it "can't happen here." ☜ Racked with a deep resistance to the rising tide of Amerikan fascism, I plead with anyone who will listen to look at the truth, to examine the facts, to understand the implications. I am faced with denial staring back at me from vacant eyes. ☜ In an instant I realize, that I, too, did not want to see, until I found out for myself. In a moment I turn from trying to convince someone of what I see, to urging them to use critical thinking to look past the comfort of the moment. ☜ In that instant, the need to change minds and hearts is released, and I retreat silently into my own knowing, to watch and wait.

BARBARA WITH

*"It is so long, the spring which goes on all winter."*

PABLO NERUDA

# AN INCH DEEP, A MILE WIDE

How was I to know he would be my future ex-husband? His eyes were so kind the day we met. His easy-going personality was not my usual attraction. Drawn previously to bad boys, this "nice guy" signaled an entirely new era. 〜 For 18 years we danced, fished, traveled, and ate, sharing bed and table, making our own maps. Unconventional met cleverly curious; intersections were formed. He brought balance; I was the wildhood. We cherished our freedom, each alone and with each other. We valued our laughter, which seemed to get us through times of disconnection. 〜 Eventually, our disconnection turned to frustration and left unchecked, morphed to angst, war, rage. Where once were shared intersections were now torn-up streets and unlit avenues leading through an unknown town. 〜 In the heat of our last battle, he accused me of being too deep. Too deep! How could he? I was, at least according to my last examination, the same depth I had been when we met: impossibly, darkly deep, like the end of the ocean. I never denied this of myself, and yet now it was an issue. 〜 In a riot of rage and frustration, before I knew it, I was slamming him in my own accusation, "I would rather be too deep than only an inch deep and a mile wide." As soon as it left my throat, I saw clearly the difference between us — his energy floating on the surface, mine remaining invisible miles below. 〜 Years later, as friends, those differences make no difference. Friends are friends. Love never dies, it only changes into a better fit for all.

BARBARA WITH

*"How beautiful your cry that gives me your silence."*

RENÉ CHAR

## SISTER'S TRAGEDY

For whatever reason we could not remember, she cut me out of her life as if I were a cancer. One minute we were thick as thieves; the next I had offended and she was gone. ✑ For many years she refused to speak to me. On birthdays, the lack of a greeting cut from her as if a real blade struck my heart. No reaching out could turn her. No reasoning would appeal to her stubborn insistence that I was somehow a threat. ✑ I missed my sister terribly. Like a child prodigal I roamed outside the family plot, a strange woman in an insane world. ✑ My life eventually became a victory. I finally found my family and a home of my own, took a long rest and began again. But still she stayed away. ✑ It was my mother, actually, who made the call. ✑ "Sandy's son has been murdered." ✑ In the void-like silence the statement echoed through my body. Universes collided, and I could only imagine where my sister was at that very moment. ✑ A day later, she ordered a car to get me from the airport. The driver pulled up to my nephew's home, the one my sister helped him build for him and his young son. There was my sister, on her hands and knees with rubber gloves, scrubbing the sidewalk where he had been stabbed outside the back door. ✑ Together, on our hands and knees, we wailed as we cleaned his blood. We will never be parted again.

BARBARA WITH

*"To confront a person with his shadow is to show him his own light."*

CARL JUNG

# ROGUE MOVERS

Sorting through our stuff, we have to pick what to send ahead to New York. I choose an online mover, and lickety-split, two guys in a rental truck drive away with our lives.  In New York, I await the arrival that never comes. Phone calls lead to infinite holds, lead to claims of "It's on its way." After a week of unrelenting obstruction, I research what I should have done before.  Several national news sources report Israeli companies setting up fake movers; loads held hostage with demands for more cash.  Weeping alone in West Hampton Beach, looking at what is lost, I see nothing that mattered except my wedding album, and I even let go of that.  In the new-found independence of one who just lost everything, I research what is equivalent to the devil for the Israeli culture. Golem comes up as a spirit that "attaches itself to those whose heads have separated from their hearts" and then one needs a Rabbi for an exorcism.  My last email to the rogue movers cheerfully mentions that I have a circle of women friends at work and how we would hate to see Golem find a way into all their lives.  Within 20 minutes, they are flying a Cuban driver up from Miami to bring my hijacked load from Chicago through New York City on Memorial Day weekend.  Sure enough, a sweet young Latino man shows up at 5:00 Sunday evening. Together we unload what seemed like way too much stuff and he tells me, "You are so nice. I am surprised. Back at the office they said you were a witch."

BARBARA WITH

*"Who knows what our bodies are really up to?"*
PAUL HERB

## DAY OF THE DEAD

The sound is heard with the solar plexus, not the ear. A "swoosh," like pushing air through a tube, signals the shift in perception. The change isn't seen with human eyes. It opens something inside — an awareness of some non-physical part of my human self that is sharing the presence of the dead person. ✏ I wasn't born with special powers. Everyone can (and should) learn to do this. The challenge is that emotions — fear, angst, anger — color perception. We ache to have that loved one back, or we're terrified to face our own death. The very presence of the formerly physical person triggers both those reactions in the living. So sometimes the dead remain silent for a while. ✏ Once we move the truth of our own dying through our body — feeling the angst, the fear, the incredible sorrow — that truth then fills up the space between our cells like a nutrient and bubbles up through a deeper, more ancient voice from within. ✏ When we listen with our solar plexus to that voice, we can feel their forms and hear their voices. Even though I am looking at the kitchen table and he is not there, I see him in my mind at the table, like a hologram in my brain. I feel his presence on the wind of my breath. As I honor my own fears with compassionate release, a new muscle memory emerges. It's him. It's really him. ✏ Then we can talk openly as I realize a part of me is already dead, even as I speak.

BARBARA WITH

*"For small creatures such as we, the vastness is bearable only through love."*

CARL SAGAN

# COMPASSION

Have you ever wondered how life is even possible? Doesn't it strike you with powerful reverence every day that we get to have this physical experience? ✑ Think of the amazing dance of great cooperation going on within your own body — so many systems of consciousness mysteriously operate brilliantly together to create human life: neuro-logical, biological, cosmological, physiological, psychological, quantalogical. Who or whatever plans and implements creation is truly a god. ✑ The separation we experience as humans — you from me from the river from the stars — is a beautiful and necessary illumination of an unfathomable depth; a well so deep we can't hear the splash of the thrown stone. We do, however, feel the ripples of that stone emerging from within our bodies and radiating outward. ✑ What life force is this that impels human life onward? What kind of great mind would think up an oasis such as Earth, and spend billions of years preparing a garden from which humanity could emerge? This garden of such beauty that could boast millions of species of fantastical animals, vegetables and minerals, and everything we need to live fully and richly — surely this is the byproduct of an act of enormous love. ✑ Let Compassion be your god. Everyone making decisions for the good of the whole being forwards us onward into even higher levels of dazzling miracles. Let us become love, for the good of all. ✑ Imagine. ✑ There would be nothing left to do but watch and be amazed.

BARBARA WITH

*"True, I talk of dreams, which are the children of an idle brain."*

WILLIAM SHAKESPEARE

# THE SUBJECT IS DREAMS

The children of an idle brain? So says Shakespeare, and who can dispute anything he has said? But now, with my idle brain fully engaged, I begin to wonder about dreams. We call every wish, every plan, every goal, every fantasy, a dream.

"My dream is to someday have my own accounting business."

"I dream of being a success."

"I dream of being kidnapped by aliens."

"I dreamed I was naked holding a bunch of bananas in the checkout line at the IGA."

We hear these statements, or those akin to them (well, maybe not the naked banana one) from our family, friends, and acquaintances every day. ⤖ The word *dream* and its derivatives can be used in many parts of speech in the English language. ⤖ For example: My dream is to work on a banana plantation. I think dreamily of banana-cream pie. Last night I dreamed I was eating banana-peanut butter sandwiches with Elvis. Dreaming is so enjoyable, especially when it involves bananas. ⤖ Now that I think of it, I'll wait to investigate the various interpretations of the word dream because for some reason, I feel the need to go into the kitchen and bake a couple loaves of banana bread.

⤖

LAURIE OTIS

*"Unexpressed emotions never die.*
*They are buried alive and will come forth later in uglier ways."*

SIGMUND FREUD

# THE RACE

I'm awake at 3:30 in the morning. Maybe it's the vivid dream I had. It's a recurring dream which plays out in different settings. This time I was on a street in my home town back before the local movie theater had succumbed to video tapes. ➳ I think I was going to "the show," as we called it, when I noticed a friend across the street. This is where the action is always the same: we catch each other's eyes and start to run, as if racing, this time down the familiar street. Of course the race doesn't end before the dream; that would be like a falling dream actually ending with blunt force contact and death. ➳ I always race with the same person: a man I've been in love with for years but rarely see. In my waking life, we occasionally run into each other in the grocery store, he shopping with his wife while I, as usual, am alone. If she happens to be busy down another aisle, we have embraced, as friends do, and shared an intimate look. Once, at the funeral of a mutual friend, we embraced and kissed in front of our fellow mourners, comforting each other in our sadness. I feel guilty when I remember this, as if we had taken advantage of the occasion. ➳ Sometimes I feel that we should meet for coffee and talk over old times. Would that be so bad? Would he be betraying his wife? I guess he would. It's best I just keep racing with him, in my dreams.

➳

LAURIE OTIS

*"I have a dream."*

MARTIN LUTHER KING

# SOME CHANCE OF COMING TRUE

Whether speaking to a vast crowd from the steps of the Lincoln Memorial or to a single inter-viewer for a publicity shot, the message is the same: don't give up your dreams. Of course a dream takes a great deal of persistence in order to become a reality. ✑ Martin Luther King Jr. had millions of followers, historical precedence, and an all-encompassing respect for humanity. His job was to get the word out to the whole country and to establish societal awareness of an existing inequality that shouldn't be tolerated. He experienced many setbacks and failures on his quest, but his dream had legitimate expectations. It was feasible and attainable, and he never gave up. ✑ Madonna started out as a poor girl from Michigan who was an aspiring dancer; had talent, imagination, and a passion for performing; and hungered for recognition and success. She also experienced rejection, but she paid her dues and became a star. Her dream had legitimate expectations. It was feasible and attainable, and she never gave up. ✑ What I'm saying is, working to change the world or trying to be a rock star takes more effort than most people are willing to expend but if a person is able and has passion, this kind of dream has a good chance — or at least some chance — of coming true. ✑ I don't mean to compare King and Madonna's dreams or imply that one is more important than the other, or more important than anybody's, for that matter. As far as I know, there's no scale of importance for dreams — from heads of state to homeless.

LAURIE OTIS

*"Old age is no place for sissies."*

BETTE DAVIS

# FIRST WILL COME DAFFODILS

Do we grow too old to dream? Could having a dream be one of the abilities we lose as time chips away at our joints, organs, and minds? Just because my knees ache, can I no longer dream of walking the stone paths of the ancient Inca city of Machu Picchu? Does my sometimes muddled confusion sound a metaphorical death knell for my writing of the great American novel? ⤺ Oh, it isn't that I still have a bucket list. Lord knows I haven't seen everything I'd hoped to see or accomplished everything I'd planned in my youth, but I'm satisfied with my travels and think there are still a few modest accomplishments in me before I'm completely addled and confined to my house. ⤺ I think it's the mortality factor. When we're young, the sky's the limit; but at my age, dreams change and we have to settle for those that don't require a lot of time and are not quite as grand as a flight to Peru. We lower our expectations, so to speak (which, incidentally, is psychobabble's most recent recipe for happiness: okay, been there, done that). ⤺ So here's to lowering my expectations. Maybe I'll dream of the coming summer's garden, making lists of plants and seeds and pages of instructions for the young, strong people who now do my outside work, since I've reached a stage where I need help to dream. ⤺ I think I'll just lean back in my chair. Wow! I'm happier already! (Eerie music starts and my voice sounds as if it's coming from the bottom of a well.) First will come the daffodils and tulips and apple blossoms, and then it'll get warmer and next … .

LAURIE OTIS

*"A garden I tend whose blossom never existed."*

PABLO NERUDA

# DAY DREAMS

When nighttime thoughts slip into day,
Invade my life, gain my attention,
I stop the din and sink again
Into the land of "might have been."
It's a shadowy place that keeps alive
Those dreams too old to mention.

I could have married a farmer's son,
Stayed at home, to never roam.
Or lived my life as a rich man's wife,
With all I'd want, and free from strife.
Sometimes I sit behind a desk and sign my name;
Or tread the boards and curry fame,
When nighttime thoughts find me alone.

Oh seek me not, you wraiths of night;
The sun's too bright to give you sway.
Do not intrude with your sighs of regret
My voice must not utter the words, "and yet … ."
For had dreams like these really come to be,
There's one thing for sure: I would not be me
When nighttime thoughts slip into day.

LAURIE OTIS

*"The poem is the point at which our strength gave out."*

RICHARD ROSEN

# END OF THE LUPINE SEASON

*Gudrun is singled out for teasing at school and finds herself having to walk through a gauntlet of taunting bullies. Overcome with shame, fear, and anger at the injustice of it all, she suddenly and unconsciously leaves her physical self behind; a jarring experience.* ➤ Tonight she wanted to think hard about how she had seen Jalmer defend her at school. She knew he hadn't, but she also remembered completely removing herself from the whole encounter while she had imagined swift retribution justly administered. The feeling had been exhilarating. Gudrun reasoned it would be so easy to repeat that exercise in any difficult situation, saving herself the taint of embarrassment while remaining calm and unruffled. ➤ On this day, Gudrun had discovered the land of fantasy where she would dwell, off and on, for the rest of her life. Her smile broadened as she continued to test her powers. At first she waited to lose herself in her thoughts until she was in bed, but the practice grew addictive; and sometimes she would gaze into space in the middle of class and leave the schoolroom behind as she soared, floating and twisting, in her storyland. ➤ Then came adolescence, when hormones coursed through Gudrun's body with as much fervor as those that caused the girls at school to primp and simper, betray their friends, and generally live a miserable existence worrying about dates, or the lack of same. It was at this point that Gudrun invented her lover who remained faithful for life, even cradling her in his arms at the moment of her death, allowing her the dignity of a fearless passage and shielding her one last time from reality, whose cruelties he had enabled her to evade.

LAURIE OTIS

*"I am sure of nothing so little as my own intentions."*

LORD BYRON

## CALIFORNIA DREAMIN'

The summer people have gone, hitched up the boat and driven down our dusty, gravel road as if they were off to town or Bay View Beach. At first I didn't notice it much. Oh, it was quieter, but I was cocooned in the glory of autumn and too busy worshipping each tree as it blazed, then shed its withered leaves. 	I didn't think much about it until one night when I was awake at 3:30 a.m. and glanced across the short expanse of land that separated our houses. No comforting light shone from any of the windows. I've always thought that some member of that household shared my occasional insomnia. If I were up at night, I'd often see an answering gleam across the way. *Reading,* I'd think. *I wonder what book. Maybe we should have a cup of tea.* But I never asked about the book or tea. 	The next day I wandered into their yard. Their friendly golden retriever didn't greet me. The empty tire swing twisted in the wind. No bathing suits or beach towels decorated the deck rails. The lawn chairs were folded and piled against the porch. 	I stood for a moment, musing about summer sounds that would waft through my windows on a warm breeze: music, a slammed screen door, clinking glasses, or the laughter of friends at a cookout. I should have walked over and joined them with a bottle of wine in hand. But I never offered wine or company. 	The temperature has fallen below zero for several days now. I'm almost out of the strawberry jam I made last summer, and starting to think life is too hard here, alone in the winter. When they return, I should make cookies and ask them for coffee; but when the sun and the birds return, I probably won't deliver either.

LAURIE OTIS

*"Sitting still is a pain in the ass."*
NOAH LEVINE

## ON THE MAT

The curtain rises,

a performance looks the same to the observer

but it is different every time.

I return because of the feeling after.

Before …

only

jitters.

I cannot hide.

There is no performance,

only the truth of the moment

on the mat.

REBECCA P. COHEN

# MAY

*"When you flip the switch in that attic,
it doesn't matter whether it's been dark for ten minutes,
ten years or ten decades. The light still illuminates the room
and banishes the murkiness, letting you see the things you couldn't see before."*

SHARON SALZBERG

## SHADOWS

Light is needed

to see the darkness that

illuminates

the beauty of a shadow.

What is the photo negative

of any moment

that

mixes

light and dark?

REBECCA P. COHEN

# MAY 2

# GIGGLES

Belly laughs from a child,

a smile that embraces the room,

laughing so hard with friends you cry.

What can you do today to create a smile?

Imagine what makes someone else come to life.

Brilliant moments of laughter

are happening in millions of places

right at this moment.

Let

that

energy

lift you.

REBECCA P. COHEN

*"The important thing is not to stop questioning.*
*Curiosity has its own reason for existing."*
ALBERT EINSTEIN

# CURIOSITY

Neutralizes anger

Removes judgment

Connects us

Informs

Lightens and enlightens

Beckons

Inspires

Innovates

Is

Love

REBECCA P. COHEN

# MAY 4

*"It's time to start living the life you've imagined."*

HENRY JAMES

## LESSONS OF MANIFESTING

There is no crystal ball,

only an intention.

Make a wish, blow the dandelion

*whoooooooh …*

and take a small or big step,

in joy or courage.

Then the next, and the next …

give thanks.

You are on your way.

REBECCA P. COHEN

*"He judged the instant and let go; he flung himself loose into the stars ... ."*
ANNIE DILLARD

# NOTICE

The settling in

to what is.

The push and pull

are clear.

My pattern

shows up again.

What will happen

if

I

let

go

?

REBECCA P. COHEN

# MAY 6

*"Anything that excites me for any reason,*
*I will photograph; not searching for unusual subject matter,*
*but making the commonplace unusual."*
EDWARD WESTON

# ZOOM IN

You have to look.

Mist has meaning

in droplets of moisture

Seen

if you observe.

Sunshine.

Daylight

igniting

billions of tiny crystals.

REBECCA P. COHEN

*"Do not now seek the answers, which cannot be given you*
*because you would not be able to live them. … Live the questions now.*
*Perhaps you will then gradually, without noticing it,*
*live along some distant day into the answer."*

RAINER MARIA RILKE

# SURRENDER

As I get older, I have begun to see the freedom in surrendering. Years spent resolutely "driving my bus" whenever, wherever, and however I wanted has taken its toll. My mantra lately is to allow space for change. The tricky part has been realizing that the change I am making space for may not be the change I had envisioned; that I can't determine the terms of my own surrender. True surrender — I am discovering — is trusting that what is coming next is greater than anything I could have dreamed for myself.    It's no cake walk, deciding to surrender to what's next, but it gets easier as I practice, and practice, and practice. I've learned the world does not end if I'm not in charge. And, in fact, it seems to run a little better when I'm following the bread crumb trail to the next bus stop and not worrying about whether the bus will run out of gas or I will forget to brake. All the time I used to spend plotting and planning is now spent watching the horizon and appreciating what I have — a much better way to move through the world.

MARY DOUGHERTY

*"Sell your cleverness and buy bewilderment.*
*Cleverness is mere opinion, bewilderment is intuition."*

RUMI

# LOOK UP

Look around. A simple cessation of physical movement, a pause in our mental checklist creates space for wonder, and connection to the magic that lives within and around us. ✎ I put my garden to bed for the winter yesterday afternoon. Between pulling, cutting and pruning, I spent 30 minutes in full-out wonder at the symmetry and engineering of a milkweed pod. It's perfectly designed to birth and give flight to seeds that ensure its survival into the next year. The beauty and intricacy of something as humble and seemingly ordinary as milkweed is remarkable, and as I watched their seeds interact with the wind and sunlight, I realized, once again, that this world is full of magic.

✎

MARY DOUGHERTY

*"In a hole in the ground there lived a hobbit.*

*Not a nasty, dirty, wet hole, filled with the ends of worms ...*

*with nothing in it to sit down on or to eat:*

*it was a hobbit-hole, and that means comfort."*

J.R.R. TOLKIEN

## LOOK DOWN

Lake Superior has a fantastic way with the weather, and one morning a thick blanket of fog rolled onshore. The photo opportunity quotient was off the charts so I set out to capture a little soggy, foggy magic. The sun burned brighter on my drive to Houghton Falls, and though the sheets of fog were thinning out considerably, I was committed to my photo mission. The shots were bumping around in my head: brownstone cliffs shrouded in fog, pines appearing out of a white sea, ravines filled with mist. Wrong. The breeze picked up and pushed the fog back out to sea. There were no haunting fog photos in my immediate future. ✎ I sat on the trunk of a fallen hemlock near the lake and considered my next steps. I heard rustling and snapping across the stream and saw a large grey squirrel, running full speed across the tree trunk ... right at me. *Wonderful,* I thought, *first no fog and now a maniacal squirrel hell-bent on attacking me.* As I clumsily scrambled out of his way, I tripped and ended up on all fours, face to face with a perfect yellow mushroom. I was so busy chasing fog that I had missed an entire world beneath my feet. Time flew as I spent the next few hours on my hands and knees amongst the inhabitants of the forest floor. ✎ It's good for the soul to spend a few hours bathed in wonderment. It's as easy as looking down, and following the directions of a bossy squirrel.

MARY DOUGHERTY

*"Why, that dog is practically a Phi Beta Kappa. She can sit up and beg,*
*and she can give her paw — I don't say she will but she can."*
DOROTHY PARKER

# A DOG NAMED GEORGE

Like most good things, it happened at the grocery store. We were at a swim meet and I had forgotten to bring the Gatorade, so I hurried to the store, anxious to redeem myself and prove I'm not "that Mom." The doors opened and there it was, a picture of three eight-week-old Labrador retriever puppies. Keeping my redemptive mission in mind, I wrote the phone number down and decided to think about it a bit before I added dog number four to our family. I made it all the way to the cereal aisle before I started dialing.  ≈  Three hours later, we were headed home with a 12-pound yellow Labrador puppy sitting on my lap. The closer to home we got, the more my impulsive puppy purchase seemed a little, shall we say, rash? It really hit home as I pulled into the driveway and realized that there is no way to gracefully introduce a new family member to a husband who isn't into four-legged surprises. Let's just say, it was a very long weekend.  ≈  Six years later and well out of puppy stage, George is a card-carrying member of the Dougherty clan. He arrived on the scene with a fair amount of chaos but I wouldn't change a thing.  ≈  Sometimes those impulsive, seemingly insane decisions work out. You go to the store for Gatorade and come home with a puppy. Some decisions, like finding your perfect canine wingman, are best made with your heart, not your head.

MARY DOUGHERTY

*"It may be that when we no longer know what to do,*
*we have come to our real work and when we no longer know which way to go,*
*we have begun our real journey. The mind that is not baffled is not employed.*
*The impeded stream is the one that sings."*

WENDELL BERRY

# THE LONG WAY AROUND

Who needs a map, when you have an iPhone? You plug your coordinates into the phone and a friendly voice will guide you, step by step, to your final destination. Except when you're looking for a waterfall in the middle of nowhere, without a cell phone tower for miles and only a vague idea of where you are headed. That's when it gets a little tricky. ⤳ My son Will and I started out with Spring Camp Falls as our destination but since we had no idea how to get there and no cell phone service, our route was far from direct. In the midst of our amateur orienteering, we drove through remarkably beautiful country, swapped George (our yellow Lab) stories, bickered about Will's music choices, and breathed the same air in the same space for a little while. We eventually reached our destination and I was so glad we had taken the long way around. ⤳ Choosing an unknown path can be tricky but it reminded me that the moment I think, *I have no idea what the hell I'm doing* is the moment I begin to do exactly what I should be doing. Obstacles are not deal breakers, they are a chance to recalibrate and keep one's eyes peeled for the sign pointing to the next destination. Throwing out the map might be the best thing I've done.

MARY DOUGHERTY

*"Do one thing every day that scares you."*

ELEANOR ROOSEVELT

# THE EDGE OF FEAR

I'm not the biggest fan of any situation that results in heart-pounding, sweaty-palmed, dry-mouthed fear. I usually prefer the sunny side of the street — until some one or some thing pokes me and says it's time to shake things up. Then I charge headlong into uncharted territory with my heart pounding, my palms sweaty, my mouth dry as the Sahara and no one to blame except myself. That's when the rubber hits the road.  Recently, I found myself in front of a crowd of 200 with a page and a half of notes and no idea how I was going to keep from fainting dead away. Turned out that the edge of my fear was the edge of accomplishment. The first five seconds almost brought me to my knees but after opening my mouth to utter the first few words, I settled into a space filled with a sense of competence I didn't know I had. How do we find what's lurking in the shadows of our spirit? By stepping out of our comfortable boundaries and into the murky unknown. Maybe fear is really just a flashlight, illuminating the crevices where our strength lives.

MARY DOUGHERTY

## MAY 13

*" ... when women were birds, there was the simple understanding that to sing at dawn and to sing at dusk was to heal the world through joy. The birds still remember what we have forgotten, that the world is meant to be celebrated."*

TERRY TEMPEST WILLIAMS

# FARE THEE WELL

I composed many letters to my son Jack for his high school graduation, and each time I thought I had it nailed, I would remember one more story I didn't want to be forgotten. How do I sum up nearly 19 years of shared experiences in a meaningful way that isn't 300 pages long? It's an impossible task — our stories inhabit tucked-away artwork, handmade Christmas ornaments, photos of birthdays long past, special baby blankets, and pieces of beach glass. The sheer volume of memories is a testament to the amazing life we've watched unfold before our eyes. ☙ He's the boy who made me a mom for the first time; the three-year-old who played ice golf at the St. Paul Winter Carnival; the six-year-old who lost his tooth on the way to Bayfield and wrote a note so the tooth fairy could find him; the nine-year-old who made a braided jute necklace on Mother's Day; the 12-year-old who, after cleaning out his dinghy on Stockton Island, still let me in the boat with our 140-pound Newfoundland, Guinness; the 16-year-old who worked beside me for the first two years at my restaurant and now, the 19-year-old getting ready to move to Madison. Our shared heartbeat for those precious nine months before he was born and our intertwined paths for the past 19 years transcend the written word. It boils down to this: don't forget to be amazed, astounded and completely bowled over by joy; the rest of it always figures itself out.

MARY DOUGHERTY

*"I must study politics and war that my sons*
*may have liberty to study mathematics and philosophy."*

JOHN ADAMS

# AWAKENING A QUEST FOR JUSTICE

Discrimination rips apart a civil society and damages the soul. In 1954 in *Brown v. Board of Education of Topeka*, Chief Justice Earl Warren wrote that separation of children by race "generates a feeling of inferiority as to their status in the community that may affect their hearts and minds in a way unlikely ever to be undone." That decision energized the modern civil rights movement. ✑ At nine years old, I didn't know about the Supreme Court or understand the meaning of segregation. However, a conversation with my best friend introduced me to the hurt of injustice and motivated me to work for a more just society. ✑ He argued he could not get a haircut at my barber. "Of course you can," I maintained, "Pinky is a good friend." "You don't understand," he proclaimed. "Pinky won't do my hair because I am a Negro." ✑ The difference had never mattered to me. We were classmates and played together. I had eaten at his home and he had been welcome in ours. We were the same. ✑ I felt his pain. Why did it matter that he was a different color? It wasn't fair and certainly wasn't right. In that moment, I felt the dagger of discrimination and pain of prejudice though I couldn't spell the words. My life was changed forever. ✑ I didn't know the barriers to be overcome nor did I have a clear vision of how I was going to change people. All I knew was that I would spend my life trying to make sure that people treat each other as equals. ✑ The challenge remains today, but I have hope. Separate and unequal liberty will perish. United and respectful, the promise of an equal America will prevail.

BOB JAUCH

# MAY 15

*"There is nothing noble in being superior to your fellow men.*

*True nobility lies in being superior to your former self."*

ELIJAH WOOD

# A SUPERIOR ACT OF SPORTSMANSHIP

The winless Superior High School football team lost again but came out of the game learning some of the most important lessons in life. ✎ Vince Lombardi said, "Winning is everything." Apparently, he hadn't met Coach Bob DeMeyer, who taught his players to strive to win, play hard, do their best, and hold their heads high with pride no matter the outcome. ✎ The team was behind 47-14 when the Menomonie coach called a timeout, met with the officials, then walked across the field to speak with Coach Bob. ✎ "We are going to throw a pass to our right end, a young man who has autism. We aren't sure he will catch it, as he has dropped every pass during practice. If he does we hope your boys will be gentle when they tackle him." ✎ "Tackle him," exclaimed the winless Coach who exhibited the supreme act of sportsmanship. "Why don't we let him score?" ✎ He met with his players who lined up for the play. The quarterback threw the pass and the young man caught the ball. Not ever having caught a pass he didn't know what to do until his team-mates encouraged him to run for the goal line. ✎ For 66 yards, Superior players feebly dove at his feet while he ran past them. They were the first to celebrate his touchdown. ✎ A week later at a home game, the team was supported by a packed house of appreciative fans who cheered as if they had won the Super Bowl. With a winless season, these athletes reminded us that playing a game with class leaves a more lasting legacy than the score.

✎

BOB JAUCH

*"Respect is what we owe; love, what we give."*

PHILIP JAMES BAILEY

# SEEKING RESPECT AND MAKING A DIFFERENCE

I visited a 7th grade special education class to teach students about government, and left inspired by their appeal for government to eliminate hurtful words in outdated laws. "We are tired of being called retards by others who do not know us. It is a hurtful word and we would like you to pass a law getting rid of the term *mental retardation*." They only wanted what everyone else desires, to be accepted for who they are. "We know we are different but we believe we are special," they told me. I agreed with their hopes: hurtful words like *imbecile* and *retard* were dehumanizing and not acceptable in our society. "We need to change the law," I encouraged them. "However, we must remain mindful that changing a word won't necessarily change the cruel way in which some treat others." I emphasized that each of us are unique and we should use our gifts to be better and to make a difference; that they should be proud of who they are, "You may not be able to change everyone in life, but each of us can take small steps to make meaningful improvements to help in the lives of others." They were smarter than their years. They knew that bullying would continue; however they were not going to wait for someone else to correct a wrong. They stood tall and took it upon themselves to be architects for change, believing that changing the law can help to change attitudes. The law was changed and "mental retardation" was removed. The students proudly attended the signing ceremony. In seeking to respect difference, they made a difference.

BOB JAUCH

*"It is easier to build strong children than to repair broken men."*

FREDERICK DOUGLASS

# A CHILD'S GAZE FOR PEACE

The stillness was broken by Buddhists humming prayers for peace. ∿ It was January 16, 1991; the world was on the verge of war in Kuwait. As the leader of state lawmakers, I presented flowers at the Hiroshima Peace Memorial established in memory of the nuclear horrors and to advocate world peace. ∿ Having just completed a sobering tour through the museum, I felt a deep sadness for the suffering of thousands of men, women, and children who were innocent victims of the virtual destruction of their city. Walking through the museum left a profound impact on me. The photos gave life to those who perished, and meaning to their suffering. I heard the echo of their pain and their fervent plea for peace. ∿ The museum told a story that did not place blame. It was designed to show respect and renew a cause for a more peaceful world. Japanese citizens live in the shadows of nuclear aftershock — it is no wonder that they maintain such a passion for peace. ∿ World leaders had drawn a "hard line in the sand" for the next day at 5:00 p.m., promising to expel Iraq forces from Kuwait. As we stood in a place with a dark past we worried about the dark clouds of war. ∿ My attention focused upon a young child kneeling next to her mother. Her look of innocence has inspired me to always commit to making a difference in the lives of children whose faces I will never see. She remains nameless to me but the memory of her continues to motivate me to serve a cause, making life better for our children's children and their children too.

BOB JAUCH

*"I learned compassion from being discriminated against.*
*Everything bad that's ever happened to me has taught me compassion."*
ELLEN DEGENERES

# COMPASSION IS NOT A SIN

We live in the United States of a deeply divided America, polarized by politics, separated by economic opportunity, and fearful of a world in conflict. ✑ Too many feel powerless and lack a sense of hope for themselves and their children's future. ✑ Amidst the turbulence there is a need to scale seemingly impossible peaks and cross the political and economic gulfs that divide us. ✑ We need to renew a sense of purpose that guides us to work for the common good. Working for the betterment of others is not a spiritual goal, it is a social prerogative. ✑ We stand on the shoulders of others who sacrificed for our good and we owe the next generation and their children dedication to the value that we are stewards of their future. ✑ I was privileged to meet the Dalai Lama who is one of the world's most influential leaders. He encourages us to look within and find the means to affect lives for the better. ✑ It was a magical moment. I was uplifted by his smile and energized by his gentle touch. His inner peace inspired me to discover mine. Spending only 30 seconds with him renewed my spirit and restored my sense of hope. ✑ Looking into his eyes, I grabbed both his hands and said, "Thank you for reminding us that compassion is not a sin." ✑ He beamed with the love that makes the world whole.

BOB JAUCH

*"I am not bound to win but I am bound to be true.*
*I am not bound to succeed but I am bound to live by the light that I have.*
*I must stand with anybody that stands right and stand with him while he is right."*
ABRAHAM LINCOLN

## CROSSING THE LINE

In 1840, Abraham Lincoln jumped from a second story window to stop a vote. As president, he was soundly criticized for his courageous leadership, yet today he is admired as one of America's most beloved presidents.  Four years ago, little did my 13 Democratic colleagues and I know that when we went to Illinois to prevent passage of anti-worker legislation in Wisconsin we would live by Lincoln's words and actions. Our departure from Wisconsin meant there would be too few lawmakers to take a vote on issues that the people had not fully weighed in on. The decision was not easy but we took a stand for a cause that was just and right.  We didn't leave our state to weaken democracy, we left to strengthen it. We figuratively and literally crossed lines to give citizens a chance to exercise their voices and allow democracy work in a process that seemed destined to ignore it  It was a painful ordeal. Our beloved state was bitterly divided. Our critics called us cowards and demanded we return. Despite intimidating phone calls and threats to recall us from office, we felt obligated to stand firm to protect principles far more valuable than our own political success.  Our decision to risk our political future lit a candle, and hundreds of thousands of citizens carried the torch of justice to protest the assault on workers. Sadly, their voices were ignored by a majority deaf to reason and fairness.  Worker rights were diminished but infinite hope will sustain us.

BOB JAUCH

*"Love consists in this, that two solitudes protect and touch and greet each other."*

RAINER MARIA RILKE

## MY MOTHER'S FINAL JOURNEY

It was a good day to die, with the autumn trees glowing and the sun shining. It had been an unexpectedly long journey. Two weeks earlier my mother said, "I am going to die today" but it was just the beginning of a process, one she faced with grace and humor. ✎ Sustained by sips of water she remained comfortable and frequently asked, "What time will they pick me up? Are you going to drop me off? What time does this show get going? Why is this taking so long?" and, "How do I get in?" ✎ Each morning she lifted her arms for hugs, greeting the nurses with a smile. Those loving individuals were her angels. ✎ My mother wore beautiful moccasins. On her chest was an eagle feather attached to a red healing bag containing sage, cedar, tobacco and sweet grass. Once she raised the feather toward heaven in an attempt to guide her spirit. ✎ She brought me into this world and I was blessed to support her departure. At the moment my mother's breathing slowed, my wife was miles away reading to students about the completion of the cycle of life. "Freddie the leaf landed on the snow … he was more comfortable than he ever known. He closed his eyes and fell asleep … he would join with the water and serve to make the tree strong." ✎ At that same moment my mother died, her spirit traveled to the place created for beautiful souls. She faced south, viewed by Native Americans as the source of life. She was my source, my tree, my strength. ✎ Her evening had come; a union with the mystery and power of life.

BOB JAUCH

# MAY 21

# POLAR VORTEX

NEWS FROM THE FRONT: We braved last winter's arctic blast — the coldest weather in a century — living in wall tents and wigwams in the rugged Penokee Hills of north-western Wisconsin. We're occupying Iron County public land to stop a billionaire coal baron from West Virginia from digging a 22-mile-long open pit mine in our water-rich territory.  ≋  We kept from freezing by burning dry, hard rock maple in our woodstoves, ate lots of wild rice, deer meat, and squash, hauled water from artesian springs, and played cribbage at night. Except for kerosene light and candles, the only lights within several miles were the moon and stars. During our seasons in the bush we made birch bark baskets with Melvin Gasper, gathered wild rice with Larry Ackley, sang songs of praise and swam in Tyler Forks. We built a relationship with Rusty "bear whisperer" Buck, a fifth generation Finnlander logger and our Iron County neighbor.  ≋  One -37° degree morning was so cold that spilled coffee exploded before it hit the ground. We put out suet for the birds, and within moments a flock of chickadees arrived. They shared the food, contented and happy near the wild heart of life.

≋

NICK VANDER PUY

*"The world begins at a kitchen table.*
*No matter what, we must eat to live."*

JOY HARJO

# SWEET VICTORY

NEWS FROM THE FRONT: Sitting around the Odevero-Koosman farm kitchen this morning, savoring the last caramel sticky buns and speaking of aha moments during the fight to save the Penokee hills, Pete Russo, Chair of the Ashland County Board asked, "Do you remember when we first met?" I said, "You betcha. Joe Rose and I almost got into fisticuffs with you at a mining impact committee meeting at the Ashland County courthouse. And I remember, when you came into the hallway afterwards, I might have started a bare knuckle match, but with tears in your eyes, you told me you'd found out a week earlier your grandmother was Mohican. And you'd learned that her name was Morning Star Woman."  ⮜  Right at that moment I knew we were going to be victorious stopping this Penokee mountain top removal.

⮜

NICK VANDER PUY

# MAY 23

*"Redemption lives in knowing*
*that you might also hear our hymns of joy when we too*
*marry ourselves to the earth."*

ROBIN WALL KIMMERER

## RICING

NEWS FROM THE FRONT: Scouting a wild rice lake this morning. Last night we slept in the car at the landing. An eagle flies by as we launch the canoe. The plants are flowering, which usually means we can harvest in another ten days or so. Two trumpeter swans launch as we enter the bay. Some mud hens and rice birds clatter ahead. The water levels are excellent for access. A muskie surfaces as we check out a site for rice camp. It is so good to be alive on a wild rice lake in late August.

NICK VANDER PUY

*"It is time for all the heroes to go home*
*if they have any; time for all of us common ones*
*to locate ourselves by the real things*
*we live by."*

WILLIAM STAFFORD

# WILD TEA

NEWS FROM THE FRONT: Motoring back today from the Iron County finance meeting in Hurley, Wisconsin, Clif "Papa Smurf" Gann and I hung a right (north) on Upson Lake Road. We were the first vehicle on the fresh snowfall. We cut into some fresh fox tracks paralleling the road for more than a half mile, then pulled into the artesian well just before the Upson Lake landing. About 100 gallons per minute of the finest water on earth gushes from an eight-inch pipe leading down to the creek. Magical events happen at this artesian well and have been happening here for millennia. Right now we're sipping on chaga and wild ginger tea made with this elixir. We are rich beyond compare.

NICK VANDER PUY

# MAY 25

*"The mist was all gone from the river now
and the rapids sparkled and sang. They were still young as the land was young.
We were there to enjoy it, and the great machines seemed far away."*

SIGURD F. OLSON

## MAKWA

NEWS FROM THE FRONT: Our occupation in the Penokees raised awareness about the destruction which would occur from Penokee mountaintop removal. We revealed Treaties between the Lake Superior Chippewa and the federal government that remain a bulwark against destruction of our motherland. The legal concept of ceded territory is something the mine barons hadn't rubbed up against until now. We are the stronghold.  ⋚  Last night a smallish white *makwa* (bear) visited my dream life. We got down on all fours together, played and wrestled. Light biting. This morning when we rose, we hiked into Brownstone Falls at Copper Falls State Park near Mellen. It is even more extravagantly beautiful in the winter. Some of the fringe ice looks like white coral.

⋚

NICK VANDER PUY

## MAY 26

*"Eagle calls and bone whistles echo among lanyards of black ash
intertwined with cedar. Wolves, bear, turtles and cranes watch
from the four directions. She takes her first step. It's spring."*

MIKE WIGGINS, JR.


# SIGN

NEWS FROM THE FRONT: We made a pilgrimage today to Grant's Point on Madeline Island (*Mooningwanekaaning-Minis*). We drove the ice road with hundreds of other cars. First stop was the small tribal park near the marina.  When artist Janet Moore walked out on the beach at the public landing on Grant's Point, she gazed across the barren channel ice toward Long Island, Houghton Point, and the Penokees and said, "This is a place that can rip your heart out." I thought about taking her over to meet my old chum Johnny Ruff on Ruff Road, but gazing ahead, sitting with a red blanket over his shoulders, in wool pants and mukluks near a maple tree, was the wizard himself. There was Johnny Ruff, meditating on the scene, his mind on eternity. I gave him tobacco. He didn't recognize me at first, then his piercing blue eyes focused with a gentle smile, "You know, Nick," he said, "I saw deer eating maple buds this morning. When the sugar starts coming up that's the first thing they do." We caught up on old times.

NICK VANDER PUY

*"We now enter a straight 25 miles in length, full of islands, then proceed to a rapids ...*
*We make cottages and learn the truth of what the wildmen say — that once we arrive,*
*we should make good cheer of the fish they call assikmack, or whitefish."*

PIERRE-ESPRIT RADISSON

# ADIKIMEG

I am a poor fisherman, living off the products of this great inland sea.   When my father, Sgt. William Van Der Puy (USMC), came back to his hometown Sheboygan, Wisconsin after the Korean War, he left Camp Pendleton, got on a train in San Diego, California and pulled into the depot in Sheboygan.   During the war he dreamt about coming home and fishing for perch on Lake Michigan off the North Pier, so he did just that. Still wearing his military khakis, he walked down to Stockinger's bait shop on Ontario Avenue. He purchased two cane poles, some #6 Eagle Claw hooks, a minnow bucket, and several dozen shiners for bait.   He fished for perch every day for two weeks. He'd put them in a wicker creel, scale them in the kitchen, get some hot grease going in a black, cast iron fry pan, bread the perch with flour, and make a fish fry. When he didn't catch perch he'd stop by the fish shanties in the harbor and purchase some whitefish.   He'd serve these fish on a red and black tablecloth to his parents, John and Dena Van Der Puy, and his girlfriend, Betty Ann Esser. I'm sure they enjoyed some potatoes, coleslaw and some frosty brown bottles of Kingsbury beer, too.   About a year later I was born. I am made of fish.

NICK VANDER PUY

*"The family is the nucleus of civilization."*

WILL DURANT

## FAMILY PHOTO

We had been in India for nearly three weeks when we went to visit a very rural village. Most of the men had left this particular village in search of work in the cities and never returned. The women, children, and remaining men were highly self-sustaining with small mud huts for houses, gardens to grow their own food, some electricity, and big, very big, smiles.  ≈  It was 2008 and this was the first time these villagers had met people from a country other than their own. The big attraction turned out to be our digital cameras. No one in the village had ever seen a picture of themselves, and thanks to the digital camera's ability to show pictures instantly on the viewfinder, this became entertainment for the evening.  ≈  I was invited into a woman's home, and after showing me around the two small rooms that comprised her entire house, she asked me to take a picture of her and her two teen children. She stood between them with a huge smile on her face and I took the photo. When I showed it to her, she stared at it for a long time and pointed, smiling at the likeness of her children and herself. Her eyes then welled up with tears. The pride in her eyes is something I will never forget. It struck me that of all of the things we take for granted, family photos throughout life are certainly one of them. I left that evening forever changed, forever and newly grateful for so many things.

≈

JEN FANUCCI

*"It is not in the stars to hold our destiny but in ourselves."*

WILLIAM SHAKESPEARE

# LEAVING INDIA FOR THE FIRST TIME

It was the end of our tour in India. The leadership group I had been learning from and growing with for nearly two years had allowed me to live out my dream of visiting India. We were about to spend our final days along the Bay of Bengal. The entire trip had been a dream: the sights, the smells, and so many moments had changed each one of us in deep and indescribable ways. ⮜ We exited the airport at our final destination in Chennai and a familiar, smiling face greeted us. A tour guide from earlier in the trip had decided to meet us for our last few days. This person, from the first moment we met, was someone I could not imagine being without; a pull that can't be described. There was something I was to learn from him or needed from him. Or was it simply India? Had she taken hold of me? ⮜ The last morning came and we sat as a group discussing favorite moments in this foreign land and our feelings about going home. The entire trip had overwhelmed me but at the same time made me feel more at home than anywhere I had ever visited. I tried to explain my feelings to the group but instead I wept. Separating from India seemed an impossible task. I knew deep inside that I had more to learn and experience. Something told me that my life was completely altered — a strange, wonderful, and terrifying feeling. ⮜ It would be several years and many life changes before I returned to India and to the tour guide who would become, over time, my closest friend. Both would prove vital in setting the stage for an entirely new life.

JEN FANUCCI

*"One of the secrets of life is that all that is really worth the doing*
*is what we do for others."*

LEWIS CARROLL

# TAJ MAHAL

Her name was Anne, from Duluth, Minnesota. She saw my flyer in a café advertising a "Once in a Lifetime Trip to India." She called the number I had posted and we arranged to meet at an Indian restaurant in downtown Duluth. The next day she signed up for the tour. She told me later that the fact that I asked her to meet me for Indian food had won her heart. ✎ This was my first attempt at trying out a new life. It had been three years since I had been to India but it had never left my soul. With help from a tour guide friend from those days, we made all the arrangements for a fantastic trip. As it turned out, Anne would be the only one on the tour: my first client, and first one to put her trust and faith in me. I arrived in India ahead of her and once she joined us and we took off down the road, it was magic. We took a road trip, just the four of us: my guide friend, Anne, our driver, and me. Anne expressed to me that visiting the Taj Mahal before she turned 60 was number one on her lifelong list. We were a few years ahead of schedule but that didn't matter. When we reached the Taj Mahal, Anne stood in awe and wept. A dream, a true dream, had come true. Until that moment, I never could have imagined how it would feel to witness and help in this way. The word "gift" isn't enough. I was hooked.

JEN FANUCCI

# MAY 31

*"I have noticed even people who claim everything is predestined*
*and that we can do nothing to change it,*
*look before they cross the road."*

STEPHEN HAWKING

# NEW DELHI

I stayed in India after my first tour with a client, wanting to see if it was truly the place for me. I left my husband at home, took a small apartment in Delhi, and for nearly two months, just let life take me. The experience of traveling with someone who had never been to India and who put her faith in me was still ringing in my heart. I played with the local children; learned to cook from the housewives who lived next to me; survived taking bucket showers each morning; went to temple and prayed; and spent time exploring the bustling city of New Delhi, and myself. I wasn't to have children, so it seemed, and my husband was doing battle with his own changes so I saw no harm in exploring a new life. I immersed myself in this culture. I shopped at the local markets, made my own food and lived like a local in this vibrant city. The travel bug had taken hold. I could no longer live in one small town any longer. There was just too much life in the world. I returned home to announce it was time for a separation. I had decided, as I explained to him, that at this point we needed to save our friendship, since things had just kept getting worse. We had both made mistakes and I had made some big ones. It was time to help each other, as we had always done, to find out what we really wanted in life. I had put a life change into motion and there was no turning back.

JEN FANUCCI

# JUNE

*"Freedom lies in being bold."*
ROBERT FROST

# FREEDOM

The car was packed with a few of my belongings. The rest would be put into storage. My husband had mapped out my route from northern Wisconsin to Bellingham, Washington where my family lived. It was decided I would leave before our wedding anniversary and I pushed it to just one day before. I was to take a solo road trip across the country and make the most of it by visiting national parks along the way. I was about to leave it all behind: cats, dog, house, gardens, community, and best friend, following the plan to spend time with my family and see how things felt. I fell to the ground and wept, my legs just gave out under me. I had changed my mind but he looked at me and told me it was time to go. ✑ I took my amazing solo road trip and was eventually served with divorce papers. Over three years, I worked jobs for a few months at a time, not knowing what else to do or where I belonged. I worked on a mountain in Colorado, and as a tour guide and driver across the expanse of the country. I led a small group tour to France and went to my dream place of Tuscany on a solo adventure. I washed dishes in a busy casino and then finally booked a ticket back to India. For nearly two years now, I have traveled through India and Nepal. Once something is put into motion, the entire universe helps keep you on that path if it is truly in your heart. My husband gave me a gift that day when he insisted I drive away. A gift of freedom. It was up to me to decide what to do with it.

✑

JEN FANUCCI

*"A person often meets his destiny on the road he took to avoid it."*

JEAN DE LA FONTAINE

# A NIGHT FIRE

She was a twenty-something woman from Germany with a lifetime of abuse: verbal, physical and sexual. She had come to India to put it all behind her, to find a way to heal. We met by chance while having chai at a café on the banks of the Ganges River. We talked for hours and enjoyed meeting over a few months. We were two women trying to move on in new ways. Different ages, different countries, different pain. Alone in India, but together — one woman. She was working with a guru and yogi, and went every day for a month or more to sweat out her pain and past. She had purple wool pants that she wore religiously at each and every practice and meditation. One day, she brought them to me, telling me they held all of her past pain. She wanted to give them to me, to let the pain go. I took them from her and held them for a only a moment when she began to cry and said she wasn't ready. I handed them back.   One evening, a few weeks later, she called and asked me to meet her at a private spot along the river bank, explaining that she needed my help. I met her that night and in the dark she took my hand. We walked silently to a spot she had chosen where she dug a hole in the sand, got a candle and lighter from her backpack, and pulled out the purple pants. She looked at me with her strong, intensely loving eyes, hugged me tightly, and together we lit those pants on fire.

JEN FANUCCI

*"Throw your dreams into space like a kite, and you do not know what it will bring back,*
*a new life, a new friend, a new love, a new country."*

ANAÏS NIN

# A GUAVA FRUIT

Traveling as a solo female throughout India has had its fair share of challenges as well as beautiful, life-changing moments. For some time, I've stayed in an apartment in a little community within the amazingly diverse city of Delhi. On Christmas Day 2014, a gift was given to me. It was given by a bicycle rickshaw driver. This man had taken to keeping me safe since I moved to the neighborhood. He didn't speak English but since meeting me, he tries. We have had several attempts at Hindi-English over the few months I've been here. Whenever I see him, he acknowledges me, and if I'm walking he simply doesn't allow me to, even if I tell him I want to walk.  ◈  He has missing teeth, wears one pair of socks with flip flops, even on the coldest days, and luckily has an old, warm coat and hat. I know his struggles by now; they are not uncommon.  ◈  On Christmas Eve, I was walking to the metro — not a long walk — but it was cold and he saw me. He insisted I get on his rickshaw and dropped me off near the metro stop. When I reached to pay him, he waved "no" and instead he took, out of his bicycle basket and wrapped in a cloth, a guava fruit. He handed it to me, smiled, and simply said, "Christmas." There could not have been a greater gift. Life is a constant struggle, for all of us. This gift and this man reminded me why I have chosen my path. Kindness and unexpected life-transforming moments are everywhere.

JEN FANUCCI

*"Don't go around saying the world owes you a living.*
*The world owes you nothing. It was here first."*

MARK TWAIN

# RIPPLES IN QUARTZITE

When I was a child, I wondered why there are so many different kinds of rocks. It wasn't until years later, during my first geology course in college, that I would finally get some answers. It was thrilling to learn how the Earth operates, but it seemed that rock samples in the laboratory were incomplete fragments of something much bigger. It wasn't until my first geology field trip, late in the semester on a cold, gray April day near Gouverneur, New York, that I understood the larger story of rocks. I put my magnifier lens up to the rock outcrop to study it in detail — it was light gray and composed of an infinite number of shiny little quartz grains. They had been deposited together as sand then gradually converted into sandstone and eventually compressed into quartzite, the hardest rock of all. I had seen quartzites in geology laboratories before and knew they held interesting stories, but wasn't prepared for what I saw next.  I hopped up onto a ledge at the base of a tall cliff and immediately noticed that the rock surface was rippled with narrow ridges about an inch tall. The ripples were exactly like the ones in the sand at the beach today. I knelt down to put my hands on the ripples and realized I was touching an ancient beach of the past. When I noticed that the ripples disappeared into the mountain of quartzite, I realized this surface provided just one tiny glimpse into Earth's unimaginably long history, and that I had started a fascinating journey of my own.

TOM FITZ

*"Look up at the stars and not down at your feet.*
*Try to make sense of what you see,*
*and wonder about what makes the universe exist.*
*Be curious."*

STEPHEN HAWKING

# CORAL ON A MOUNTAIN

By the time I graduated from college I had studied the granite on all the tallest hilltops of New Hampshire, but I had not seen an outcrop of limestone until I hiked in the Rocky Mountains of Montana during a geology field camp. When I reached the top of Sacagawea peak in the Bridger Mountains north of Bozeman, I looked out over a spectacular landscape very different than the one I had grown up studying in New England. The forest was thin, the water was scarce, and there was no granite in sight. The rocks were mostly limestone.　　I reached down and picked up a sample of the light-gray rock that made up the long, rugged ridge. Sticking out of the rock was a beautiful coral as large as my hand — so perfect that it looked like it was from a modern reef. I studied the coral with my lens and then looked out at the Bridger Mountains and realized what had to have happened to that coral. There it was in my hand, a coral that had lived on an ocean floor, now 9665 feet above sea level, more than 600 miles from the sea. The coral was still and silent, the mountains were huge, seemingly permanent features, but there it was in the rock, a coral on a mountain top, clearly telling a story of unimaginable change.

TOM FITZ

*"The sky is filled with stars, invisible by day."*
HENRY WADSWORTH LONGFELLOW

# LIFE AND DEATH IN LIMESTONE

I was nervous the first time I led two vans full of students west to study the rocks in Wyoming. I was excited about my first job teaching a geology field camp, but I was recovering from a case of Lyme disease that had shaken my thinking on health and life and death. I was not as strong as I had hoped to be, but was savoring the fact that I could at least hike again. Near the end of a long day in the field, I sat alone on a gravel bank above a dry stream bed. Between my boots was a small limestone pebble with the imprint of a shell. I picked up the pebble and saw that the entire rock was made of shells — hundreds of shells all together in one pebble that fit in the palm of my hand. I had studied fossils before, but had never thought about the lives of the individual creatures that had lived and died so long ago. If it had taken hundreds of animals to make one small pebble, then how many animals did it take to make a mountain of limestone? Each shell represents a life; an animal that lived, ate, mated, and eventually died on the ocean floor, its shell adding to a growing layer of limestone. Mine is just one more short life, but it is part of a beautiful ongoing dance between organisms and Earth that provides the materials for life. It was comforting to know that although my life is small, it is part of a big, ongoing story. I am fortunate to have this moment, to be part of — and to partially understand — Earth's evolving story.

TOM FITZ

*"Men love to wonder, and that is the seed of science."*
RALPH WALDO EMERSON

## UNTOLD STORIES

We stopped the vans and got out to study the rocks in the narrow canyon just west of Cody, Wyoming. The rocks above our heads were layers of sandstone. The form of their layers indicated they had been deposited by water flowing over Earth's surface long ago. The rock at the bottom of the cliff was strikingly different though. It had a variety of bright pink and shiny gray crystals very different than the earthen tones of the brown sandstone above. The rock on the bottom was granite — the result of slow solidification of molten rock deep in the Earth, yet the sandstone on top must have been deposited at Earth's surface. We had seen both of these rocks elsewhere and learned their separate histories, but had not considered their stories in one narrative. The connection was there along the line where the two different rocks came in contact. The top of the granite was crumbly and weathered — a sure sign that it had been exposed to the elements, then buried under miles of sandstone. So whatever rock had existed above the granite originally had been stripped away by erosion and replaced by sandstone. But what had been stripped away? That rock was missing, gone from the rock record. A seemingly infinite number of pages of Earth's narrative had been torn out, leaving nothing but questions about what might have happened in that vast amount of time. We can read from the rock record a story of dramatic changes, but we'll never know the whole story, and that mystery just adds to its beauty.

TOM FITZ

*"The real problem is not whether machines think but whether men do."*

B. F. SKINNER

# POWDER RIVER COAL

The mine geologist told us that the Marion 8200 walking dragline shovel is the largest land-based machine in the world. It could reach out in a circle that encompassed six acres and rip up 100 tons of shale without hesitation. It worked 24 hours per day, stripping the thick layer of shale overburden off the coal seam and setting it aside so the coal could be mined. The hole that the dragline was digging was so long that trucks at the far end of the pit were tiny dots on the horizon. At the bottom of the pit was a 100-foot-thick layer of the blackest rock I had ever seen. It was a thick coal deposit in the 50-million-year-old Fort Union Formation in Wyoming's expansive Powder River Basin. The scale of the operation was mind-boggling and changing Earth's surface more rapidly than any geologic action I had ever witnessed. Although the shale overburden was to be re-leveled as Earth's surface, the coal's fate was very different. It was being loaded onto trains that traveled to power plants all over the country where it would be burned to generate electricity. The coal was an accumulation of an unimaginable number of ancient plants — ferns and forests that had captured the energy of the sun — buried and stored as beautiful black coal for millions of years. The coal would not be rock much longer though, soon it would be gas, mostly water vapor and carbon dioxide that would play a very different role on the planet than it had for 50 million years. ✺ I had studied the remnants of thousands of dramatic changes on Earth, but the story I saw in the coal mine was a change unlike any I had read in rock before.

## TOM FITZ

# JUNE 9

## IMPACT

We stopped at Hillcrest Park in downtown Thunder Bay, Ontario and climbed onto an outcrop of very odd limestone. Bill Addison, a science teacher who lived down the street, met us there to tell a remarkable story. Parts of the rock were regular limestone, but scattered within it was a myriad of little spheres and a conglomeration of many different rocks piled together randomly. The rock had been a mystery for years until Bill, examining it under a microscope, found an oddly fractured grain of quartz. Fractures like that tell a specific story because they can only be created by one process: a direct hit by a meteorite. Bill told us that hundreds of miles away in Sudbury, Ontario is one of the largest impact craters on Earth, and it is exactly the same age as the odd limestone layers in Hillcrest Park. Bill's story spread through the geologic community rapidly and together, he and other scientists revealed a detailed story of catastrophic change. The impact at Sudbury, 1.85 billion years ago and among Earth's largest known impacts, blasted a hole miles deep and threw melted rock into the atmosphere where it collected into little spheres that blasted across a vast area. Then a tsunami half a mile high ripped up the rocks of the ocean floor and threw them around like little blocks. The blast went around the globe, and in an instant the world was changed.  ✎  Much of Earth's story is one of slow change over vast amounts of time, but that is not the only way the planet can change. A lot has happened here, and not all of it has been peaceful.

TOM FITZ

# JUNE 10

# TOGETHER AT THE END OF THE DAY

The first day of mapping at a geology field camp was at Sheep Mountain in Wyoming where ancient layers of rock are in the shape of giant folds sticking up out of the desert. It is a geologic showcase containing nearly every lesson in the science; a geology textbook wide open in the vast space of Wyoming's landscape. The students spread out over the land, nervous that their classroom learning was inadequate preparation for the day's assignment of reading the Earth's story on their own. I watched from the top of a ridge and could tell from their travels that the rocks were guiding their journey, that they were asking the right questions and were headed in the right direction toward the answers. I knew from my previous studies in the region that one day was insufficient time to read the whole story, but was enough to start them on their own journey reading Earth's story.

Near the end of the day, I watched from a distance as they turned from their geologic questions and hiked back to meet at the van. I hiked down the ridge to be there and experience their excitement as they traded stories about their own revelations like those I had experienced in the field so many times. We stood together on gravel that was full of fossil shells telling the stories of creatures that lived their lives and passed a changed world to their offspring, just as we are doing today. We are all connected because we happen to share this small moment in time, and because we share a common past of unimaginable change.

TOM FITZ

*"Poetry arrived in search of me."*

PABLO NERUDA

# SAVED BY A POEM

Many years ago, I found myself plagued by the worst imaginable insomnia. Night upon night I watched the hands on that clock tick. And tick again. Night after night after week. The weeks piling up. More than a month. Then close to two months. No sleep. It seemed inhuman. I wouldn't survive. I knew I wouldn't survive, but I did. Worked all day. Slept not at all at night. The panic was thick. 〜 Nothing I tried, took, or did gave me peace. And then, weeks into this impregnable nightmare, I remembered how it felt to be a girl with a poem on her lap. I'd not written poems for years. I wasn't a "real" poet. I had no right to write poems. 〜 But I knew, instinctively, that the poems would save me. 〜 And so I took up a pen. And it was the soothing stitch of language that saved me. This calmer place where my thoughts went. 〜 The war my mind was having with my mind began to ease. The knots of my despair untangled. A word here, a line there, a thought, a dream, a daze — until I woke that dawn in my downstairs chair, half a poem on my lap. 〜 I had slept. I had put myself to sleep by creating, within me, a calm place for calm words. 〜 Poems and stories have saved me in that way ever since. Even when, as is often the case, I'm the only one who reads them.

BETH KEPHART

*"Fortunately ... the great, significant, splendid impulse for beauty*
*can force its way through every boundary."*

ROBERT HENRI

# FOUR ORANGE CALLA LILIES

In a long, white winter of ice, I needed sun. My husband was at the pottery studio. The house was still. I had been working, as I do. I stood. Left the computer. Left the house. I returned, a few hours later, with calla lilies — four stalks of peachy orange. I returned with a bottle of wine, two new cookbooks, a few ingredients, the resolve to try something new. I returned, in other words, in a brand-new mood, and the day (so previously solemn, so previously still) became a day I owned, a day I will remember, a day that went from still to lived.

BETH KEPHART

*"Three things in human life are important.*
*The first is to be kind. The second is to be kind.*
*And the third is to be kind."*

HENRY JAMES

# IN THE AFTERMATH OF A TWISTED FACT

So I wrote a story for a newspaper and I got a key fact wrong. Or — I'd done my research and those I believed were in the know remembered something one way when it might have been remembered another. ✎ The story got printed. ✎ Several days later I received a phone call. ✎ The person on the other end was not insulting, not irate, not castigating. She was, indeed, one of the kindest souls I'd ever encountered. A woman with the grace to thank me for the story, then to update me on that swervy fact. She laughed the error off. She sent me a small gift. We began a correspondence, which I daresay has become a friendship — and all because I got something wrong. ✎ Imagine if we could do this for others — offer up gifts and friendship instead of anger in the aftermath of a twisted fact.

BETH KEPHART

*"But where sympathy is reborn, life is reborn."*
VINCENT VAN GOGH

# OUR MEASURE AS HUMAN BEINGS

Think of all the things that can throw us out of ourselves, out of our own lives. Fear of being eclipsed. Fear of being unheard. Fear of being second rate. Fear of never being welcomed by the established, ultra-fine, (self-anointed?) elite. ⤳ I, a writer, battle these fears. I go to war with them. And then I remember this: our measure, as human beings, is not the number of prizes won or the number of books written or the number of gadgets sold or the number of newspaper inches our lives have been given. ⤳ Our measure, as human beings, is the number of times we actually stepped outside of ourselves and lived bright. Our measure is how gracefully we stretch our arms, also our hearts, toward another.

⤳

BETH KEPHART

# JUNE 15

*"Let France have good mothers, and she will have good sons."*

NAPOLEON BONAPARTE

## CHILD OF MY HEART

I had a hard knock. I lost my footing. I went into my own quiet swirl of — what is the word? — timidity, I suppose. The world seeming more angular and aggressive. The weather feeling personally spiteful. The long days like lost time. ⤜ The only way to heal, I ultimately knew, was to spend more time in the company of the boy, now a man, who has, since the day he was born, calmed me. I just wanted to see him. I just wanted to laugh when he did. The dark chocolate eyes of my son. I needed to see them. ⤜ I did.

⤜

BETH KEPHART

*"There's open space. Enter it."*

NATALIE GOLDBERG

# HE REACHED FOR HER

In a room of a dozen writing souls, in an old house on an Ivy League campus, a boy reached across the table for the hand of the newest student and called her brave. ⮌ In that one instant, a community was forged. ⮌ We were bound, we were whole, from there on out.

⮌

BETH KEPHART

# JUNE 17

*"More light!"*

JOHANN WOLFGANG VON GOETHE

## SHINE

Just these words, then:

Live bright.

BETH KEPHART

*"If you do not wish to be prone to anger, do not feed the habit;*

*give it nothing which may tend to its increase."*

EPICTETUS

# ANGER AND ONIONS

I watched the knife descend in apparent slow motion. The blood that followed looked like an homage to a B-rated horror film. In that moment, I realized that I had forgotten. I had forgotten all that I had learned about anger and people. I had forgotten the moment, years ago, when I learned about the power of choice, and ownership of rage. ✎ I was a young teacher. In a meeting, the principal said something outrageous and painful and I stewed over it for days. I stomped. I moaned. And I told my story over and over, each time nurturing my anger, encouraging it to grow. ✎ Then wisdom stepped in. ✎ A senior member of the history department, who had taught for decades in Asia, pulled me aside. "There's a proverb that states, 'Those who anger you, control you.'" Gently he continued, "You have been carrying this issue for days, and I can assure you that he hasn't thought about it since. Put it down. Take back your power." ✎ So I practiced, over and over, for years. I learned how to recognize my anger and set it aside. ✎ But then, I forgot. I forgot that a true practice must be well practiced. ✎ A passive-aggressive comment had been thrown my way, and instead of dodging it, I caught it. I reached out, trapped it to my chest, and held on. Tightly. As I squeezed, I encouraged my anger to grow. While I was slicing onions. ✎ When we forget what we know, it comes at a cost. Luckily, mine did not require stitches. So I was gently taught. Again. Our power comes from being the stillness, and releasing anger to the winds.

✎

EMILY MCMASON

*"There are two ways of spreading light:*
*to be the candle or the mirror that reflects it."*

EDITH WHARTON

# FIREFLIES

The moon rose up over the end of the day as I sat on the beach, reflecting on the water's lessons — for my daughter learning to swim, and for me learning to dive.  It could be a coincidence that we had set aside fear and relaxed into the unknown, trusting ourselves. But it wasn't. Because on this vacation we were surrounded by fireflies. Tiny little beacons of unconditional love. People who are our magic light, around whom we believe in ourselves just a little bit more.  How do we find them? They hide in all sorts of places. Family. Friends. Distant relations. Even sometimes in casual acquaintances. I don't think it's about searching. It isn't about looking at all.  It's about listening. Listening to the in-between-ness.  In the middle of conversations, what's going on in our heads? *What are they thinking? Will they judge me? Laugh at me? Think I'm a fool?* These are the crickets. Chirping too loudly. Let them go.  But when we are with someone, and in between the words we speak is stillness? When all we hear in the pauses is silence? Those are the sounds of unconditional love. When we aren't concerned about how they interpret our looks or our weight or our laughter or our politics or our mind, we've found them. These are the fireflies. The people to keep.  And who are we with our children? Do we cricket, criticize with our eyes or tone, sewing self-doubt? Or do we firefly, guiding them with twinkling silence? Tonight as you tuck them in, listen. What sounds do you make? What does your child hear? Breathe. Then fill the darkness with light.

EMILY MCMASON

*"Say 'yes' to life."*

ECKHART TOLLE

## THE TO-BE LIST

The chocolate pudding story has taken on mythical proportions at our house.  ⮌   I was a toddler. My dad was in medical school. There was one dish remaining from dessert the night before, and my mom, who usually embodies selflessness, ate it. By herself. But not before she, first, locked herself in the bathroom and, second, lied. "What you doing?" asked the curious toddler (because why would the door to the bathroom be closed?) "Nowthang" lied the voice around the spoon.  ⮌   We all have it: personal pudding that feeds our soul. Important not because we deserve it, have earned it, or are owed it. Important just because. Just because we love it.  ⮌   These are the things on our to-be list which is very different than our to-do list. The exercise-sleep-eat-well-floss-your-teeth list. How can I tell the difference? When something is on the to-do list and I to-don't, it feels like I just got busted by a favorite teacher, and I feel heavy with guilt. But if I skip the to-be list, I don't feel weighted down. Instead, I feel hollow, not grounded, drifting aimlessly, not sure of who I am.  ⮌   We spend so much time starring in the role of parent, that we forget. What do *I* like? High heels? Pick-up games? Late movies? When we surprisingly find a moment to ourselves, we don't know what to do. We have forgotten how to be.  ⮌   Today, I'll grab a spoon and rediscover myself. Join me?

⮌

EMILY MCMASON

*"Generally, by the time you are Real, most of your hair has been loved off,*
*and your eyes drop out and you get loose in your joints and very shabby.*
*But these things don't matter at all, because once you are Real you can't be ugly."*

MARGERY WILLIAMS

## VELVETEEN PARENTS

I first learned about beauty from a one-armed, balding monk named Father Michael. That isn't entirely true — he was actually one-and-a-half-armed. And even though he was middle-aged, balding, and round in the middle, he was beautiful. One of his favorite activities at summer camp was to read aloud. The day of *The Velveteen Rabbit* was rainy, so we sat like soggy baby birds, perched in the attic eves of the lodge. Despite the cold and clamminess, it was enchanting. I remember sitting in silence for a long time after he had finished and quietly closed the book. Even as a child, I was taken by this story and its magic; the magic of what it means to be real. And the message resonates more strongly as I become well worn with age, and I see, in contrast, the beauty of my children. They are beautiful because they are so very real. In each step, in each sound, they inhabit all of who they are — without thought of their imperfections, or how others may perceive them. They neither judge, nor fear judgment. For now. When I bemoan my wrinkles, lament gray hair, and curse my curves, I send messages about my children's bodies as well. Bodies are the natural habitats of our souls. They aren't meant to be perfect. If we embrace our strange markings, dingy spots, bedraggled whiskers, and floppy ears, we come to know what the Nursery Magic Fairy and Brother Michael knew. We are our children's Velveteen Rabbit, and because they love us, we are beautiful and real.

EMILY MCMASON

*"There are only two lasting bequests we can hope to give our children.*
*One of these is roots, the other, wings."*

JOHANN WOLFGANG VON GOETHE

# PUSH ME PULL YOU

When my husband was a boy, he spent hours playing at his grandparents' house on a toy called the Push Me Pull You. A toy long lost, even missing from any family photos. Yet the name alone intrigues me and has become one of my parenting mantras: push me, pull you.  I use the mantra as a guide during *those* moments. The times when I am exhausted. The times when their behavior has gone beyond. The times we are disconnected from each other.  The times when what I want to do most is push myself away from the situation in order to get as much distance between us as possible. What happens when I do? The discord grows. The conflict rises.  Yet when I pull you in closer, my child? It stills the water. It binds our hearts.  I have learned that the stronger the urge to push, the greater the need to pull. Pull you in until we touch. And soften. And find our center again.  It is an act of surrender. To being fully now. To stopping my fleeing thoughts and turning back to what is happening in front of me. And in this acknowledgement of reality, it shifts, and melts into something new. Something better. Something sacred.  It isn't a choice that gets easier. The instinct for flight doesn't diminish. And yet I know what to do: in trusting the knowing, I reverse direction and pull.

EMILY MCMASON

*"Little things seem nothing, but they give peace, like those meadow flowers*
*which individually seem odorless but all together perfume the air."*

GEORGES BERNANOS

## VALUE-ADDED HAPPINESS

The whole point of my paddleboard was to be an exercise in zen. ✎ But I got distracted by the view. Paddling past houses that were pretentious, exquisite, and spectacular, I wished they were mine. ✎ Then, I noticed their V.A.H. — value-added happiness: the small things that create big joy. ✎ A rope swing, well worn and frayed. Three Adirondack chairs, bleached by the sun. A brick chimney abutting a moss-covered roof. Four posts, no walls, sheltering a dining table. ✎ It isn't life's enormous things that charm me. It's the little ones. ✎ No matter the size of our house, or our family, we can find V.A.H. The speed of life is often exhausting, and I forget to stop, thinking that the faster I go, the more I'll get done and the better it will be. Turns out, I'm wrong. It is the full stop that holds value. ✎ Getting lost in a book as a child? V.A.H. ✎ The teen joy of splashing shriekishly cold water on summer's hottest days? V.A.H. ✎ The adult laughter shared over the flavor in a glass? V.A.H. ✎ What I learned from those houses wasn't about wealth. It was about wisdom. About stopping to notice. About getting down on our hands and knees, looking under the big stuff to see the delight that waits patiently at our feet. Figuring out how to hold still enough to see the dancing dust motes of joy. All we really need is a moment, maybe two. And the presence of mind to pause and create the small things: life's V.A.H.

EMILY MCMASON

*"That is what learning is. You suddenly understand something*
*you've understood all your life, but in a new way."*

DORIS LESSING

## OLD DOG, NEW TRICKS

Coco does not suffer from the stereotypical canine/car problem. There is no car chasing going on. There is only car fear.  ᗡ  We live on a quiet street but nearby is a highly traveled road with a posted speed limit of 45 mph. For six years, whenever I've walked Coco along that road she always and completely freaks out.  ᗡ  She pulls on her leash. Or hides behind me. Or runs in circles, tangling my legs. Every time a vehicle passes by, the same thing happens. And I get frustrated every time, then incrementally more frustrated, expecting a different outcome. (Who is Pavlov and who is the dog?)  ᗡ  Coco has a vocabulary of 10 words. Maybe nine and a half since "come" doesn't produce consistent results. So I didn't expect her to understand, but I knew I needed to try something new. As I heard a car approach, I crooned to her: describing the car, that it was coming nearer, that the engine would sound louder, that it was near us, then past us, then gone.  ᗡ  She walked calmly by my side the entire time. Different stimulus, different response. I tried it with the next car. And the next. It worked every time.  ᗡ  I didn't avoid the road with fast cars. I didn't hold her leash differently. I was simply there in a way I hadn't been before.  ᗡ  As with Coco, when my kids experience fear, or fall apart, or tangle themselves up, my instinct is to fix. To finish. To solve. Yet to grow in confidence, in capability, they simply need my side-by-side-ness. The soft whispers of experience. The sweet everythings of love.

ᗡ

EMILY MCMASON

*"Still round the corner there may wait,*
*A new road or a secret gate."*

J. R. R. TOLKIEN

# BEGINNINGS

I registered for a four-hour poetry writing class with poet and professor Orval Lund, fall quarter, 1990, Winona State University. I'd always loved to create through writing, so I took the chance to learn and express myself through poetry in a structured setting. ➛ It was an evening class once a week, and I would make the short walk from my dorm room to Minne Hall as the sun was starting to set. It would still be warm when class finished — autumn evenings in Winona, Minnesota are beautiful. ➛ Each week, the time in class flew by. Orv was a great teacher. If you had potential as a poet, as a writer, he let you know it, accompanied by a big smile, and it felt amazing — a direction, a fuller purpose for my life. I don't remember now much of anything I wrote that was notable, just that I was learning the bones and blood of poetry. This sustained me week to week, my walk lighter at the end of each class; enjoying the warm night air, possibilities, and dreams.

➛

LIZ MINETTE

# JUNE 26

*"All mankind is divided into three classes:*
*those that are immovable, those that are movable,*
*and those that move."*

BENJAMIN FRANKLIN

# WORK

Only, I have to keep writing, right? After the four-hour evening poetry class ended that quarter, I didn't write. Things I felt or saw would inspire me, and I might take notes, but I didn't really write again until I took another creative writing class in my senior year. Gone was that first thrill of knowing I could write. I *could* write, I just didn't. I feel now that I didn't honor the gift of that thrill enough to continue, and allowed the momentum to wither. And my small collection of writings at the time frustrated me. But I was the one causing that frustration. My initial idea of myself as a writer suffered. How to remedy? Well, write, just write — anything. Something will come. Like anything, whether art, business, or athletics, you have to — you must — practice, work at it, learn it even more, love it, hate it, and ultimately, stay with it, to succeed.

LIZ MINETTE

*"Opportunities are usually disguised as hard work,*
*so most people don't recognize them."*

ANN LANDERS

## STAYING WITH IT

I keep and take a notebook with me, each day, whether I write in it or not. But I try to find time to write, if I can, during the day or evening — my lunch hour, a spare minute, or an hour or more — to create more writing ideas for poems or stories, rough drafts, near-final drafts. The challenge is just making or finding the time to do it. Sometimes I tell family and friends, "This is my writing time. I need my space to do this." It's hard for me when the demands of other things (family needs, work, groceries, cooking, yard work) pull at me from different directions, or sit in the back of my mind, trying to get my attention. I know and try to keep realizing my writing is just as important and won't grow and live without my attention. I don't like being frustrated with a lack of creative effort, so, to remedy that, I write.

LIZ MINETTE

*"We are all apprentices in a craft
where no one ever becomes a master."*

ERNEST HEMINGWAY

## FINDING YOUR COMMUNITY

I initially found a really cool writing community by seeing, on posters around town, their monthly reading series which featured a reader followed by an open mic. Readings were held in a funky, old, former mattress factory building near Lake Superior. I started attending the readings just to hear and see these great poets read — some of whom I'd never heard of — and then listen during open mic. It was also a time and place to see and be seen, and connect with other writers. Having never read in public up to this point, I was thinking, *How do these people do this? Some of them are so good. How do I do this?* I somehow gathered up the courage to try, and remember the couple times I read as good experiences.  ⇜   Later, I joined Lake Superior Writers, based out of Duluth, Minnesota, in order to connect with other writers. A couple of their members host a monthly writer's group that I'm part of. This writer's group is so valuable because it gives us a much-needed focus for regularly creating new work. We each get to present our writing for group critique, to see what is working well in that month's piece, and what could use more attention. I'm so thankful for the feedback I've received over the years from my writer's group as it has helped me create a solid body of work. I've found strength and inspiration in community.

LIZ MINETTE

# JUNE 29

*"Avoid having your ego so close to your position
that when your position falls, your ego goes with it."*
COLIN POWELL

## OPEN MIC

Open mic nights are nights are a unique experience and important for people who want to try their work in front of an audience to see how it will be received. A while back, I hosted an open mic night, once a week, for a year. Next time — if and when there is a next time — I'll know better what to expect. I'll have a featured reader, preceded and/or followed by open mic. Get the public relations out earlier and have time limits on performances. Relax and have a good time.  Networking and getting to know people was great when I was hosting. I didn't, however, always know how to deal with negative feedback when someone believed they didn't get the response they felt they deserved. "Why do people always go up to the bar when I'm onstage?" one guy angrily demanded of me. My response now would be, "Guess you answered your own question." Still, open mics are an important way to discover new talent — maybe even your own!

LIZ MINETTE

*"I just go with the flow, I follow the yellow brick road.*
*I don't know where it's going to lead me, but I follow it."*

GRACE JONES

# GETTING OUT OF MY OWN WAY

I farm nannied, on and off, for friends for a few years. They have a lovely farm with two horses, chickens, and, at various times, pigs, cats with kittens, dogs with puppies. They also had a big Jacuzzi under the stars, a beautiful, funky home, and peace and quiet. I loved it. I wanted to write about it.  ✎   I started the shape of, and worked on a poem called *Saturday Poem*, while in Boston for work. My hotel room writing desk overlooked Boston Commons, which felt like a great place for success of a first draft, and ultimately, a finished piece.  ✎   It wasn't. I sent the poem out several times for publication to no avail. I finally workshopped the poem in a writing class at the Loft Literary Center in Minneapolis. My classmates were very helpful in letting me know how it didn't work. My syntax, dropped sentences and ideas, one stanza not following through to the other, a great ending, but stumbling to get there. I had a stack about a half inch thick of returned copies with class comments. I let the stack sit for a while and then, one night, I just sat down and started working on the poem. I looked at my classmates responses. I looked at my notes. I started putting the new draft for the poem together like a quilt. I stepped out of the way, and let the actual and real magic of the images sing and shine through on their own.

✎

LIZ MINETTE

# JULY

# JULY 1

## SATURDAY POEM

At Solstice, a full moon flags the December barn.

There is only this light on the way to evening chores.

Two horses softly walk to the fence, stand,

shoulders rounded smooth as planets.

Both are curious for anything my hands hold:

a touch, apple slices, the heat of oats.

Zoie the farm dog has come along with me. She wouldn't have it any other way.

Inside the barn, two cats, buddhas on a ledge, intently watch

Zoie's barrel-shaped body scuttle after one scent to another.

Hens thump to their roost under the heat lamp with a sound like boxes falling.

I exchange new straw for their coop's small harvest — three eggs tonight.

Cracking two over the cats' feed, I place the third in my coat,

and then Zoie and I walk the long driveway.

The moon follows, casts shadow among birch and in front of us,

as dog and human try to catch up to themselves.

Back to the house's soft watch, Zoie's last two puppies, Jasmine and Kebu,

spring from the kennel when I open it.

They greet us jumping, crushing the egg I've forgotten —

small return of sun in my pocket.

LIZ MINETTE

*"Cruelty is all out of ignorance.*
*If you knew what was in store for you, you wouldn't hurt anybody,*
*because whatever you do comes back*
*much more forceful than you send it out."*

WILLIE NELSON

## FALLEN

Powdery snow takes me back to childhood — a Christmas season when Jerry Butts and I were hunting with our BB guns.  ⟿  We were in the pines between the T Road and Denomie Creek. A small chickadee lighted down on a branch in front of us. With a shot, the small bird dropped down into the powdery snow and we ran to it. Butts picked the bird up and he studied it. I looked closely at it too. Then he looked at me and said, "You know what? This don't feel right, we shouldn't do this." I agreed. Butts put the little bird down in the snow and I left the woods with perspective that has lasted a lifetime.  ⟿  My older cuz looked 10 feet tall walking out of the woods that day.

⟿

MIKE WIGGINS, JR.

*"If you have men who will exclude any of God's creatures
from the shelter of compassion and pity,
you will have men who will deal likewise with their fellow men."*

FRANCIS OF ASSISI

# DEER HUNT

He finally stopped and touched the ground under a twisted old cedar that was drooping sprigs low. As I walked up to him, his chest slowly heaved upward and settled back down. Deeply. His eye picked me up and I saw my heart reflected back at me. Fearful, overcome. I spoke to him and I told him I was sorry. I told him, he was an ancient warrior and that he was going on a journey, that he would be alright. I told him that I would see him again on the other side. Then I said thank you for helping my family. His chest went still. ⤚  I brought him over to the edge of the highlands above Sugar-bush Creek and the Bad River Bottoms and put down tobacco as a gesture of respect. For us. He's been with me ever since. Fireflies make me think of him and the coming hunts of the new year. Ojibwe. It's what we do.

⤚

MIKE WIGGINS, JR.

# JULY 4

*" ... we ordinary beings can cling to the earth*
*and love where we are, strong for common things."*
WILLIAM STAFFORD

# BIG LAKE

I sat perched on a clay cliff above Lake Superior, awaiting daybreak as the yellowing horizon line gave way to a red, elliptical rush. Way down below me, the beach held steady as the Big Lake washed tiny rocks.  I wanted to write a story about eagles. Not just any story, but a story that would conjure feathers, and water and height. I knew I needed eagle words. Eagle words can bring up the fish below surface water, or reveal the sky side of a nest. White fluff in a cloud caught my eye as I looked out over the Big Lake. The morning sun fanned out in a golden reach, speckling the water. The cliff gave me a bird's eye view of the Earth turning and it was a good place, but I still needed eagle words.  As I peered into the Big Lake below me, an eagle story was born in thought. It slowly took shape on paper and became full-fledged as it grew bigger. I could see eagles in my mind; they were flying above the horizontal morning light. I thought harder and soon soared with them. After watching them work, I remembered where I came from. In the upper reaches of the sky, I looked down at the pitiful Indian man on the clay cliff staring at Lake Superior. I peered into the waters where his eyes were fixed and saw a shimmer of thought about baby eagles and water. It's near enough to the surface so I'm going to dive down and pluck it from the alpha waves. I'm coming back with it, even if there are no eagle words. Wait for me up here.

MIKE WIGGINS, JR.

*"Death is not extinguishing the light;*
*it is only putting out the lamp because the dawn has come."*
RABINDRANATH TAGORE

# IMPACT

One day while under a Lake Superior morning star, I truly embraced the fact that someday I'm going to die. Someday, but one day. ✍ There is a sudden, subtle ferociousness that grows inside me now that I am temporary. ✍ Under vertical sunbeams I carried my new, old eyes and I saw the subtle, ferocious winds of hummingbird-winged, spiraling tornadoes. ✍ I blinked and they were all gone in a green, rainbow flash into the sky. ✍ And you. With your eyes, your lips and your skin, surrounded by the fragility of a finite amount of life, I find myself seeing in new light. ✍ I ought not to endeavor to search anymore for the perfect sunrise or set. ✍ The sun, I shall put away. Gladly. The cloud bank can hold the moon's glow and the stars can shine on the rivers flow. The moon and stars I shall put away. Gladly. ✍ My eyes only have a certain amount of time to capture your light and there is a sudden, subtle fierceness that glows inside you, a being who is temporary.

✍

MIKE WIGGINS, JR.

*" ... the canoe yearns for the*
*land of rice and fat ducks ... "*
ROB GANSON

## WILD RICING

Thinking about them — it was not for nothing. Those ricers bending reeds announce through rhythmic swishes that the dream of the ancient ones is here and now. Those old ones envisioned a good life for us with our hearts near the shoreline and fingers in deer meat and berries. They envisioned a world for us that would have sage and cedar smoke remembered — when we need it and also when we don't. A world where drums would echo in our ears and the next season's harvest would dance at the edge of the horizon.  ⌒  If, at the end of our days, our Tribe embraces the ancestors' wildest dreams of *bimaadiziwin* (good life), and also treat each other well, we will have arrived at a good place in a good way. The people would and could feed each other and tobacco would send it forward. And tobacco would message it back. To them. – from *Mashkiziibii* (Medicine River or common use: Bad River)

⌒

MIKE WIGGINS, JR.

*"Oft when the white, still dawn lifted the skies*
*and pushed the hills apart,*
*I have felt it like a glory in my heart."*

EDWIN MARKHAM

# DAWN

Up above, four remnant stars surround the waning crescent Moon. In the east, there is coming light on the horizon. New. Hues of varying oranges and yellows and imminence are birthing low near the Earth, and the Big Lake moves to them. To the south, the elemental carvings on the red clay cliffs sit up, as the night bids good night. To the west and north, soft lavender and soft, deeper blues nestle the lower altitudes and take on the look of clouds even though there are no clouds.  ✎  It is here in this place, where even the waves sing quietly and beautifully. It is here, in these outer, watching skies, that high-flying cloud banks start to glow, pink and rosy.  ✎  The Big Lake steadily and gently readies herself and reflects back what the horizon lights are bringing out. In these fleeting moments, the Big Lake holds the Earth and sky together, creating a sky-lit nursery to greet the Sun and a new day on this planet. Soon the Sun will arrive to be washed in baby blue. She will assist the sky with this change. Through all the swirling brightening, Lake Superior is the rock.

✎

MIKE WIGGINS, JR.

*"Now I see the secret of making the best person:*
*it is to grow in the open air and to eat and sleep with the earth."*

WALT WHITMAN

## LAND ETHIC

Waterwalker Josephine Mandamin reminds us that water is life. George Newago, Red Cliff Elder, reminds us that our Treaties represent life. I know why one won't find water and clean air in our Treaties. It's the same reason one won't find water and clean air in the Constitution of the United States. Water and air are not negotiable. What extractive industry is doing to all of us around Lake Superior has to be looked at through this filter our elders put forth.  ⌒  I mentioned to a very respectful Associated Press reporter that it was one thing — as Anishinaabe — to bite our tongues and listen as Aldo Leopold was given credit for the land ethic. I accept it; that debate is passé. But I also mentioned that it was quite another and high time to crank up the "Anishinaabe water ethic" for *all* peoples. As protectors of water, it's what Anishinaabe women have been doing for a long time.  ⌒  He asked me what the difference was between the "Anishinaabe water ethic" and other views. In a nutshell, I replied, "... um ... 'bout 1000 years."

⌒

MIKE WIGGINS, JR.

# JULY 9

*"Love has nothing to do with what you are expecting to get —*
*only with what you are expecting to give — which is everything."*

KATHARINE HEPBURN

## PESTO

My pesto isn't necessarily that fabulous, but if you ask my daughter, she will disagree. She thinks my pesto is "the best in the world." I think my mother's apple pie is the best in the world and Nini's lasagna is, for sure, the best in the world. That's because, according to my daughter, we "put the love in it."  Aside from being a lovely, youthful sentiment, how many things do we regularly put the love into — everyday things done with love and care? Do I put the love into grading papers? Do I put the love into grocery shopping? Do I put it into doing dishes? No. I will never have love for doing dishes, but shouldn't I sneak love into more than just pesto? How hard would it be to enjoy, refine, and love the everyday things that have to get done? What would happen if instead of getting crabby when I pay bills, I exercise gratitude that I have the money to do it? When I pay the cable, I choose to be happy because I have the internet in my home, something that was unheard of 20 years ago. What if I put the love into that? What if I put love into the research of my writing, rather than see it as something that has to be done? What if I put the love into rewrites? Getting notes from an editor? Maybe it would make me as happy or as proud as hearing my pesto is the best in the world. OK, maybe not, but I bet it would take a lot of the sting out of things I don't relish.

## LIZ WOODWORTH

*"If you're not failing every now and again,*
*it's a sign you're not doing anything very innovative."*

WOODY ALLEN

# MISTAKES

Back in 1994, my husband and I lived in Minneapolis where our friend Michael Bland was Prince's drummer at that time. My husband, a drummer as well, really respected Michael and enjoyed hearing him play. A friend told us a great story about Michael and to this day, I apply it to many areas in my life. ✎ The story goes that the band was in the studio recording "Diamonds and Pearls." In the middle of the song, there's a horn break and a short, but powerful drum fill. In the middle of recording, Michael Bland dropped a stick, but managed to finish the fill. He asked Prince if he wanted to try it again, but Prince said, "no" because the fill was unexpected and unique. Basically, a big mistake turned out to be more interesting than the original plan. ✎ I think about that often. I always have an abundance of plans, particularly for artistic endeavors, and they rarely end up the way I first envision them. I have learned that when I fight against my mistakes and try to force my original vision, things can fall apart pretty quickly, but when I allow the mistake to guide me, the unexpected and unique show up, just like that drum fill. ✎ I have yet to direct a play that ends with the cast it began with; usually for the better. Rewriting is often more surgery than just sutures. Rather than me stressing or fretting, I try to accept it and see how it can be more interesting. ✎ We should all drop a stick now and then.

✎

LIZ WOODWORTH

*"So Pa sold the little house. ... He made hickory bows and fastened them upright to the wagon box. Ma helped him stretch white canvas over them."*

LAURA INGALLS WILDER

# DEAR PA INGALLS

When I was young, I read your daughter's books. Laura put you on a pedestal, as we do when fathers pass away. You seemed a responsible, caring father who put his family first. Then I read the books to my daughter. My feelings have changed. Now, you seem fairly selfish with poor decision-making skills. Let's look at some of your errors in judgment. ✎ **1.** You moved your happy family from the *Little House in the Big Woods* to a dwelling of mud. Things were good in Wisconsin; you had maple syrup parties and barn dances! Caroline didn't want to go, but you made her. ✎ **2.** During the dangerous trip with three small children in a covered wagon, you crossed a river while it was flooding. Good thing your horse could swim. ✎ **3.** You left an elderly couple on the prairie alone after their horses were stolen and you insulted them on your way out, calling them greenhorns. ✎ **4.** You had to move your family *again* because you built your homestead in Indian Territory. ✎ **5.** Despite clear signs, you didn't plan for "The Long Winter." Laura cut her hands daily making straw bundles to burn. All you had to eat was grain. Carrie almost died. ✎ **6.** You moved again to a gold mining town. No church? No school? No problem. Make your wife open up a hotel that serves food to drunken scoundrels. Good job. ✎ **7.** You are incredibly racist. I get the context, but still, super racist. ✎ Perspective and time changes views on anything, and more often than not, the writer of the story has more power than the subject. Lucky for you, Laura was kind.

LIZ WOODWORTH

*"Make no mistake about why these babies are here;*

*they are here to replace us."*

JERRY SEINFELD

# TURNING 50

Although I have more than a year before I turn 50, I'm already pondering this epic milestone. At 48, I've already outlived my brother, my uncle and my grandfather. (The men in my family don't fare as well as the women. Don't worry, most women in my family live well past 80.) Half a century! It certainly gives one pause. And don't think it is just the current, youth-obsessed America that is the only community that thinks 50 is a big deal. Just turn to Leviticus, where 50 is described as your jubilee year! Fun Bible fact: on your jubilee year you're encouraged to free your prisoners and your slaves. "A jubilee shall that fiftieth year be unto you: ye shall not sow, neither reap that which groweth of itself in it, nor gather the grapes in it of thy vine undressed." Basically, you get to retire and celebrate the fact that you lived this long. I personally don't even get to start thinking about retirement for a long, long time. Also, last time I checked, we didn't own slaves, but I am saving up for a Roomba vacuum cleaner. ⇌ As I get closer to 50, I've learned and earned my life lessons. I can say "no" without as much guilt. I have more confidence following my gut and first impressions. Simply put, I make better choices. As my flesh relaxes and settles, so does my judgment of myself and others. I find I treat others more kindly and with more understanding. I find I don't lose my temper as often, which is a blessing. I'm getting softer, smarter, and just better. Hello, 50. Good to see you.

⇌

LIZ WOODWORTH

*"Cheers to a new year and another chance for us to get it right."*

OPRAH WINFREY

# MY HUSBAND'S SCAR

My husband has a well-earned scar on his forehead. He got it when he was 18 and stupid, and didn't use a seat belt. Up until then, he had zero scars on his face: no acne, no chickenpox, nothing. Then he went through a windshield of an International Scout on the Fourth of July. He lived. He has a scar.  He learned a lot from that scar. He's learned that people who judge on looks alone are jerks. Now, he always uses seat belts and refuses to ride with anyone who doesn't. He's learned that life is precious and he's learned he is a very lucky guy.  I love that scar, because he grew from it. That is perhaps the thing I admire most about my husband. He learns from his mistakes the first time, and he also changes his behavior to avoid further mistakes. He tries (and succeeds) to be a better person with every mistake and every step. He inspires me every day.  So many of us make mistakes and blame others or circumstances; we continue to blame everything else but ourselves. It's okay to blame ourselves when we deserve it; it's great to learn from our mistakes, but I think the most important part is to then change our behavior. That's harder than just learning from mistakes, to actually change habits, routines, and behaviors in order to be a better human being. It's so much easier to blame something else, but then no real change will ever happen. Make your scars count.

LIZ WOODWORTH

# JULY 14

## CANCER CHRISTMAS

I feel guilty about my cancer. I have friends who have lost body parts, hair, speech, and even lives to cancer. I have a scar on my left breast. That's it. If cancer is a war, I was the journalist who stayed in a five-star hotel to cover it. I saw a fraction of the ugly truth and then got to come home and look the hero because "I went there." 　 I didn't lose a body part, I didn't lose hair, I didn't lose a life, I didn't lose money, I didn't lose my lunch, I didn't even lose sleep. My cell borders were clean so even my radiation went from six weeks to four, allowing me to avoid the nasty burns many other cancer patients suffer from. 　 My biggest pain was the hour-plus drive for radiation, but even that was made easy, because friends drove me. After treatments, we would find an hour to shop or have a cocktail. Friends routinely brought me food and gifts. My daughter started to call it "Cancer Christmas." I stayed positive and knew in my heart I would be okay. 　 There was no reason, there was no clear cause, there was no big take-away. I have pondered and looked and thought and reflected on why I barely got this disease while others have died from it. Sometimes things just happen. Sometimes only your toe gets wet, while others get leveled by a tidal wave. Sometimes you don't have to learn the big lessons, but be grateful for dodging the mess. I am so grateful for the experience and for my guilt.

LIZ WOODWORTH

*"I once had a rose named after me and I was very flattered.*
*But I was not pleased to read the description in the catalogue:*
*no good in a bed, but fine up against a wall."*

ELEANOR ROOSEVELT

## MY DAUGHTER'S FEET

My Chinese-American daughter can wear my size eight shoes and she's only 12. She has beautiful, big feet. My father used to say, "They build better foundations on churches than outhouses."   ⮜   I recently read about a 102-year-old Chinese woman who is the only survivor of the horrid practice of footbinding. It gave me pause. I even blogged about it. I couldn't help but think of my own daughter's feet, and of the horrors and pain of that practice. I am so grateful she lives in the here and now.   ⮜   What people tend to forget is that under the guise of beauty, footbinding had a much more practical use. Plainly put, these women couldn't run away from their situations. Women with bound feet were captives. They couldn't walk easily, let alone run. They were at the mercy of their husbands.   ⮜   Of course, there are other examples of this kind of practice in other cultures; something that is used to make women more desirable but ultimately messes with their bodies so much that making a hasty retreat from a nasty situation would be impossible. The most horrific is female circumcision. It has a similar result. Those who survive the ritual cannot usually run, or walk quickly; they "shuffle."   ⮜   High heels, corsets, neck rings, all these practices do that as well, making it difficult to literally run away from a bad situation. The women in this world have made so much progress, but we have miles to go. I doubt we get there any quicker in heels.

LIZ WOODWORTH

*"The strength of a nation derives from the integrity of the home."*
CONFUCIUS

# MORE AND MORE, CLOTHED IN CLOUD

There are people who know this: what it is to be clothed in cloud, fog, rain.
They stand and clouds run through them. No effort, only being. That to be housed
is to wear a home. A house needs cleaning, tending, drains must be fixed, gutters
unclogged, windows replaced, floors swept, and swept, and swept again.

There are people who blanket for snow and wind, and some rains but that is all.
They wear the sun more often than not, more often than you or I. They wear the sun,
and the light of moon and stars, they sleep in cars, they sleep in graveyards of graffiti,
their turtle shells, their moth-like wings of woven sleeping bags and too-big someone
else's shirts, their homes less house-like, more homeless.

MAGGIE KAZEL

*"One must still have chaos in oneself to be able
to give birth to a dancing star."*

FRIEDRICH NIETZSCHE

## AVOIDING TSUNAMIS

As she tried to unlock it, the door nearly fell onto her small but mightily pregnant body. It avalanched down, old and heavy, porch snow following. ✎ I surveyed a desert inside: empty, no furniture, except for two laundry baskets in a corner and the one scared girl. Through her sobs she explained. Pregnant. Due any day now. And hooked. On heroin. Promised help with furnishing the apartment, but that fell through. Scared. Lonely for her mother back up north. Then there's the unborn. More crying, and choked attempts at speech. ✎ Out with it, finally, I understand why: she'd been raped. Loves the baby, but ... she stops talking, which is probably good: her anguish will surely bring torrents, and we don't want to lose her in a tsunami of grief and fear. The number of natural disasters in this tiny apartment were profound. My voice low, I keep talking about how it was her lucky day, as I was a grown up "rape baby" obviously put there to help her see we needed to keep moving. ✎ I had come looking for an Elder who needed a ride, but found her instead. We shoved baskets through that godforsaken window — she had baby clothes and was not about to lose them. She hopped over ice floes, careful to stay upright, keeping baby safe. Nearly May and still we have to skate or slide! She asked for food, a place for her baskets, a ride to the hospital. Almonds found in the glove compartment, worldly possessions snug in the trunk, and this I know: we avoided the tsunami. We arrived, soaked but alive, in time for baby, Grandma and all the cousins, too.

✎

MAGGIE KAZEL

*"What is a poet? An unhappy person who conceals profound anguish in his heart but whose lips are so formed that as sighs and cries pass over them they sound like beautiful music."*

SØREN KIERKEGAARD

## BLIND FAITH BABY

"Keep some money stashed in case you need to run." I had done that. ✎ I drove first to the all-night grocery store for diapers and to call a battered women's shelter. I called them all and every single one was full. I remember they said, "Look for a cheap motel" and I drove to one I thought would work. It was almost 1:00 a.m. ✎ The night clerk tried not to notice I could not stop shaking, and I tried to hide it and act calm. He saw me empty the money out of my pockets, and count it up carefully. He distracted the baby with cooing noises so I could fill out the registration forms. I said, "I have enough for one night." ✎ He counted and collected the bills and then pronounced, "Well, I'm clocking you in at 2:00 a.m. — that means you didn't really arrive yet, so you get to stay for two nights." When I realized what he was doing for me, I started to cry. He looked at me and whispered, "This motel is full of women and children just like you. Every weekend." I was stunned. And then he turned to my baby, who was turning all the knobs, and said, "You like that music? That is Blind Faith. They came out way before you were ever born when I was in Viet Nam. Yep, that's Blind Faith and they are really good. You've got good taste, baby." ✎ He knew how to spot and care for a casualty, without touch, without questions, adding only music, floating from an old boombox.

MAGGIE KAZEL

*"Nothing heals us like letting people know our scariest parts.*
*When people listen to you cry and lament, and look at you with love,*
*it's like they are holding the baby of you."*
ANNE LAMOTT

# HANDS WAVING COCOA

Baby, I still see you running on the Rez, escaping us kitchen-sweating adults, under tables and chairs, chocolate on your face, your dress. Giggles of luscious, taste bud news, chubby legs stumping, and the whump-whump-whump baby moccasin sound, as you make for the screen door. We can't catch you: you whir around our sludge; this grief has undertow. ➥ All of us are in shock, your Auntie was so very young, and your Elders in their grief gently guide us through this change. Four long days of cooking and eating and cooking some more. Four nights of vigil in the living room, getting ready for her journey away from us. Auntie's been leaving, she's gone and we are still here, not quite as hopeless as we were four days ago. When in you come, your feet padding lilt, your hands sticky silly, your face a full moon of unbelievable joy. That baby garblewisdom fills the air, and everyone's enchanted. This is when we start to notice — this means we aren't holding our breath anymore. The actual air has returned to the room, evidenced by these eruptions of lifesaving belly laughs, as we are mesmerized by, as we revel in, your hands waving cocoa.

MAGGIE KAZEL

*"Simplicity is nature's first step, and the last of art."*

PHILIP JAMES BAILEY

## POTS, PANS, GENEROSITY

The night staff generally stuck to the office, unless they needed to fix a light bulb, or help a mom when her child suffered a high temperature or new cough, but tonight turned out differently. The baby in my care nodded off easily, and it was my turn for washing dishes, so my plans were terra firma, unexciting. But I noticed something palpable, a subtle change in how I felt. I was functioning beyond mere survival, joining in with the household tasks and the evening's social gatherings. I no longer felt like I'd barely get through the day. I was taking my time drying the pots and pans, and I was singing out loud, because I liked the acoustics in the kitchen. Feeling so much better I could sing with real heart, and the most wonderful thing happened. The night staff said she followed the music to find who was singing, and then she asked, 'You have the most beautiful voice, do you sing in a choir?' That look in her eyes and the tone of her voice gave away how genuinely moved she was. ⤳ I used to sing in a duo and in a choir, too, but these parts of my life were far behind me. She had no idea that her comment was spilling rain onto a patch of desert that didn't expect to be revived. She didn't have to walk into the kitchen, she could have gone back to the office after her nightly rounds. That night of pots, pans, music and generosity, something profound, yet invisible to those around me, occurred. She gave me a part of my life back.

MAGGIE KAZEL

*"A dreamer is one who can only find his way by moonlight,*
*and his punishment is that he sees the dawn before the rest of the world."*

OSCAR WILDE

# LATE, HOT, TIRED

Heat exhaustion has set in, I realize, as I get ready for bed. I'm trying to remember — the snake is in the cage, the thing that looks like an aquarium, minus the sweet, small fish. What about the hamsters, or gerbils, those friendly-looking rodent-type creatures living in the boys' room. And did I feed the dogs? Really, the woods runner one, too? Oh, mercy. But the biggie is — did I feed all five kids?  ⌒  Remote woods, hotter than July, kids all asleep, and in the kitchen window a face appears, like a bright, fevered moon, but animated, golden brown, and smiling. It is after midnight. Who is this? Hands waving, mouth moving, she makes her way to the door. She's mother of two of the sleeping and wants to see them. Now. I'm too tired to feel shocked but my MamaGuard is up, in case. I search out the oldest, gently shake her awake. "She's here," I say, "you wanna see her?" The daughter rises, finds brother, and they kitchen-table-huddle with the moon-vision turned mother.  ⌒  And it goes like this: so much was broken, but the threads are weaving. Even sleepy, family memories are made. Words whispered, hugs given, and as quickly as she comes, she goes. Late. Hot. Tired. But in this moonlight, it seems, anything is possible, and everyone may mend.

⌒

MAGGIE KAZEL

*"When it is dark enough, you can see the stars."*

CHARLES BEARD

# THE GLITTER LADY

She walked in, head-to-toe glitter. All that glitters, was her. Impossibly straight back, rigid posture, very polite, even formal ... and the crowds parted. It was as if she'd walked off a stage, into our alley, then through our humble doors. There we are, two staffers up to our eyeballs in men, women, and children, huddled in from the rain, with various stages of sobriety, anxiety, and discontent. Much strain, simmering anger, very, very little peace. And in she pops. With a parasol, no less. Glitter eyeshadow, glitter rouge, glitter in her wet, wet hair. "I am looking for housing." Pause. "Am I in the right place?" Glitter hose, glitter shoes. "Yes, yes come on in," I say, and I offer coffee, a place to sit down. Such a small, cramped place, yet suddenly, a wide berth on either side of her. On some days, this would bother me, because it seemed as though they were outcasting her. But today, no. They were absolutely certain, without eye contact or words, that she needed help worse than all of them put together, and without any articulated agreement of any kind, she was gently guided to the front of the line. It was as if they knew, and they wanted her to have the most help possible. Tipping their heads, pointing her gently to the front of the room, then kindly looking away, not staring. As if she was the most fragile of all their beloved relatives. Glitter reflected millions of tiny pieces of light. Here in our hovel, the storm raging outside, us dripping and downhearted inside. Then this soul-piercing light. Then the room lightens and warms.

MAGGIE KAZEL

*"'Pan, who and what art thou?' he cried huskily.*
*'I'm youth, I'm joy,' Peter answered at a venture,*
*'I'm a little bird that has broken out of the egg.'"*

J.M. BARRIE

# DEPARTMENT OF LOSS PREVENTION

I took one of those Facebook quizzes, this one breathlessly titled, "What emotion are you suppressing?" I figured my suppressed emotion would be rage, grief, or maybe even some other awful emotion I hadn't even thought of like hysterical disenchantment or aggravated ennui. ✎ I clicked through and answered the questions, although I'm not sure how they get my deepest truth from what kind of pizza I like and which flowers are my favorite, but I'm sure the quiz people know what they're doing. ✎ Waiting as my results were compiled, I braced myself to feel the heavy truth of my suppressed emotion. The answer popped up: "You are suppressing *joy*." ✎ I leaned back in my chair and laughed, "Holy shit! I *totally* suppress my joy!" ✎ Suppressing joy is like my own internal Loss Prevention Department trying to protect me from some future hurt. Loss Prevention wags its finger and cautions, "Don't be joyful, because something will come out of the clear blue sky and slap you down." ✎ The thing is, circumstances will come out of the clear blue sky and slap me down regardless of what protections I put in place. Life contains great joy but also significant slappage. That's just the way of it. ✎ I can either be joyful in this moment, or not. Being on high alert for things dropping out of the clear blue sky does not prevent them; it just creates a joyless life. ✎ And you know those loss prevention types … they never let you have any fun.

BRIDGETTE BOUDREAU

*"People who think they know everything*
*are a great annoyance to those of us who do."*

ISAAC ASIMOV

# I MISS CERTAINTY

There was a time I knew right from wrong.  ⤺  There was a time I knew what you should do, and what I should do.  ⤺  There was a time when I knew things like relationships should always be worked on; that you should always try really hard and be good; that hard work was its own reward.  ⤺  There was a time I was certain that you shouldn't be so judgmental, and I judged you for it. After all, you're so damn judgy.  ⤺  I miss certainty, being able to rest in the knowing of how things should be. I miss knowing that there were lines made of black, and that it was clear exactly where you crossed them. And that crossing them was oh so bad.  ⤺  More recently, I've crossed a line or two, and they were decidedly gray; on this side of the line, I'm not so certain about things.  ⤺  Over here, I've done wrong things that felt so right. I've done right things that felt so wrong.  ⤺  Over here, I'm not sure what you should do. As for what I should do, I can only feel my way forward in any given moment. That's been working pretty well.  ⤺  As for you being judgmental, to be honest, lots of times I still think you shouldn't be. Because I can be pretty damn judgy.  ⤺  There was a time I was certain I wanted my life to look a particular way. Then I was certain it should look this other particular way. Now it looks like neither one of those ways. And I'm more peaceful and happier than I've ever been.  ⤺  Of that, I am certain.

BRIDGETTE BOUDREAU

*"Don't mistake the weather of your mind for the sky of your being."*

JEFF FOSTER

# HUNGER

I was at shamanic ceremony recently (as one does) and shared that my intention for the ceremony was to access my creativity. The shaman looked at me in that penetrating shaman way and said, "You know it's your self-consciousness that blocks your creativity, right?" I did not know. ✎ Apparently shamans don't believe in soft-pedaling it. ✎ As the ceremony unfolded, I spent a few very frustrating hours trying to envision the perfect three-step process to access my creativity. I would think to myself, *Step one, breathe. Yeah, that's good. Okay, now step two, let the self-consciousness go … shit!* I have no idea what step three is; I never got past step two. ✎ By evening, everyone else was deep in meditation, but I kept hitting the wall. Finally I'd had it, so I muttered to myself, "Fuck this! I'm going outside!" ✎ I wandered outside and oh … the light! The moon was half full, and in the rural setting, it was just me and the vastness of the Milky Way. I was at one with it all. ✎ In that moment, I realized that I was starving. I was hungry for experiences, for movement, for that vastness. I was — and still am — hungry for life. ✎ That movement, that giving up of how I thought it should be, and following my desire — my hunger — to go outside, was my creativity in action. ✎ As I stared at that sky, the insights from the evening coalesced in my mind. *Self-consciousness blocks the hunger! The hunger is the creativity!* ✎ It's not about eradicating my self-conscious thoughts; my mind tape will always play in the background. It's about letting my hunger move me. ✎ What a trip.

✎

BRIDGETTE BOUDREAU

*"I do not understand the mystery of grace —*
*only that it meets us where we are and does not leave us where it found us."*

ANNE LAMOTT

# GRACE

I do this thing where I try to protect the people I love. I'm like the Secret Service. Please, allow me to jump in front of you and take that bullet!    What looks like altruism and devotion is really a manifestation of my ego. When my loved ones are struggling and I swoop in there with all of my life-coachy solutions, I'm saying to them that I'm better equipped to handle their problem than they are. Worse, I'm saying they're more fragile than I am. To my horror, this adds up to something like, I don't believe in them.    Ew.    When I dig deeper, I see my need to fix is the outward manifestation of the little kid in me who took responsibility when bad things happened.    Recently, two of my dear friends were arguing. In a radical departure for me, instead of trying to fix it, I got the hell out of the way.    Then something incredible happened: Grace entered. Grace brought them more intimacy. Grace showed me that none of it had anything to do with me.    I don't know better than you. You are not fragile. I believe in you.    Further, I believe in the intelligence of life: that everything is being set up perfectly for us, all of the time. We are conspiring with life to create the circumstances that allow us to learn our life lessons. We set things up on the external stage of our life so we can integrate, heal, and connect with our wholeness.    The bonus (or maybe the point?) is that when I step out of the way of the intelligence of life, Grace enters. Perhaps she's been there the whole time.

BRIDGETTE BOUDREAU

*"Courage is just fear plus prayers plus understanding."*

EDDIE ALBERT

# WRITE YOUR PRAYERS

Write your prayers

on a little slip of paper

each night.

Tell the gods what your heart wants.

Where you want help,

where you're tired of going it alone.

Read them again the next night.

See how your prayers have been

answered.

Always.

BRIDGETTE BOUDREAU

*"Steadfastness, it seems,*
*is more about dogs than about us.*
*One of the reasons we love them so much."*

MARY OLIVER

## TOO MUCH GOODNESS

Scruffy, my 14-pound Terrier mix, adores chewy bones. Each time I hand her one, she tenderly takes it from my hands as if an embarrassment of riches has rained down upon her. ✑ Then she starts pacing around the house with it in her mouth. I hear her little nails clack-clacking and she tries to figure out what to do with this unexpected largesse. Soon, the whining starts. ✑ Too. Much. Goodness. ✑ Next, I hear a scratching sound on the couch. She'll place the bone carefully on the couch cushion after she's excavated her imaginary hole, and then kick, kick, kick, to cover it. ✑ This can go on for hours; sometimes she doesn't even eat the bone. I'll look over and she'll be lying forlornly on one side of the room, the bone on the other. It's all too much. ✑ I do the same thing. Except my go-to move is to not even take the bone from the proverbial hand. I tell myself I won't like it or I won't get to keep it. Even when it's being dangled in front of me. ✑ "Would you like to be a writer?" *Nooooo! Too scary! Too hard! How will I ever write a book?* ✑ "How 'bout now?" *Okay, maybe I'll try it.* (Takes the bone.) *Oooh, it's too much! I can't do it! I can't stand to look at it!* (Buries book in the couch.) ✑ Eventually, I realize the book — or other heart's desire — is just too delicious to keep in the proverbial couch cushions. I pull the bone out, take a deep breath, and gingerly take a bite.

BRIDGETTE BOUDREAU

*"We don't realize that, somewhere within us all,*
*there does exist a supreme self who is eternally at peace."*

ELIZABETH GILBERT

# THE ALTAR

Life requires you to sacrifice what was for what wants to be.
There's no wading. You must dive. Headfirst, blind,
unsure if there's cool water to catch you.
Not because life is punitive, but because you must have faith.
By placing that thing that always felt safe, your go-to move, on the altar,
you're telling life you're ready to receive the gift that awaits.
"Bring it on!" your sacrifice says. Some call this "letting go," but that sounds so nice,
so genteel, so easy. To me it feels a little bit like dying.
Part of my ego has to go; it kept me safe up to now,
but it keeps me smaller than I'm meant to be.
When I put that thing I can't take with me on the altar,
I hesitate … the awful liminal place, the altar,
my knife raised high, hand shaking.
Finally, I plunge the knife, and to my astonishment,
the altar disappears. The landscape is entirely different, yet familiar.
I am very much alive and resting in peace.
My heart recognizes this place: I am home.

BRIDGETTE BOUDREAU

*"Thousands have lived without love, not one without water."*

W. H. AUDEN

# ILLUMINATED BY STAR FIRE

Stars look down with fiery hydrogen eyes on the miracle of water
as aboriginal people drum rhythms that vibrate the transcendental Oversoul
of the headwaters and backwaters and groundwaters and feeder streams.
Fish and men swim against the current to keep their species alive.
We are water flowing north and south.
We are water wombs and semen,
brooks and streams and puddles with frogs.
Water people flow and rush and rage when false prophets are praised
and laws condemn us to death.
We make waves that crash upon the rocky shores of unyielding, jagged corruption.
We are two-legged, four-legged, winged and finned, feathered and furred,
of rainforests, deserts, lakes, and oceans.
We are ice crystals, frozen waterfalls, ice caves, blue ice, and crashing wave art galleries,
rivers circling with playful otters,
playful and prayful, we are hopeful water creatures blissfully dependent and vulnerable,
still illuminated by star fire, still caressed by winds.

MAUREEN MATUSEWIC

*"Dread has followed longing,*
*And our hearts are torn."*

WILLIAM BUTLER YEATS

# JUST A RAVEN IN AN OUTSOURCED SKY

The raven flew purposely toward me as I stood in the yard of my simple home in the woods. To my amazement, the black bird barrel-rolled twice above my head and simply kept going. I searched for some meaning in this private sky show, but arguing with a cast of characters pushing for an open pit mine in my homeland had filled my days, mind, and heart with doubt and sadnesss. I concluded the bird was just a raven in an outsourced sky. I went back to thinking about my neighbors who prayed to their gods to allow them to trade the watershed and hills and clean air for jobs. Lobbyists served high-capacity cocktails to the governor and his minions who encouraged grandmothers to fill their grandbabies' bottles with industrial waste. ᕮ I, once a wandering forest child who sang to the birds and animals, had a mind that was infected with this political pollution and could not see to accept the gift of the raven. ᕮ Months later, as my husband lay sleeping; I studied his face and saw past his gray whiskers to the peach fuzz of our childhoods when we were innocents who wandered the woods together. A small poem formed in my heart and the evil spell was broken. ᕮ I realized that moments in life are a series of poems about love, sunlight, and laughter. Instead of trying to solve political dramas, I could open myself back up to the beauty and mystery of the powers that rule the wildflowers and the waters, and the gift of the messenger — the raven in a loving sky.

MAUREEN MATUSEWIC

# AUGUST

*"I can be jubilant one moment and pensive the next,*
*and a cloud could go by and make that happen."*
BOB DYLAN

# WATER LILIES

White water lilies with lemon meringue centers on the fringe of a mucky lake.

The quiet surface reflected the sky and shore,

van Goghed by the sun and wind and water,

shielding the ancient civilization where insects cling to slimy stems

and transparent piles of fish-egg eyes rock back and forth with the currents of life

watching and waiting for that moment to hatch so that they can feed or be fed.

A duckling bobbing innocently on the water

is jerked once from underneath, then again,

dragged under never to return.

A muskie, I suppose.

Shocked, I turn to the sky and listen to my heart beat.

MAUREEN MATUSEWIC

*"Constant kindness can accomplish much.*
*As the sun makes ice melt, kindness causes misunderstanding, mistrust,*
*and hostility to evaporate."*
ALBERT SCHWEITZER

# THE DOOR NUMBER 3 CLUB

When I picked Maggie to be my dog, it was because she was the right size, short-haired, sweet, and subdued. She was in a cement stall in the shelter's door number 3 with the rest of the pit bulls and misfit dogs. She belly-crawled over to us, sweetly and submissively, winning our hearts and a reprieve, scars and all.  ⤳  Five years later, her spoiled life consists of snuggling and kissing friends and relatives beyond politeness, chickens cooked just for her, and sitting in laps despite being clearly too large. But sometimes, when I casually reach out to pet her unexpectedly, her skin jumps in fear. A few times, frustrated that my love has not healed her, I've said, "Really, Maggie? You are afraid of me?"  ⤳  I understand now, since my little girl self had a recent, simple dream. In it, the girl was looking at one of the little, white wooden garages that lined the alleys of my home town. The sun was shining, the grass was green. It was quiet, like a photo. As she stood there, the garage doors began to open, and memories begin to drip in pieces from the dream to my half-awake state. I rolled over, pulled the blanket over my head, pushed the memory back and clearly heard, "Little girls should not go into little white garages."  ⤳  This is the dream of door number 3 where members greet each other with twitches and fear and love.

MAUREEN MATUSEWIC

*"God is trying to sell you something, but you don't want to buy.*
*That is what your suffering is: your fantastic haggling, your manic screaming over the price!"*

HAFIZ

# CENTERED

The Sun is the center of our solar system, but the Moon and North Star take turns center stage at night in the Northern Hemisphere. Closer to home, the Penokee Hills center us, as they always have, drawing us to walk in their forests and cross their clear streams. My thoughts slow to accept and enjoy whatever is in my path: yellow trout lilies and purple violets; sweet grasses warmed by the sun; jagged outcroppings; ice sculptures and forest creatures. In this altered state, one can feel the vibrations of ancient trails and people who were here long before men defined the legal boundaries of Wisconsin. ✎ Penokee people feel homesick when they are too-long separated from the hills and waters that flow north into Lake Superior. They are drawn from all over, with feelings for this magnetic place. It is easy to understand why people feel deeply for their homelands, and confusing why others have sacrificed their centers, filling themselves with desires for money and short-lived power. Some use misguided quotes of their gods as weapons, ignoring the loving messages in the same books and the loving messages of the Sun, Moon, and stars. ✎ The hills and the Penokee people have been threatened by boundary creators who hold the price of ore and appetites of the world at their centers. Unquenchable thirst for power positions them as leaders of greed. ✎ Meanwhile, the Penokees remain constant. Plants rest under the snow, water flows slowly now, waiting for the spring thaw.

✎

## MAUREEN MATUSEWIC

*"Make the most of your regrets; never smother your sorrow,*
*but tend and cherish it 'til it comes to have a separate and integral interest.*
*To regret deeply is to live afresh."*
HENRY DAVID THOREAU

## TOO LATE TO SEND A CARD?

Walking through a thrift store, I saw an antique china cup decorated with red and gold flowers that reminded me of my lost friend, Karen. An unexpected feeling of loneliness came over me. In our mothering years, we were good friends who spent time together as our boys played. But, life separated us physically and when she had an affair that I didn't understand or approve of, it was the end of our friendship. My older self would have asked questions, especially, "Why didn't you tell me that you weren't happy?" Her sister told me she's been married to a new man for about 20 years and is happy. *Is it too late to send a card?* ✎ Reading through old poems, I came across memories about my little brother Pete, who murdered a woman, then killed himself, six years ago. ✎ Sometimes I blame Alaska for tempting him with its beautiful, dangerous land, darkening his mind with her darkness, drawing him into despair. But I know it's not Alaska's fault. ✎ Sometimes I blame Pete. *We were right here! How did you hide the craziness?* I shake my fist and shout, "Look what you did!" It's more than just Pete's fault. ✎ Sometimes I blame myself, for not being anywhere near "right there." ✎ There is no excuse for love not shared. ✎ It's been six years. Time does not heal all wounds; you just don't pick at the scars as often. ✎ Giving love and respect freely allows you to roll around memories sweetly. ✎ Holding back hurts.

✎

MAUREEN MATUSEWIC

*"It's a rather rude gesture, but at least it's clear what you mean."*

KATHARINE HEPBURN

# THE HAIRCUT

Christie and I usually make small talk when she cuts my hair, but this time we were quietly eavesdropping on a drama in the next chair. An angry, older woman with pinkish duckling hair was harassing her hairdresser — hired to fix the old woman's self-inflicted bad haircut. ᕦ The old woman said, "Why do you keep touching the right side of my head? The left side is longer!" ᕦ The young woman stepped back. She eyed the woman and said patiently, "I am trying to even out your haircut. Do you want me to stop?" ᕦ "No! I want you to fix it, but I don't want it any shorter! I need to get a curler in it!" ᕦ My husband, who was waiting for me, looked up from his magazine. Our eyes met and we tried to hide our amusement. ᕦ In short order, the young hairdresser finished and the repaired haircut looked respectable. The woman pulled a hat over her head abruptly and silently paid her bill. Christie whispered, "Look at the floor. There's hardly any hair." A few fluffs lay on the floor like pink rose petals. ᕦ As soon as the old woman left, the frustrated young hairdresser let loose a verbal bomb, "She fucking hacked her hair and then was mad at me?"ᕦ We all chimed in to support her patience and kindness. But her outburst was a reminder of too many times in my life when I held back while being mistreated, only to blow later, sometimes regretfully. ᕦ Older and wiser, life has taught me the value of shrugging things off or saying, "Fuck this" up front and moving on with my day.

ᕦ

MAUREEN MATUSEWIC

# AUGUST 6

*"The language of friendship is not words but meanings."*

HENRY DAVID THOREAU

# FRIENDSHIP

Friend: "What are you reading?"  Me: "What's-her-name's blog on unleashing your super hero. I really like her writing even though I don't like the self-help feel to some of her stuff. I think I'm reading it because of my own vocational questions.  What are *you* reading?"  Friend: "I'm reading, 'What if your cat eats tinsel?'"   Friendship — it's what happens between the lines.

HEIDI C. KING

*"What happens when people open their hearts?*
*They get better."*
HARUKI MURAKAMI

# THE HEALING

I
cut.
Cut off.
Cut out.
Cut through.
Cut to the quick.
I am a cut above.
My heart tells me
I'm ready to
let go
of
c
u
t
t
i
n
g
.

~

HEIDI C. KING

*"There are four kinds of people in the world ...*
*Those who build walls. Those who protect walls. Those who breach walls.*
*And those who tear down walls. Much of life is discovering who you are."*

P. S. BABER

# WALLS

Our town is small, but we have a first-rate nursing home. Since I live less than a mile from the home, I often stop there on my daily walks to say hi to my friend Elsa. My visits frequently occur during the residents' dinner time, so I slowly became friends with Elsa's tablemate, Violet. At first, the only thing I knew about Violet was that she'd had a stroke and struggled to find the right words. ✎ Over time, I became proud of myself for breaching the wall to friendship with such a complete stranger. ✎ One day, Violet and I had a conversation that went like this: "Hey, Violet, what's that patch over your eye for?" ✎ "I don't know," mused Violet, aware of the patch but equally unaware of its purpose. ✎ "Hmmm," I pondered. "Maybe I could just ask the resident nurse what happened. Oh, but they won't tell me if they know I'm not your family. (Pause.) Can I just say I'm your family, Violet?" ✎ With sincerity so pure it knocked down the wall I'd just been chiseling through, Violet walked straight into my soul: "You don't have to *say* you're my family, you can *be* my family!"

✎

HEIDI C. KING

# AUGUST 9

*"A child of five could understand this.*
*Send someone to fetch a child of five."*
GROUCHO MARX

# TRUTH

Is it simple?

Is it deep?

So close

You've always known

Yet not till now?

Then yes,

It's likely

Truth.

HEIDI C. KING

# AUGUST 10

*"You people have names [said the cat].*
*That's because you don't know who you are.*
*We know who we are, so we don't need names."*

NEIL GAIMAN

# INVISIBLE

I used to think the world around me made me invisible.

I was invisible because I was a girl.

Then I was invisible because I was a woman.

Then I was invisible because I did not have great power.

Now I know

I am invisible

Only when I cannot see

Myself.

HEIDI C. KING

*"Walking is good for solving problems —
it's like the feet are little psychiatrists."*

PEPPER GIARDINO

# WALKING

My sister tells me that many famous people take a daily walk as part of their schedule — that walking unleashes their creativity. My roommate regularly asks me after my own daily walk, "So what fell into your head this time?" Studies show that people who walk have more creative and higher numbers of ideas. And, wouldn't you know ... Adam and Eve "heard the sound of the Lord God walking in the garden in the cool of the day." Let's go!

HEIDI C. KING

*"We are here to awaken from our illusion of separateness."*

THICH NHAT HANH

# THE SUN ROSE FOR ME

The sun rose for me

For me alone

I swear

Red ball of fire truth

You cannot tell a lie

You tell each one the same

"I rose for you alone"

Red ball of fire truth

You cannot tell a lie.

HEIDI C. KING

*"... and then, I have nature and art and poetry,*
*and if that is not enough, what is enough?"*

VINCENT VAN GOGH

## MILLION-DOLLAR BIRDS

The morning after Christmas, I surveyed the living room and assessed the cleanup postponed from last night's potluck. Six "friends without families" had gathered here. A generous host, I'd given each guest a million dollars. The bills came from the paper goods aisle of the grocery store, a neat stack glued together along one edge, easy to tear off and distribute. Oversized, printed on one side only. Except for food and each other's company, the bills were the only gifts.  ⤙  We'd all laughed and chatted over wine and dinner. Except one of us, a man whose preferred social mode was silence. I'd long ago stopped trying to coax him into conversation. He was the Buddha in the group — placid, self-contained, quiet as a cat.  ⤙  Looking around the room that morning, I noticed something small next to the plates and glasses on the corner end table. Had a guest forgotten something? To my surprise, I found two origami sculptures, each folded perfectly into that Japanese symbol of good luck — a crane. Each made from one-half of a million-dollar bill. Where the silent one had sat last night, tuning out the group.  ⤙  My heart warmed and opened. "Million-dollar birds," I said to myself, smiling. "My good fortune, a treasure." The Buddha had turned his party into a meditation on folding paper, and planned to leave his work behind. The gift I'd given was now returned in new form, doubled in value. I felt visited by the Magi.  ⤙  I carried the million-dollar birds to a special spot on the bookshelf, where they remain today, valuable as ever.

⤙

DARLENE FRANK

*"Do everything with so much love in your heart*
*that you would never want to do it any other way."*

YOGI DESAI

## SELECTIVE COMPASSION

The four of them walk slowly across the driveway: my neighbor Felicia with a woman close to her on each side, and her husband, who had moved out months ago, following right behind. Felicia holds her arm across her chest. Their serious mood makes me wonder what's wrong. ᖇ Then I notice the stuffed animal in her hand, the helium balloon on a string. Hospital, I think. Broken arm? ᖇ "Did you have an accident?" I ask. I want to offer sympathy but not probe. ᖇ She shakes her head, points her hand down toward her female parts, and grimaces. ᖇ "Oh, I'm so sorry. I hope you'll feel better soon." We pass and go in opposite directions. ᖇ A moment later, judgment rears. That look of helplessness, poor me, that I caught in her face and gesture. She feels sorry for herself! All the unneighborly feelings I've harbored toward this woman come alive. I imagine the guilt she'll make her children, brother, mother, husband endure taking care of her. My sympathy is gone. ᖇ And then my better self speaks up: "So, you practice selective compassion. To some you will give, to others you will not." ᖇ How ashamed I feel. I, who profess spiritual principles and even lead a group on the same. Heartlessness lives next door to my heart. ᖇ I remember that day often now, especially when I see someone who reminds me of Felicia or her family, and I deliberately call up compassion. It's still selective. But my better self shows me, on cue, a drop-down menu. To whom shall I give love: ONE. SOME. SELECT ALL. The first two options are grayed out. Only the conscionable choice remains.

DARLENE FRANK

# AUGUST 15

*"I'm living so far beyond my income*
*that we may almost be said to be living apart."*

E. E. CUMMINGS

## MONEY MANTRA

"Julia doesn't *ever* need to worry about money." Walking at the beach, I repeated this like a mantra. It had been on my mind for days after my friend Alice described a woman she knew. The firm way she'd said it — *never* needing to worry — had attached itself to my brain unlike most passing remarks about money.  ⬳  Like most people, I'd imagined relief from financial concern, but it was a mere mental exercise. This time I had a goal — to actually experience this feeling. So I repeated the mantra about Julia and imagined it was true. For me. Forever.  ⬳  It felt incredibly good. Wholesome. Delicious. Voluptuous. I felt so free and happy, I wanted to sing.  ⬳  I continued to walk and stayed in the feeling. Everything around me looked brighter. The feeling seemed not to come from my thoughts any more; it had taken me over and I made no effort to sustain it. It carried me along on its wave.  ⬳  The feeling had gone beyond happy. It was joy.  ⬳  Even more mind-blowing, this joyful feeling had nothing to do with money. It was independent of any relationship to income and bill paying. This meant I could feel the same happiness about something other than money. Maybe about anything.  ⬳  Happiness — joy — was a feeling I could summon. I had just done it.  ⬳  This experience changed me. I am happier now, and able to bring on this feeling that radiates joy — joy that feels completely natural.  ⬳  Do we ever need to worry about money?

⬳

DARLENE FRANK

*"Beauty is a fragile gift."*

OVID

# THE ELEVATOR GIRLS

When I was 38 years old, I worked a few months as a technical writer at a bank in San Francisco. Daily, on the elevator ride to and from my 10th floor office, I noticed girl after girl whose face seemed extraordinarily beautiful. I know the girls were women, but I thought of them as "the elevator girls."  Where did they come from? I wondered. How could they all share the same kind of beauty? What gave them an identical glow?  I had never seen so many splendid-looking women in one place. Each elevator ride became a sojourn through a small gallery of beautiful faces: resting my eyes on one after another, noting the skin's texture and the bones of the face, the silhouette of the head, the precise outline of the eyes, each mouth a unique soft shape of color. It was their skin that gave me the most pleasure — smooth, flawless, unmarred.  But daily, this puzzle: What made them so beautiful?  One morning, as I walked the dim hallway to my office, I knew the answer — the elevator girls were young, only in their twenties. I was looking at youth! At 38, I had finally learned to see the beauty of youth.  I wondered if the girls knew what a gift they bestowed on the world. If they carried themselves proudly, aware of their luminous sparkle.  In my youth, I had missed my own beauty.  I want to tell every young woman: Youth, by its nature, is beautiful. Appreciate who you are now. And to all women: Notice your beauty today. It will never come again in the same way.

DARLENE FRANK

*"What is the good of your stars and trees, your sunrise and the wind,*
*if they do not enter into our daily lives?"*

E. M. FORSTER

# TREE IN GOLDEN GATE PARK

Walking one spring afternoon in Golden Gate Park, I was stopped by a large, old tree. I was well outside the umbrella of its limbs when I felt the force of it. I knew I had entered the tree's huge energy field, the sacred space this tree claimed. ⤳ I stood for a few moments in the church of its leaves, and took in its vast arcing form, its loving wings. Its lowest branch began so far above the ground I could only dream of reaching it. ⤳ The park was quiet. Few people were about. The tree's energy blended with my own and I offered a silent prayer that surprised me with its archaic phrasing: *Angel tree, I do thee worship.* ⤳ In the late afternoon sun, I took keen delight in the wind in my hair and the brush of silk inside my coat pockets and the white spring flowers in the grass. Into all my body flowed the blessings of this tree. ⤳ Touched by the magnificent spirit of the tree, I breathed my thank yous and walked on through the park.

⤳

DARLENE FRANK

*"The body is your only home in the universe.*
*It is your house of belonging here in the world."*

JOHN O'DONOHUE

# FULL MOON

We sat on the rocks by the lake on a warm summer night in Maine, my host Joan and her daughter and friends from the free school where she taught, and I. White shimmering lines on the water mirrored the full moon's face.  "I always find the moon so sexy," Joan said.  Sexy? The moon? That white, cold, distant, unreachable shape in the sky? Maine was as spectacular a landscape as I'd seen by that point in my life. But the moon? The Maine moon was nothing special. No moon was.  I was in my early twenties, still in college. It had been a bad summer all around between me and my host, and I left early. But what did I know at that age — about myself, how to leave gracefully, or the moon?  Decades later, on the opposite coast, I walk next to the ocean with a friend, the sky dark, the moon hidden behind fog. Lights from the pier illuminate our path. Suddenly, to our left, in a cleft where the hills meet in a broad V, a patch of fog clears. I catch my breath at the sight. Feel a warm rush in my body. The huge supermoon — that extra-large full moon — has risen over the hills and is now exposed. A flourish of clouds conceals the lower half of the moon like a silky skirt wrapped around a dancer. A magnificent goddess, she rises further, radiating power.  I stand transfixed by her size, her bold glow against the dark sky. She steals my breath. I long to take the moon into my arms. Make her mine, forever.

DARLENE FRANK

# AUGUST 19

## BREAKFAST NOTE

Morning silence, neighbors gone, no noise until the delicate smash of egg upon the floor. How easily its cool shape slipped from my hand. I watched it fall, in near sleep — so fast — its crash a single note at a perfect pitch. That note of impact replayed all day to me, like a temple bell. Drew my wandering fragments of attention back to Now, where brief whispered melodies hinted at secrets I might one day know. Did something inside me break free that day? Gently fracture, no warning, just its time? A haiku moment clearing all debris, summoning up infinity. Here, broken, is new form, such that I even wished a second egg might fall, to hear that sound again. Invitation to a world where knowing slips away, and dreams might disappear or new ones enter, with the splitting of a fragile shell.

DARLENE FRANK

*"We cast a shadow on something wherever we stand."*

E. M. FORSTER

## BLUE MILL TAVERN

We were all in Iowa together: my two big brothers, my two big sisters, and me, the baby. On a hot, humid July afternoon, we piled into a van to tour our variously shared childhoods. We drove by schools, houses, and ball fields, telling stories of our youths — liberally embellished by the brothers. With a 17-year age difference from youngest to oldest, we didn't all share the same memories and experiences.  ⤝  When we drove past the Blue Mill Tavern, we all started telling about the times we sat outside that bar, waiting for the prodigal dad. Over the years, the car may have changed from Buick to Chevy, and the names of the bars may have changed but we all remembered being a kid in a car waiting for a dad who might not appear for hours. As the youngest, my stints were usually solitary. The others were closer in age and would sometimes sit together and goof off. I was shocked to find out that they sometimes had the audacity to walk home if the wait got too long; I had never considered the possibility of leaving the confines of the vehicle.  ⤝  It was a shared experience still vivid 40 years later that defined us as a family and as individuals. It shaped us — making us funny, tough, and ultimately okay.  ⤝  The next time we returned to Iowa there were there only four of us. One of my brothers had died unexpectedly of an aneurism and we had come to scatter his ashes at the site of many brotherly exploits. On our way, we drove by the Blue Mill Tavern.

ELIZABETH MADSEN-GENSZLER

*"Every moment and every event of every man's life on earth
plants something in his soul."*

THOMAS MERTON

# NEW HOUSE

When I first moved to town, I had a regular walking route and a need for surprise — no mean feat when the route encompasses a rectangle that is roughly 16 by 5 city blocks. To my never-failing delight, one aging sidewalk's entire square would tip dramatically from side to side as soon as I stepped on it. I knew the street but I worked to make sure I never exactly remembered the block. This gave me endless amounts of surprise and delight. ⇝ As if that wasn't enough excitement, there was another street I loved that intersected with the tippy sidewalk street. Somehow I could manage to surprise myself yet again by making sure I changed my route just enough that I didn't hit this street too often. It was lined with huge elm trees, was only four blocks long, and ended in a T with another tree-lined residential street. I loved the way it felt, to turn the corner and see the lush corridor of trees ending with a row of small houses. Along the street was a lovely craftsman-style house and a magical and mysterious red brick house. The brick house had a big yard and an aging, wrought iron fence. Though the house was beautiful, there was also something wonderfully off-kilter about it. ⇝ Over the years, the elm trees succumbed, the sidewalk was replaced, the red brick house received renovations, and months after my husband died, I realized the new house I found to live in was one of those I had seen when I had gazed down the street with so much pleasure.

⇝

ELIZABETH MADSEN-GENSZLER

*"I remember the first time I heard a teenager say LOL. Just what?*
*But it means 'laugh.' Why don't you just laugh? What are you doing?"*

J. K. ROWLING

## 271 CLOSE FRIENDS

I deactivated my Facebook account 10 days ago. During the first days, I felt the same lethargy, headache, and angst that accompany quitting caffeine or sugar. Information about other people is a drug of choice and simply put, I'm snoopy. ✎ Before the Internet, I knew stuff about people because I have the kind of face that causes strangers to tell me weird, personal stories. Then I met Google; I felt like I had found a soul mate. Google knew how I thought. Google knew stuff that I wanted to know, even before I knew I wanted to know it. I am a Google savant. It enabled me to know so much about others that I needed to pretend ignorance of the pedigrees and lawsuits of mere acquaintances. So, there I was, living happily with Google and our periodic visits to Wisconsin Circuit Court Access. ✎ Then I got a Facebook page, and a mother lode of personal information about people I barely knew dropped in my lap. I didn't even need to work for it. Because of these people I barely knew, I had access to pictures of the feet of people I had never met and could read about these strangers' vacations, illnesses, relationships, and political leanings. ✎ With my 271 closest Facebook buddies, I started feeling lonelier than I ever had before. I spent hours every evening looking at pictures of what other people were eating, and reading about their cool parties and great jobs. ✎ I went cold turkey and deactivated Facebook. There are things I miss, just not the feelings of envy and resentment and the pictures of feet.

ELIZABETH MADSEN-GENSZLER

*"Always remember that you are absolutely unique.*

*Just like everyone else."*

MARGARET MEAD

# THE SPECIAL ONES

We thought that *we* were the special ones. Then we found out that everyone who came by to sign the card had a story and he had made all of them feel special too. ᕍ He wasn't the best at fixing things but he was so good spirited about it that we cheered him on, so the next time he might get it right. When he caught a towel on fire in our microwave, it just seemed so cute and goofy that we could only laugh as the office filled with smoke. He kept apologizing and we assured him it was fine. The next day he brought us a homemade blueberry pie. ᕍ When he was clearing snow with a small plow, we heard a big crash as the glass on our front door shattered. He was so apologetic and worried that we wouldn't be able to bring ourselves to even tease him about that mishap. ᕍ Unlike the stereotypical male, he was unafraid to call co-workers and ask for advice on fixing things. They, like us, seemed to find it disarming. ᕍ Every time we submitted a work request, he would stop in to say hello and tell us what he was doing and how long it might take. He had retired from another career, came to maintenance as a part-time worker, and managed to make an impact on everyone he met. ᕍ Several months ago, we found out he was quite ill and while we don't yet know the outcome, we were reminded how special he made us all feel.

ᕍ

ELIZABETH MADSEN-GENSZLER

*"If you're poor and you do something stupid, you're nuts.*
*If you're rich and do something stupid, you're eccentric."*
BOBBY HEENAN

## SMALL STUFF

I like the small stuff. It's the small stuff that often makes life bearable.  It amuses me every single time I shred a piece of paper because the office paper shredder looks like a vagina with sharp metal teeth; I love that my dog's feet smell like corn chips; I am enchanted that twice a day there is a chance to see the clock show 11:11; and I was over the moon when a bunch of fire hydrants in town were painted in hues that made them look like rosy-nippled, robot women.  There are so many things in life that I cannot control — and don't even work to control — but my endless ability to be charmed by the small stuff is something I nurture. I don't exercise enough, I don't eat right, I weigh too much, and spend too much time watching television, but I work to make sure that I can still see the quirky magic in the world. For me, the answers aren't in nature and religion. I find nature to be nicely accented by a billboard or two and I am unnerved by all religions except that snake-handling one because of its odd combination of danger and sexual tension.  The people in my life who love me view my love of all the small stuff sort of like the antics of a trained chimp. My teenage daughter smiles indulgently when I excitedly tell her how much the dried hair balls coughed up by the cat remind me of dreadlocks. Viewing life through a slightly off-kilter lens keeps me coming back every day for more.

ELIZABETH MADSEN-GENSZLER

# AUGUST 25

*"If a dog jumps into your lap, it is because he is fond of you;*
*but if a cat does the same thing, it is because your lap is warmer."*
ALFRED NORTH WHITEHEAD

## SOCKS AND PEOPLE

My dog and my teenage daughter don't especially like each other. When she was packing to go away to college, he swallowed seven of her brightly colored Hello Kitty ankle socks and one expensive orange-patterned, SmartWool® sock. The day before she left, he urped them all back up. The eight socks and the dog were whole and relatively unscathed except for fading on the SmartWool® sock. I washed the socks several times and packed them in her bag. People commented that the dog must have been sad about her leaving. I knew that wasn't true. Sometimes bad things just happen to good socks.

ELIZABETH MADSEN-GENSZLER

*"Loneliness adds beauty to life. It puts a special burn on sunsets
and makes night air smell better."*

HENRY ROLLINS

# ROSEMARY

Rosemary is a transformative scent; it is the scent of expectation. It reminds me of the things that I have lost and the things I long for still. ⤶ Scent is evocative. A wafting smell can take me back in time or forward in expectation. My mother smelled like Avon's Cotillion perfume mixed with the exhaust from a deep fat fryer and my father smelled of creosote leaching from railroad ties. I believe I fell in love with my late husband because of pheromones and I will never forget the alluring smell of the wildly squalling daughter placed in my arms in an orphanage in China. ⤶ Now, I live in a house without other people and I miss the day-to-day smell of a shared life. I love the smell of my dog and two cats and it might be specieist, but I miss the sweet smell of the top of a child's head and the musky smell of a husband. ⤶ These days I try to content myself with rosemary. Cutting rosemary and throwing it into a pan of onions and garlic simmering in olive oil makes me feel alive and connected. Yet, as much as I love the scent of rosemary, I never fully care for the plants. Every year, I have visions of growing lush rosemary plants all summer long, then bringing the plants inside and keeping them alive through the long winter. In reality, I start the plants and tend them sporadically; I end up with a collection of sad, spindly plants that I harvest and use too infrequently. Sometimes it seems like my life would be different if I tended the rosemary. Hope, like rosemary, springs eternal.

ELIZABETH MADSEN-GENSZLER

*"If you have not slept, or if you have slept, or if you have a headache, or sciatica, or leprosy, or thunder-stroke, I beseech you, by all angels, to hold your peace, and not pollute the morning."*

RALPH WALDO EMERSON

## REVERENCE REMEMBERED

I was sipping coffee when I read this Emerson quote, chuckling to myself about having thunder-stroke, whatever that is. *Amusing, but this doesn't really apply to me,* I thought as I moved on to another morning reading. My mind went back to leprosy, though, and how lucky we are that ... wait a second. Was that me who was complaining to my husband yesterday morning about the newspaper delivery man (he's always late on Sundays!)? Was that me who was griping about my sore back? My restless night's sleep? Well, yes, but surely *polluting* is too strong a word for simply talking. Or is it?  ⤙  I considered other ways that I sometimes foul up the morning. Furiously scribbling a to-do list before my eyes are even fully open. Rattling off the day's agenda to my daughter, as if she, in pre-school, is invested in smooth orderly transitions. Letting the threatening weather report nudge me into brooding. Not seeing, not revering. Well, Emerson, you've got my attention now.  ⤙  Cradling my coffee mug, I look out over the fresh white snow, wedding-cake perfect under the pink glow of the rising sun. As unpolluted as anything I've seen. My daughter will soon walk sleepily into the kitchen, eyes peeking out from behind an armful of stuffed animals. I will hug her. I will welcome her to this beautiful day. We will look outside together and marvel at the brightness, holding our peace.

EILEEN M. KENNEDY

*"A sense of blessedness comes from a change of heart,*
*not from more blessings."*

MASON COOLEY

# SPRING FORWARD

We moved to a suburb of Chicago at the very onset of winter. Not just any winter: the record-breaking one where we, gob-smacked, were introduced to the term *polar vortex*. We moved from a warm place — one that didn't offer weather that could actually frighten you. I didn't like my new home and I felt like I might never run out of adjectives to describe my loathing of it. "This place!" I lamented, over and over. It's hard to describe the futility of wanting to grab a geographical location and throttle it. ✑ When the calendar announced the first day of spring, Mother Nature, sassy thing, kept dumping snow on us. Record-setting floods followed the snow. A record-setting number of "days without sun" followed the floods. One day I was looking out at the apocalyptic landscape, poised to record my fury in my journal. The seething insults did not come. Instead, defeated, I wrote, "I simply cannot hang my happiness on whether the sun shines." ✑ It would make a great ending if everything changed from that day. It didn't. There was, however, just enough of a surrender to slightly ease the resentment in my heart, which made the next day more tolerable, and the day after that a little more so. My process of acceptance was like Chicago's progression towards spring: slow and sloppy. But these tiny shifts were seismic; they got me through days I formerly thought impossible to endure. ✑ Finally, one day flowers greeted me and the air was less biting. I felt a bursting gratitude that eclipsed the resentment, and that's when I knew I had crossed over to safe territory. The vortex had not pulled me in.

EILEEN M. KENNEDY

*"With only a change in one's perspective,*
*the most ordinary things take on inexpressible beauty."*

KAREN MAEZEN MILLER

## CHAIN REACTION

The skies were gray but not threatening yet. *As long as it doesn't rain on me it should be a good ride*, I thought, donning my bike helmet. Miles down the bike path, I heard the ping of raindrops on my helmet, which rapidly increased to a drumming beat. *Figures*, I groused to myself, *now my ride is ruined*. I turned around to head home and my bike suddenly came to a lurching halt. Trying to steady myself, I found that I was stuck — to the bike. Something was caught and the bike and I were now one. We shuffled together to the side of the path. Leaning down to examine the problem, I found that my pant leg was entwined with the chain and had been sucked into the chain ring.  Standing there alone attached to my bike in the rain momentarily caused a frisson of panic. Other bikers, wise to the weather, had stayed home. I tugged on my pant leg and stared, tugged and stared again. Then I let out a tension-breaking giggle, a recognition of my ridiculous state.  After much jiggering, I was rewarded when my pant leg broke free. Unfortunately so did the bike chain. I carefully hooked it back on the sprockets (yes, I had to look that up), then wiped the grease on my newly freed wet pant leg.  Absorbed in the bliss of self-reliance, I was impervious to the rain. What I did notice was a simple new thought that became almost sublime in my jubilant state: even if it rains on me it'll still be a good ride! Eureka! (Well, that, and don't wear baggy pants on a bike ride).

EILEEN M. KENNEDY

*"To know what you prefer instead of humbly saying Amen to what the world tells you you ought to prefer, is to have kept your soul alive."*

ROBERT LOUIS STEVENSON

# WORK RELEASE

Another looming corporate deadline but this time I'm panicked. I don't understand parts of what I'm tasked with doing. Death by firing squad if I mess it up. I seek help. My boss responds to my confusion, "I guess you're up shit creek without a paddle." ☙ Frustrated to the point of tears, I take a walk. Everyone looks yellow, like they are made of parchment paper; jaundiced under the buzzing fluorescent lights. Another stressed executive in a suit takes my arm for a moment to complain about policy. Or something. I'm not sure because I'm not listening. I'm looking at the corporate career before me. This is my future, and I feel myself fading. ☙ I've been at this game for almost a decade. Excited at first, I am now weary of wondering why life always seems like it's over there some-where. Funny, I always saw myself as origami paper, delightful squares the color of spring flowers, able to be turned into anything at all. ☙ My spirit rebels and starts siphoning off money from my checking account to my savings. When I've gathered enough, months later, she lets me know. It's time. ☙ I give my notice. It's still hard to resist the pull of security. I have to explain over and over why I'm not crazy. Even to myself. My spirit puffs up her chest and reminds me: "You are origami paper, not parchment." ☙ So I escape. I leave all the familiar and start off on something new. It was impossible to explain to others about the origami paper, so I just kept saying, "I must." Yes, I know it sounds crazy, but I must.

EILEEN M. KENNEDY

*"A thing is complete when you can let it be."*

GITA BELLIN

# FLIGHT RISK

En route to Florida, about mid-flight, my five-year-old daughter erupts into a screaming, kicking, werewolf-on-the-loose fit of madness. My husband, sitting next to her, exhausts the checklist of things a parent does when their child is spiraling out of control. Panic wells up in me. My hand presses into my husband's shoulder. *Fix this,* it urges. ⟳ I see the turned heads. I can hear the whispers. "Why aren't those parents doing anything?" Attention-shy, horrified by public scenes, I swallow the sharpness of their judgment, like so many fish bones in my throat. Mortified, I sink into my seat. ⟳ Suddenly, my daughter lunges over and sends the contents of my tray table scattering into the aisle. The action is so abrupt, so unexpected, that it shatters my paralysis and I am gifted with an exquisitely simple realization: I can do nothing to fix this. No waiting out the tantrum in the car, no sending her to her bedroom. An airplane offers no refuge. ⟳ I collect my wrappers and cups from the aisle and exchange a meaningful look with my husband. The fish bones dissolve in my throat, making it easier to swallow all those words that yearn to be shouted; those words that will make them understand: "We really are good parents! We've tried every-thing!" I feel the lightness of letting go of what my fellow passengers think of me. I make friends with embarrassment and I invite her to sit quietly with us, holding hands, waiting.

EILEEN M. KENNEDY

# SEPTEMBER

*"Without the joy of brotherhood and sisterhood, we cannot go very far."*

THICH NHAT HANH

## COMMUNITY CENTERED

Have you ever seen little kids make friends? One kid sees another kid and says, "Let's play." The other kid nods and then they run. While running, they make up a game. They are mermaids racing for sea treasure; they are airplanes coming in for landing. This process takes all of three minutes. ⬳ There is no hesitation at this age, no pausing to review a mental checklist of ideal friend traits. These kids band together in pure common purpose: "I want to have fun. Who's with me?" As I watch my daughter make another new best friend in the kids' room at a pizza joint, it occurs to me that we adults really muck up this process. ⬳ Recently moved, newly friendless, I am in my adult head too much. I pause, consider, and analyze as I search for friends, then I wonder why I don't have a gaggle of them yet. It's the hesitation, of course. Decades of programming take over, sorting strangers into my kind/not my kind. ⬳ In his book *Fear,* Thich Nhat Hanh encourages each of us to build a *sangha*, a community banding together for the common purpose of relieving suffering by sharing with one another our joys and sorrows. He reminds us that group energy is stronger than our individual energy. He doesn't advise us to find the "right" people nor wait for the "right" moment. He could not be clearer when he urges us to do it now. Enough thinking, just run. ⬳ I see the great promise in this type of community. To build it, though, I must become a little kid again. I want compassion and support. Who's with me?

⬳

EILEEN M. KENNEDY

*"It takes courage to release the familiar and seemingly secure,*
*to embrace the new. But there is no real security in what is no longer meaningful.*
*There is more security in the adventurous and exciting, for in movement there is life,*
*and in change there is power."*

ALAN COHEN

## IT'S ABOUT TIME

We are back home in Charlotte, NC for a family event. Eager to see everyone after almost a year's absence, we jump into social activity. The harried schedule eventually makes me ill. At first I think I have a virus, but then I suspect an allergy attack — the kind that used to plague me when I lived in the south, popping up at odd times of the year, making my body feel like it was fending off armed invaders. ✐  I carry this ailment back to Chicago with me and wrestle with its meaning. I am convinced there is a message and I only start to get better when I finally get it: I don't miss those allergies. I dreaded them. For the past year and a half since we moved to Chicago, my yearnings had me believing that all I wanted in the world was my old life back. Sure. With the exception of the allergies. And the scorching hot summers. And the burden of my old house. My old life, writ perfect, please. ✐  Time allows for healing and change, even when we are sometimes fighting actively against it, or at best simply not noticing it. Time has made me accept that the things from the past I've been leaning on just can't hold me up anymore. I note my tendency to refer to Charlotte as home, but I realize now, with clarity free from longing, it is not. It's time to get my vocabulary up to speed with my reality. So, I offer a correction: I visited Charlotte; I came back home to Chicago.

**EILEEN M. KENNEDY**

*"But when you practice contentment, you can say to yourself,*
*'Oh yes — I already have everything that I really need.'"*

DALAI LAMA

# NOT PEDALING AS FAST AS I CAN

"I don't want to be a lifer like that one behind you." This was written in an email from one of my employees to another, and, yes, it was about me and it bothered me, *a lot.*  The email was from a young girl, going to school at night to become a teacher, so I knew this job was just a pit stop on whatever road her life was going to take. And, admittedly, I have also looked at co-workers and thought, *They are everything I don't want to be.* Certainly this isn't what I thought I was going to be. I didn't stand next to friends who were dreaming of being ballerinas and state, "I'm going to be a mid-level customer service manager and someday get a parking spot in the underground garage and feel like I've won the lottery."  But this where I am. It's not my dream job, but steady work, and I'm actually pretty good at it.  I imagine myself to be coasting — a bicycle going downhill, taking in the sights, feeling the wind blow by, and occasionally getting up enough speed to even pull a "look ma, no hands" maneuver.  All of this takes no effort; I don't have to pedal or exert myself. It's a comforting, familiar ride and there are no surprises: I know where and how to avoid all the bumps in the road.  Maybe someday I will want the scenery to change, and I know I will need to start pedaling then. But for now, I'm going to coast and enjoy the ride.

DEBORAH THOMAS

*"Imperfection is beauty, madness is genius and it's better to be
absolutely ridiculous than absolutely boring."*

MARILYN MONROE

# PERFECT IMPERFECTION

My husband comes home from a bad day at work with a smile on his face, happy to see me. I come home from a bad day at work and take to the couch immediately, covering myself in the fluffiest blanket I can find because I need to "decompress." Today, despite what my husband will tell you, the earth will not fall off its axis if I load the dishwasher with large plates in the front, blocking smaller plates in the back. Also, if you weren't already aware, freshly laundered socks and underwear will survive without being put into the back of the drawer — as he insists — shifting the older items to the front to insure even wear. ✎ To keep things fair, I need to advise you that I, Deborah Thomas, can go to sleep in a perfectly made bed, and eight hours later, find the comforter on the floor and the top sheet across the room. Then complain I am cold. ✎ I once made a pie and thought the recipe was merely a suggestion. I never made a pie again, nor was I asked to. ✎ And I insist that all chairs be put under the table when you are done eating and all cabinets closed because I'm pretty sure that's how Martha Stewart lives. ✎ I love our quirks and eccentricities. They are a daily reminder that I am loved and get to share my real life with this amazing man. Imperfect though we are, we are perfect together and that's all that matters. ✎ Tonight, I dutifully handed over the remote so he can play couch commando and channel surf at lightning-quick speed. ✎ I wouldn't want it any other way.

✎

DEBORAH THOMAS

SEPTEMBER 5

*"Everyone says social media is some kind of unicorn. But maybe it's just a horse."*

JAY BAER

## UN-SOCIABLE MEDIA

I have a love/hate relationship with social media. I love being able to share amazing moments in someone's life. In an instant, I can see my friend's son hold up his college acceptance letters and know that he aced his applications. I can share in someone's perseverance and triumphs and be inspired by them. I smile when I think of the classmates I've gotten to know who I never really knew before. It's only now I get to see their passions, talents and gifts: who sees art through the lens of a camera, who dedicates their time to making sure children are safe, who loves music and the joy it can bring. I've reconnected with people who bring me such joy and comfort and love. ✎ These are the gifts from social media I am profoundly thankful for and enjoy. And then there are the days I have to covertly visit someone in another state, lest I post that I am within 50 miles of a social media friend and did not announce my visit. Or I learn that someone stubbed their toe. Yaaaawn. ✎ I see advertisements for items I was looking at online just the night before. Creepy! (I was supposed to be looking for a gift for my husband and now there's proof I was looking for a new pair of boots instead.) ✎ I've witnessed keyboard courage run rampant, and common sense take a back seat. And I am absolutely, 100% guilty of both. ✎ When I read this to my husband, he replied, "10-4, good buddy." I guess some of us have a little ways to go on appreciating the magic of social media.

DEBORAH THOMAS

*"The pen that writes your life story must be held in your own hand."*

IRENE C. KASSORLA

# THE GREATEST SHOW ON EARTH

My stepdaughter ran away to join the circus — for real. I can't say this was a surprise. She grew up as a nationally ranked indoor rock climber and spent her spare time coercing us into paying for trapeze lessons and circus camp. She's a natural-born daredevil who was once the starring act in her circus camp finale, where she hung upside down from the ceiling in a straitjacket. I'm assuming she learned this using the chandelier in the dining room. I don't want to know any more than that.  "She said she wants to join the circus!" I yelled to my husband. I got the "please, relax" look. Coincidentally, this was the same look I got when she built a trapeze swing in her room. (I gave her A+ for effort and creativity, but D- for not taking my nerves into account.) A few weeks later she was offered the circus job. "Well?" I demanded of my husband as my terror rose. "Now what?"  We had raised her to be a good person and only wanted her to do something she loved, be able to support herself, have health insurance and security. Done, done and done. She *had* been listening all along.  And off she went. Watching her courageously leave home at nineteen to live her dream, I was blown away. This fierce determination to live life on her own terms inspires me every day to try to live mine the same way. When you live your dream the way she does, every day is the Greatest Show on Earth.

DEBORAH THOMAS

*"Let us all bask in television's warm glowing warming glow."*

HOMER SIMPSON

# FOR YOUR VIEWING PLEASURE

I watch a lot of bad TV. My husband refers to my TV choices as "tragic TV." It goes something like this: someone's wife/husband/mother has left/had an affair/murdered/faked their own death and now the girlfriend/business partner/neighbor/cop will stop at nothing to prove that they/he/she committed the crime and bring the perps to justice. ➤ Or, if it's within two months of the holidays, someone ends up showing someone else — on every show — the true meaning of Christmas. ➤ I also watch "probably not really" reality TV. Any show that features bad housekeeping, bad children, bad parenting or mob wives? I'm all in. And if there's a *COPS* marathon on? We've hit the mother lode! (Any *Law and Order* show counts as an acceptable substitute to the *COPS* show. This statute can be found in Chapter 11, Section 3, Paragraph 3 of Deb's Rules of TV Viewing.) ➤ I watch these shows while snuggled in my favorite blanket, next to my dogs, in my favorite place on earth: at home with my husband. I don't learn anything from them but I'm not looking to; they are my escape from watching the nightly news that sometimes scares me and sometimes breaks my heart. "Tragic TV" is a much more enjoyable choice, with fantasy, reality and sometimes silliness all rolled into one.

DEBORAH THOMAS

*"Among those whom I like or admire, I can find no common denominator,*
*but among those whom I love, I can; all of them make me laugh."*

W.H. AUDEN

# PRESCRIPTION: LAUGHTER AND LOTS OF IT

I was recently experiencing a difficult time and much to my dismay, my husband and friends would not let me isolate myself. This is my usual modus operandi: I take to my bed and ruminate over what's bothering me until it hurts to laugh, have fun, or smile, and I relive the bad day relentlessly, over and over in my head.  ⮑  This time, since my husband and friends wouldn't take no for an answer, I reluctantly agreed to join their gathering. Turns out I laughed harder that day than I've laughed in a long time. At some point during the evening, we started to search videos online. We watched videos of news bloopers. We watched videos of people doing silly, mundane things. I had tears coming down my cheeks from laughter. This was side-splitting laughter, and I could not get enough.  ⮑  When we were getting ready to leave, I told my friends, "This was just what the doctor ordered." It certainly didn't take away my problems but I did learn how very fortunate I was to have people like my friends and family and husband who were there to lift me up when I needed it. People who knew I wasn't 100% that day wrapped their arms around me with the laughter and support I needed.

⮑

DEBORAH THOMAS

*"Eureka!"*

ARCHIMEDES

# MY SIMPLE, POWERFUL AHA MOMENTS

Never use the front windshield cleaner in your car when the sunroof is open.  Sometimes, it's okay to let "them" win and keep your sanity.  Dealing with problems as they arise is much better than storing everything up inside of you, then exploding over something stupid. (It's much easier to justify getting upset over your job or money than trying to explain why you busted a gasket over tomatoes on your hamburger (even though tomatoes are gag-inducing and frankly, I've every right to be wigged out at the sight of them).  Count to ten before sending an email. At least if you are me and HQ sends you an email with six people copied about the fact you bought aluminum foil for the lunchroom instead of encouraging your employees to use Tupperware for their leftovers. (This aha was confirmed when I got home that day, recounted this egregious situation to my husband, and he listened carefully, paused, then replied, "You didn't count to ten, did you?")  Contrary to popular belief and my husband, you will not go blind if you watch TV in something other than high-definition  My sister was right when she told me not to quit the job I had been promoted to when people who didn't get promoted were being mean to me. She told me I'd regret it, but I don't think she meant regret like when I took something of hers without her permission.  And of course, my parents were right about everything.

DEBORAH THOMAS

*"Life is but a day:*

*A fragile dewdrop on its perilous way*

*From a tree's summit."*

JOHN KEATS

# THE SUN ALWAYS RISES, USUALLY

I was waiting for the shower water to warm up and noticed that at 5:30 a.m. the temperature dropped half a degree to 26°F. It was dark outside and I started thinking about the sun. I have always assumed the day will begin, the sun will come up, and it will start getting warmer. But standing there watching the temperature drop, I wondered how I could be sure the sun would come up today, just because it did yesterday and the day before that. What if it just stayed away, or died or something, and the temperature just kept dropping? I was unsettled. ⌐ I assume so many things will just go on happening the way they always have. But what if today I'm in a wreck on the way to work, or I get to work and find I don't have a job anymore, or I find a lump somewhere, or my wife or my kids are injured or die? Or there's another 9/11, or a tree falls on the house, or I get sued, or shot, or fall down the steps? ⌐ And then I think how much more relaxing it is to not focus on all the things that have to go right for it to be just another day. In a way, I feel guilty that I am not taking the time to consider the potential threats to my settled life. Then I remember that no matter what happens, I will deal with it, because that is what we do. I slide the shower door shut and reach for the shampoo. The water is warm. The sun is almost up, probably.

STEVEN WIEBE-KING

*"In the end we shall have had enough of cynicism, skepticism and humbug,*
*and we shall want to live more musically."*
VINCENT VAN GOGH

# A LITTLE THING

I was recently driving home after work from Petersburg, VA to Richmond on I-95. As usual, the 6:00 evening traffic was heavy, a 78 miles-per-hour, white-knuckle barrel o' fun. I noticed the car just ahead of me was being squeezed by a merging tractor-trailer and had nowhere to go, so I risked being rear-ended, and hit the brakes to let him get out of the truck's path. Then I created a little breathing room for the trucker to ease into my lane in front of me. He flickered his lights in gratitude. ∽ I had actually just been trying to save my own butt from high-speed reconfiguration, and was jolted into remembering that those other hurtling steel cages out there were all being driven by humans, and that one of them had just thanked me for what appeared to be a bit of courtesy on my part. I found this inordinately rewarding and comforting, which was a bit puzzling to me. Why? Why do I find it strange to have a flush of satisfaction at a small token of appreciation on the highway? A flash of anger is an understandable reaction to random road rudeness, so why not a little burst of pleasure at an act of kindness? Yes, why not! ∽ I am reminded that my world is the sum of small acts, good or bad, and I can tilt the balance a little toward goodness.

∽

STEVEN WIEBE-KING

*"Much might be said on both sides."*

JOSEPH ADDISON

## EMIL'S CALLUSED PINKY

The other day, Emil, a mason who has plied his trade for six decades, and I were constructing a concrete retaining wall. I was pondering just where to place a PVC pipe to serve as a conduit for utility wires to pass through the wall, when Emil said, "Steve, see the side of this knuckle on my pinky? It's callused and has no sensation. Years ago when I worked constructing reinforced concrete safe rooms, I spent countless hours with a chisel braced on this knuckle as I hammered holes through the concrete. Why don't you just make a hole in the wall afterwards when you know where you need it?"  ⬿  To me this seemed like a totally backwards approach to the problem. Why not spend some time up front, instead, to save significant time and trouble later? But Emil is completely fine with not worrying about things until the problem actually shows up.  ⬿  I thought about how much this episode revealed about both of our personalities. I always want to be thinking ahead and planning, avoiding problems by anticipating them. He, on the other hand, is content to deal with things as they develop; working through problems as they surface, not thinking too far ahead.  ⬿  From Emil, I can learn that it is possible to deal with life's issues as they arise, and not waste too much time trying to anticipate and avoid them, especially since that's often a losing battle.  ⬿  And if Emil had planned ahead a little more, he might still have some feeling in his pinky.

⬿

STEVEN WIEBE-KING

*"I might not be able to be someone who never ever gets the urge
to push people or throw sand at them, but I try to be that person."*
ALLIE BROSH

# THE OTHER CHEEK

Violence was not in my vocabulary during my Mennonite youth, except of course when it came to siblings. At any rate, conceptually I was on board with nonviolence, but it took a couple of charged episodes to drive the point home. ➝ In the summers as a teenager I would often spend the day wandering on foot or on rusty bike, looking for fossils, Indian arrowheads, and trouble. One day, a sometime friend of mine decided somewhere between a ride to the gas station Coke machine and nowhere that it would be a good time for a fist-fight. He kept trying to goad me into throwing the first punch but when I did nothing, he backed up to wind up a good slugging, forgot his bike was lying on the road behind him, and took a hard fall. By the time he disentangled himself from the bike, the steam had gone out of him and he pedaled away, nursing his self-inflicted wounds. I remember watching his silhouette recede over the hill, thinking how awesome nonresistance can be. Vanquished! ➝ The other episode was in junior high when it was my turn to be class leader, line everyone up after shop class, and hold them until given the signal to release them down the hall to lunch. The class bully — who no doubt by now is in Leaven-worth or dead — gave me a cold stare, strode out of his place in line, and hit me so hard I thought for sure my arm was shattered. I was too shocked to react, which he fortunately interpreted as resolve, or something else mysterious, and after a long staredown, he quietly walked back to his place in line.

➝

STEVEN WIEBE-KING

*"Have no fear of perfection — you'll never reach it."*

SALVADOR DALI

# PERFECTION

We need to have the sewer line from our house to the street replaced. There are several ways to do this, from open trenching (least expensive) to trenchless (most expensive), so I asked the contractor what he would do if it were his house. He said, "I had to do my own. I did it the best way, because I own the business. I had a large oak in the front yard that was over the sewer line, so I bored under the tree to save it. Everything was great: yard intact, tree untouched. A few months later a big storm came up, and a huge branch fell and split the trunk right down the middle to the ground, and I had to cut the tree down."    It seems that no matter how hard we work to control our lives, life has its own plan. So when I start getting worked up over just how perfect something has to be, I try to remember that time has a way of undoing the most valiant of efforts. Maybe a little less fretting over the sewer could leave a little more time to smell the roses.

STEVEN WIEBE-KING

*"And on the pedestal these words appear: 'My name is Ozymandias, king of kings:*
*Look on my works, ye Mighty, and despair!'*
*Nothing beside remains.*
*Round the decay*
*Of that colossal wreck, boundless and bare*
*The lone and level sands stretch far away."*

PERCY BYSSHE SHELLEY

# STICK IT, SUSAN!

We were, as usual, late for church, and I was frustrated by a slowpoke driver ahead whose vanity plate read: SUSAN. Finally the passing lane cleared, so I gassed it into the left lane, yelling, "Stick it, Susan!" just as the driver of the car ahead hit the brakes to take a left turn, and I was inches from slamming into it. The combination of me barking and the ABS shudder from my panic braking tore the kids out of their heads-down iPhone reverie, with them yelling, "What the ---" in a symphony with squealing tires and sweat popping off my brow. When I weakly explained the sequence of events, "Stick it, Susan!" became instant classic shorthand for how defeat can be so quickly wrested from the jaws of victory. ⟳ I grew up hearing, "pride goeth before the fall," and sort of understood. After the Susan episode, I really understood.

STEVEN WIEBE-KING

*"To know of someone here and there whom we accord with,*
*who is living on with us, even in silence — this makes our earthly ball a peopled garden."*
JOHANN WOLFGANG VON GOETHE

# HYSTORYECTOMY

Recently at my radiology job, I received an X-ray request labeled with the misspelled indication of "hystoryectomy." This brought to mind a conversation I had with my wife, Jill, a few days earlier. Her dad has memory issues, so when she visits him, he is amazed to hear that he has weekly visits from his wife and from Jill, thinking that it has been years since they've been by. He is crushed to realize that by the next time she visits, he will once again think eons have passed in the interim.  ✍  This yields the uncomfortable realization that we are the sum of our memories, and if our memories fail us, who are we? Not the person we and others thought we were. We are rooted in the remembering of what happened today, yesterday, a year ago, a lifetime ago. Of who our loved ones are, and were. Of who will be with us this evening for supper, and who will visit with us next week, and who lives next door, and who lives in the next state. When all that is stripped away, it seems we are lost, wandering shells, needing constant reminders of who we once were, like a pinball hurtling from bumper to bumper with lights flashing and bells ringing as bits of our history are slung back out to us. And a desperate quiet when the ball slides down the alley past the flappers.  ✍  I am reminded to treasure each little interaction, all the small and big experiences, and all my loved ones. Maybe, just maybe if I hold them really tight, I can hold on to me.

✍

STEVEN WIEBE-KING

*"I go to nature to be soothed and healed,*

*and to have my senses put in order."*

JOHN BURROUGHS

# SENSES

There was a little bird on the trail today. ⬟ One dog had run ahead, bounding through the woods, mind set on exploring her favorite brushy acre. The other had her nose deep in the loam, shoving her little tan face as far in as she could, in the happy, obsessed hunt for a critter that had recently passed through. ⬟ As I slowed to keep an eye on her, there was a quick flutter and whir of wings, and my eyes instead turned to a nearby twig where a small bird sat watching us. We had interrupted its day, and it didn't intend to fly off, so I stilled myself, and we regarded one another quietly. ⬟ The winter-white, late afternoon sun filtered through the trees and as everything came to a hush, my ears awoke. I heard the sound of a thousand weightless, brittle, dead-but-clinging leaves tapping one another on the shoulder, as if trying to collectively remember something long forgotten. I heard the far-off, low roar of an airplane and of course, the earth-dampened squish of leaves and dog snorts. Then, as the light fell on its dappled breast puffed against the cold — the little bird still regarding me with jet black eyes and head tipped in curious observation — I heard the softest trill, saw a tail flick, then another soft trill. Over and over: *trill?* flick, *trill!* We stayed, communing for many full, rich moments. I soaked them in, grateful for my senses.

LAURA NEFF

*"Tell me what you pay attention to, and I will tell you who you are."*

JOSÉ ORTEGA Y GASSET

# LEGACY

It was day three of a family gathering and the nearby Dayton Farmers Market became the answer to "What the heck do we do now?" Cousins and siblings fanned out through the stuffed aisles, loitering in shops with names like "Reflections of Yesteryear." A few family members had split off in pursuit of some tchotchke or another, and I was slowly trailing along behind Dad. ᔓ Parkinson's had shuffled his once-sure steps, and he was far enough into Alzheimer's that we never knew whether he'd be lucid or completely confused. The aisle we walked held so much country kitsch that it was becoming a blur. Suddenly he stopped, straightened and turned, smiling brightly with eyes twinkling. He sought my same-brown eyes and pointed eagerly toward a nearby wall. "Lookie!" The old, metal sign was small with scratched yellow and blue paint, boasting a brown milk jug in the center and proclaimed, "Golden Guernsey, America's Table Milk!" A sweet little sign, easy to miss. But not for Dad. For him, it was a ticket straight to the heart, where memories of the family's Pennsylvania dairy farm were cemented; the farm his grandfather had built with his own hands and passed down to his son, and then to Dad, who loved his Golden Guernsey cows. Here, in this cacophony of clutter: a moment, a memory, and a lesson. ᔓ "You've got to pay attention to what's around you," Dad implored, knowing I would have walked right by. ᔓ A deeper look passed between us as our hearts swelled and broke at the same time.

LAURA NEFF

*"Love isn't something you find. Love is something that finds you."*

LORETTA YOUNG

# MELTING

The black-coated momma and her tan pup had taken up residence in our ramshackle barn that January. Out the kitchen window, we glimpsed them darting in and out of the woods, furtively nosing through the compost. Tamped-down nests in the hay evidenced nightly attempts to stay warm. I tried to approach, but only a wide berth let them feel at all safe. ⤸ "Do not give them names," my husband emphatically stated daily. "The minute you give them names, it's over. And we do not need a dog right now. Okay? Look me in the eyes. OKAY?" ⤸ Robert's last dog had been Seika, a husky he'd loved dearly and held in his arms on her last day. Though it had been years, he still couldn't talk about her passing without tears welling up. Barriers were built against that pain and, understandably, he didn't relish the idea of experiencing it again. ⤸ But as it became clear that the dogs had nowhere to go, I cracked. Robert watched as I sat in the barn day by day, quietly earning their trust, fingertips tentatively brushing fur. He saw the bag of dog food appear next to the kitty kibble. And he knew what was up when the temps dipped below 20° and I went to work layering old towels on the bathroom floor. ⤸ I, too, knew what was up as man slowly sidled up to dog; as cheek eventually leaned in for tentative, slobbery kiss; as hand reached out to gently rub the offered belly. And then, one day, this text: "How about 'Jane'?"

LAURA NEFF

*"Go out and walk. That is the glory of life."*

MAIRA KALMAN

# PACE

It was a rare sighting, but on this day, as my errand-running little green Kia sped down the road, her puffy, cerulean blue jacket caught my eye. ✎ The Woman Who Walks was glancing across the road, pausing with half-hidden delight, as if seeing something no one else could. The grocery bags hanging from her hands seemed momentarily forgotten and she smiled to herself before moving on along the grassy roadside. Those of us speeding by, I was quite sure, were just part of the landscape. ✎ She is an enigma in our just-outside-of-the-city-enough-to-be-considered-rural part of town, and I've seen her walking often during the eight years we've lived here. Miles and miles pass under her feet, usually the same route, and I always wonder who she is, why she doesn't drive. Don't those grocery bags get heavy? She looks to be in her forties or fifties. Does she have any family? ✎ What strikes me most is her pace. In a world of tweets and posts and emails that can practically arrive yesterday, walking slows us to the pace of nature. We are Nature, after all, and this rare, ambulatory woman, whoever she is, lives in the flow of it as she moves her legs, step by step, yard by yard, mile by mile. I never see ear buds or a phone; nothing to distract. Just a few grocery bags, lots of walking and looking, and, I presume, thinking, pondering, and more deeply experiencing the world than I.

LAURA NEFF

*"No one can figure out your worth but you."*

PEARL BAILEY

# PERSPECTIVE

Somehow or another, our wine-infused conversation had turned to the topic of artistic expression, and I'd confessed my hobby. Instantly, they started beating their hands on their knees, drinks sloshing, raucously hollering, "Let us see! Let us see!"  Goaded into action, I was soon walking down the dark hall of my rented duplex, giant sketch pad in hand, taking a deep breath. I'd never shown anyone the soul-soothing art created at night and on weekends, but these two friends had proven themselves to be true and trustworthy. A shy longing for acceptance of this part of me on paper made it worth the risk.  They sat perched on the edge of their seats as I set the bottom edge of the pad on the floor, and, hands trembling just a touch, raised the cover. Page after page I flipped, watching their faces for any kind of reaction as they read the bold, hand-lettered inspirational quotes and took in the vibrant, colorful images woven in and out of the words.  When their silence became too much, I started filling the space with rapid-fire words, nervously pointing out mistakes, highlighting flaws, then watching, baffled, as they turned stunned eyes to mine.  "You have no idea how good these are, do you?" one asked. "But, wait … what?" I stammered. And the clincher, "I wish I could take you out of yourself so you could see how beautiful this is."  Twenty-odd years later, I still carry that heartfelt wish as a touchstone, a reminder when I begin to shrink. "Own your gifts," the past whispers. And I do.

LAURA NEFF

*"Your life does not get better by chance, it gets better by change."*

JIM ROHN

# GO

The tiny conference room was ugly: smudged yellow walls, scratched furniture, obsolete technology discarded in a corner, and not a window to be found.  ⬚  I was completely collapsed in my chair, reeling with ennui as the rest of my corporate team met together many states away. The offsite meeting had been planned for months, but it was also my first day back at work since Dad's funeral. I wasn't about to fly cross country after the emotional roller coaster I'd been on, so I joined instead by teleconference.  ⬚  The conversation was what I expected: drastically unimportant compared to the rest of my life, but cloaked in corporate urgency and significance. Hours in, someone said something particularly inane, and the contrast to the meaning-soaked days I had just lived became crystal clear. My torso shot forward and, almost involuntarily, I smacked the red-orange mute button so no one could hear what was about to burst forth, and then ... "What the *$#! am I doing?!"  ⬚  If I learned anything from my dad, it was to not compromise. To live with purpose. To connect with what was most important, and to guard that with my life. It all cracked open in that moment.  ⬚  As the audio droned on, no one the wiser, I grabbed my FranklinCovey planner and frantically whipped through the pages until I found a blank one, my mind ablaze with questions like, *Five years from now, how do I want to feel? Who do I want to be with? What skills do I want to be rocking?*  ⬚  The clarity poured out, and when I left that tiny conference room for the last time, I never, ever looked back.

LAURA NEFF

*"Dwell in possibility."*

EMILY DICKINSON

# CHOOSE

Bessie, our 32-foot, converted school bus easily took up four spots at Zilker Park. We'd just pulled into Austin, Texas that day, exploring Town Lake with the bikers and joggers, and eyeballing nearby restaurants for dinner options. ✐ It was month three of what would become a 10-month tour around the U.S. and British Columbia. We were already as rich in adventure as our paycheck-collecting friends back home were in stress headaches. And since a converted school bus is an instant conversation starter, we made friends wherever we went. ✐ On this particular day, as we bustled around getting settled for a few days in the area, we heard a timid knock on the glass door of our bus. ✐ "Hello? Is anyone here?" ✐ A woman's face appeared as she entered, at our welcome, taking in the curtains, dining table with its facing bus seats, built-in couch, kitchen, cabinets, and bed. ✐ "Whoa. What are you guys doing? Do you live in this?" ✐ As we explained that we were on a sabbatical of sorts, following our noses as we toured the country and explored, I watched her entire body sag. The more we shared, the more she folded in on herself, and as we paused, she sadly whispered, "I wish I could do that." ✐ Something in me snapped-to in that moment, forever altering my perspective. "But, you can! All you have to do is decide, and then make each small decision leading up to that big one coming true." ✐ She looked up, breathed deep, and smiled with hope.

LAURA NEFF

*"Gratitude is the fairest blossom which springs from the soul."*

HENRY WARD BEECHER

# I COULD

I could look at the bad things that happened to me that day, or I could be thankful for all the things that didn't happen to me.  ⤚  I could look at myself in the mirror and see how imperfect I am, or I could gaze at myself and notice how amazing and different I am in my own special way.  ⤚  I could think of all the things that I had wanted to do, wanted to see, wanted to be, and say, "Wow I am a failure," or I could think "Wow, look at all the things I have accomplished and look at all the things I have done. I have an amazing, perfect, normal, totally awesome life."  ⤚  I could choose to be thankful. So I will.

⤚

WARNER COHEN, AGE 10

*"Once the travel bug bites there is no known antidote,*
*and I know that I shall be happily infected until the end of my life."*
MICHAEL PALIN

# TRAVEL

Travel is a great adventure. I would rather go to a place I haven't been than a place I have visited before. New places have more surprises and interesting things to learn about them. I've been to many new places, and here's what I discovered:

Malta: hot sun, like a jalapeno
Israel: delicious, local falafel that I could eat every day
Petra: riding a camel, like
being inhumanly tall on uneven and bumpy feet
Dead Sea: floating in the salty, buoyant water
London: all of the Turkish delight, like being in Narnia
Paris: a feeling of fun
Rome: fresh pasta and the crowded Coliseum
Venice: sensing the dreams of the ancestors who lived there before
Milan: the generosity of the kind and talented chef
Mexico: the blue waves and foamy surf

Learning, surprises, chances … where will I go next?

WARNER COHEN, AGE 10

*"Look! A trickle of water running through some dirt!*
*I'd say our afternoon just got booked solid!"*
BILL WATTERSON

## HAPPINESS

Walking through a grove, bright

with lots of flowers. Sitting there,

strolling along for many hours.

Thinking to myself no shame,

no disgrace, I have found

my happy place.

WARNER COHEN, AGE 10

*"You can discover more about a person in an hour of play*
*than in a year of conversation."*

PLATO

# BLIZZARD

The forest canopy shielded us from the most serious snow, so it was quiet but still enough snow to make plenty of places for the enemy — Harmond and Vince — to hide. At the sound of any snapping twig or falling branch, I cringed. ✎ A snowball streaked towards Hayden from behind a fallen tree. "Watch out!" I bellowed. "Take cover!" I took the hit for Hayden and we scurried to a big evergreen. "Do we know where they are?" heaved Hayden as he struggled to catch his breath. A quick shape from the shadows ran to a heap of snow. "Over there!" I hollered. We ran to the heap of snow and fired our ammo. With all the voices screaming and snowballs flying, it dawned on us that we only saw one person at the snow heap! That was when Vince came up from behind us and shook the big tree we were standing under. Snow rained down on us from the tree. ✎ "Boys, time for hot cocoa and cookies!" my mom yelled from the house. We all ran inside laughing.

✎

**WARNER COHEN, AGE 10**

## SEPTEMBER 28

*"I have but one lamp by which my feet are guided,*
*and that is the lamp of experience."*

PATRICK HENRY

# TURNING POINTS

The first time I saw my favorite stuffed animal. Soft, and a feeling of safety.

The first time I played soccer. I knew I could kick the ball that far.

The first time I built an igloo. Spring ice over snow, perfect for building blocks.

The first time I had a nightmare. Why are dreams so creative and scary?

WARNER COHEN, AGE 10

*"It's not what you look at that matters, it's what you see."*

HENRY DAVID THOREAU

# WHAT I BELIEVE

There are three important things in life:

To achieve what you want to accomplish,

To help others in some way, and

Happiness comes from within.

WARNER COHEN, AGE 10

*"In every conceivable manner,
the family is link to our past, bridge to our future."*

ALEX HALEY

# MY SEEDS

Family:

Mom and Dad

Harmond

Grammy and Grandpa Nick

Grandpa Neal and Terry

Papa Ron

Aunt Lisa

Uncle Chris

Aunt Marni

Uncle Johnny

Cousins Augie, Jesse, Reagan, Jack, and Caroline

Aunt Anna

Aunt Elana

Dog Sampson

**WARNER COHEN, AGE 10**

# OCTOBER

*"i imagine that yes is the only living thing."*
E. E. CUMMINGS

## STAYING PRESENT AND SAYING YES

A few years back, I was house sitting for a friend, caring for her chickens. The homing quality of chickens has always impressed me, the way they roam about during the day, returning to the coop to roost at night. For many nights during my stay, locking the chickens in at dusk was a simple task. As the sun set, I'd open the wooden peek-a-boo door at the coop's edge and count their downy bodies, locking the small doors behind them.  One evening I returned home late at night, and realized that after locking them in, I had forgotten to latch one of the doors. All seven chickens were unprotected, vulnerable to predators. I needed to place them, one by one, into the wooden interior part of their home.  The task involved crawling into their wired pen with a flashlight and kneeling in wet sawdust and excrement. In that moment, I was flooded with frustration, livid at these living things for being unable to protect themselves. Somehow, despite my haze of anger, I remembered my breath, realizing that the task was momentary, passing, that I had to be present to it instead of resisting reality. In this instant I heard an echo of a mantra I'd learned from Buddhist meditation teacher, Tara Brach: "Yes to this also."  I love that reminder: I always have my breath and surrender to call myself back.

RAGE HEZEKIAH

*"Nonsense wakes up the brain cells.*
*And it helps develop a sense of humor,*
*which is awfully important in this day and age.*
*Humor has a tremendous place in this sordid world."*

DR. SEUSS

# THE NECESSITY OF SILLINESS

My life is just not that serious. I forget this constantly. ✎ On my altar, I have a picture of myself at four years old dressed as a Care Bear. I'm in a ridiculous, sequined blue leotard, grinning and waving jazz hands. It's my absolute favorite picture of myself because I look ridiculously happy. I treasure that picture, sitting before it every morning as I meditate. ✎ When I look at that little girl, I somehow remember favorite parts of myself, and I wake up to what a weird little goofball I am. ✎ Sometimes I have to practice taking myself less seriously. For me, it means wearing costume glasses in public and blowing bubbles in traffic. It means impromptu dance parties in my car. It means finding things to laugh about and not worrying about my volume. It means bringing myself closer to the buoyant little Care Bear I once was, and loving the wholeness of who I am today.

RAGE HEZEKIAH

*"When you take a flower in your hand and really look at it,
it's your world for the moment. ... Most people in the city rush around so,
they have no time to look at a flower.
I want them to see it whether they want to or not."*

GEORGIA O'KEEFE

# FINDING HOME

City living is not for me. But after years of living on farms in Vermont and California, a desire to be closer to my family brought me back to Boston. Despite living in a lovely, quiet neighborhood, the city feels loud and busy, and often leaves me longing for rural life. But what continues to amaze me is how much I can still enjoy little pleasures of country living within an urban landscape. ✍ Recently, after a brutal dentist appointment, I was walking in Harvard Square looking for a little reward. I thought I'd buy myself a gift for exhibiting such bravery for those hours in the chair. Looking up, I saw a red-tailed hawk gliding peacefully in the air. I stood on the cobblestone sidewalk, entranced, and a stranger approached me to ask if I was watching the hawk. Side by side in the midst of city bustle, this woman and I stared up into the sky, watching the bird's fluid motion together. A welcome message that I have everything I need, and I am never alone.

RAGE HEZEKIAH

*"The gardener is not afraid."*
KAREN MAEZEN MILLER

## HARVEST TIME

If once you were a gathering,

If once you were a small circle of arms touching

gently, linked extremities, elbows kissing biceps,

forearms in quiet conversation —

If once you were a gathering,

what have you become?

Bury those old bones

in the backyard, allow

a gentle bend of knee, surrendering

what doesn't serve you.

Your body still

warm, ripe, held

and opening into air.

RAGE HEZEKIAH

*"You are imperfect, you are wired for struggle,*
*but you are worthy of love and belonging."*
BRENÉ BROWN

# SURRENDERING SHAME

I only recently learned that I'm a perfectionist. There were hints, of course — I had a subscription to *Martha Stewart Living* as an adolescent, and was a surprisingly errand-driven teenager. But I didn't realize just how much I was striving for perfection until somewhat recently. ☜  In my final year of graduate school, I wrote what I thought was an impressive poem annotation for my workshop. In preparation for the paper, I typed copious notes on my laptop, and it took me several hours to complete the four-page analysis I turned in. To my surprise, when it was handed back to me, not only were the words "See me" scrawled on the first page, but a circled "B-" as well. That's several long steps down from perfection. ☜  I felt riddled with shame, clueless, stupid, and — here's the big one — unworthy. Somehow receiving this grade seemed like an evaluation not of a single paper, but of my whole self, indicative of my worth. ☜  A dear friend lovingly suggested I try to own it, to let the grade be enough, and be okay with that discomfort. She told me to put my "B-" on a pin and wear it around, and I did. Pinning this little letter on my chest somehow freed me from my shame. This small action caused me to surrender all the static and just allow myself to believe I am enough.

☜

RAGE HEZEKIAH

*"I wish you water."*
WALLACE J. NICHOLS

## SEEKING RELIEF

Wood smoke plumes into a brumal sky, exhales

into dawn, as winter leaves me needing

to believe in breath again. I draw a bath,

fill the basin with Epsom salts, patchouli oil,

subtle gifts to bring relief. Submerging my tired body

in a well of warmth and comfort, I remind myself

I am worthy. This is enough. Outside, city dwellers

breed a new hostility, angry in the frigid air

as if the bitter weather is personal. I am one of them.

But in the haze of fragrant steam, my own anger

evaporates. I duck below the water's surface, blowing bubbles

as though I'm four years old again. Rolling onto my belly

I kick my feet, splash, and find myself

giggling, letting go, remembering I am safe.

RAGE HEZEKIAH

*"Let gratitude be the pillow upon
which you kneel to say your daily prayer."*

MAYA ANGELOU

# FINDING GRATITUDE

There are days when I am capable of fully loving the little things. ⬠ Sometimes, going to my local bank on a Friday and finding an open container of store-brand Oreos by the deposit slips is enough to make me beam. Or the quick magic of pulling into a full parking lot, just as someone is putting their car in reverse, making a space available for me. These things can feel like tiny miracles that help me feel so held and provided for — but only if I'm focusing on gratitude. ⬠ Some days even when there are little gifts all around, I don't see them because I'm in my head obsessing about how the woman at the Goodwill cut in front of me in line. Or I'm baffled by the incompetence of other drivers. Or I hate the weather. Yet I know that when I'm able to find gratitude, my life instantly becomes better. It doesn't mean all the minor annoyances of daily living disappear, but when I'm truly able to be grateful, it almost seems like they do.

⬠

RAGE HEZEKIAH

*"The passion in the earth's whisper*
*grew so loud*
*I woke."*

MEISTER ECKHART

# STARGAZING

The Beloved weeps in diamonds,

etching the ancient and dewy

caves of the heart

with arcs of wonder,

renouncing the relentless dark

with unearthly splendor,

ciphering the enigma of why

I am here.

USHI PATEL

OCTOBER 9

*"Clouds come floating into my life, no longer to carry rain or usher storm,*
*but to add color to my sunset sky."*

RABINDRANATH TAGORE

## CHOOSE YOURSELF

Being a poet wasn't the dream. Poetry was the unexpected reason I started to dream again and then my dreams became true.  For so long, I drove myself nuts trying to matter, to have some epic impact, but I kept falling short. Then one stormy evening, I was feeling the weight of the rain — lost, stuck, as though I was failing. I needed a change. I made a decision that night to start a better relationship with myself, to be completely honest with myself.  The poetry started flowing.  In that space, I could forgive, heal, and experience compassion — first for myself and then others.  Even more poetry flowed.  The poems were an external expression of an inner triumph and naturally became a comfort and inspiration to others.  I believe everyone has a gift, something that flows uniquely through them. Sometimes I searched the entire world looking for mine. Sometimes I exchanged it for a sense of security and safety. Sometimes I ignored it or didn't believe I had it.  What I was looking for was closer than I thought; as close, in fact, as it could get: *I* was what I was looking for.  When I chose myself, my gift — the one I had been searching for — naturally chose me. The choice demanded a personal exploration and self-confrontation that returned me to myself.  When I did the personal work, the words followed. When I did the personal work, the art followed. When I did the personal work, the opportunities followed. And then, my entire life could become a gift for others too.  In choosing myself, I experienced incredible freedom. A freed voice. The freedom to create any reality I wanted. The freedom to be me.

**USHI PATEL**

*"Change rooms in your mind for a day."*

HAFIZ

# HOME

*Wake up and write a little every morning.* I remember hearing this in morning meditation when I asked the question of where my anger came from.  My thoughts find a home in my hands as the paper compassionately receives her guests. There are no more strangers now because we made time to cook together. In the kitchen, we mess with recipes that feed a lazy appetite and prevent us from being naked. In the dining room, we dirty the French table linens in defiance of every choice made to appease the expectations of others — expectations they never had. At the base of the hearth, we toast to silly arguments that we misunderstood as a personal assault. In the study, we cry for time leaked on ignorant debates about the magnitude of rightness. In the bedroom, we share each other's gaze and revel in our power to transmute. ⇌ Hand to pen, pen to paper. A most peculiar healing.

USHI PATEL

*"You only have to let the soft animal of your body*

*love what it loves."*

MARY OLIVER

# BECOME THE ART

When I was writing my first poetry book, my editor, Zack Rogow, said, "If you are going to write about bees, then go and sit and listen to bees for hours. That is how you will ripen as a poet." ✎ As I sit with the bees, I feel myself becoming a better listener and observer. As I study their movements and constant quest for nectar, I learn beautiful habits and behaviors for my own life. I am the strange one who hums in unison attempting to match their drone, noticing that somehow that vibration wakes up sleepy parts of my brain and churns stagnant worlds in my body. ✎ When I feel stuck, dry, and anxious, I go to nature to listen. When I feel content, open, and inspired, I go to nature to listen. In about 20 minutes, I become the thundering hive and words honey my seriousness, my need to "have it all together." Buzzed, I decode my life in a one-night stand with the divine. ✎ Somehow they've named this hangover poetry.

✎

USHI PATEL

*"How can you describe the true form of Something,*
*In whose presence you are blotted out?*
*And in whose being you still exist?*
*And who lives as a sign for your journey?"*

RABIA AL BASRI

# THE PLEA

Heart, I miss you. I have decided it's time to get serious about us.  I regret that I ignored you and kept you in the corner. I doubted your motives. So much of what I see and experience in the world doesn't match or fit what you say — especially the grumblings of newscasters, pundits, and self-proclaimed experts. Don't get me started on the psychics, astrologers, and spiritual counselors. So many voices discount your urges. So many choose the ego as their mistress. I too have been guilty of indulging that pleasure. Today is different. We are snuggled and close. Your breath soothes my neck while your body swallows me. This is what I want. I want to know you. I want to look in your eyes and feel their safety. I want to understand how you made the poet-saints insane. I want to play hide and seek. I want to read to you from the sky's library. I want to eat with you at Earth's table. I want to exchange secrets over the wine you made. I want to build a magnificent life with you. Heart chuckled, "Isn't that what we've been doing?"

USHI PATEL

*"Greet Yourself in your thousand other forms
as you mount the hidden tide and travel back Home."*

HAFIZ

# THE HIDDEN TIDE

When I look into the horse's eyes, I feel that I am peering into the soul of the Universe. When I am peaceful within, the horse nudges my arm with his nose. "I am ready. Let's ride!" No words need to be spoken. No loud gestures. Just peace. Everything communicated is felt, not voiced. Understood, not urged. I mount. ⁀ Sam is a gentle Arabian giant who worked hard all his life. I trust his strength and stride, but I do not yet trust myself. He knows. I have been fumbling, trying to figure this out. ⁀ But today, it was different: there was peace within, the result of morning meditation, a walk, and a slow and long cup of tea with myself. This peace endowed great control, sight, and ease. For the first time in my horse-riding journey, I rode the horse and the horse did not ride me. For the first time I rode the horse with command — of myself — which energized his instinct to please me. I was experiencing surrender and trust. ⁀ Life is a horse. When I ride a horse, I have to surrender to the movement and flow of the horse, and at the same time, keep my muscles and posture in place so I don't fall. There is an invisible force at work in my life, yet I still must do the work to be in flow with that force, or I will fall. Align to the source within, center, make peace, and let everything unfold from there.

⁀

USHI PATEL

*"The river of love runs in strange directions.*
*One who jumps into it drowns, and one who drowns, gets across."*

AMIR KHUSRAO

# THE ORIGIN OF BEAUTY

Hey ego.
What if I go slowly today,
so I may
quietly slide down the Beloved's eyelashes into
the endless, moonlit pool of wonder below?
So I may soften in the tranquil embrace of the
warm, glimmery waters in her loving eyes that
pour liquid beauty from the
gentle sphere of the rosy evening sky;
coloring the saffron skin of peonies and orchids
brought to the altars of saints,
refreshing the soil's warrior queens and
silk-wrapped newborns at the
fringe of courage,
washing the mind's canyons of twisted echoes from
ugly acts of old, and
hushing the plea from the ocean's blue crests and tides for
flute notes and dancing gold.

USHI PATEL

*"It was only a sunny smile, and little it cost in the giving, but like morning light*
*it scattered the night and made the day worth living."*

F. SCOTT FITZGERALD

# CATCHING THE ARC

I noticed her smile as I drove past the bus stop on 15th Street. An Asian woman with gentle wrinkles on her cheeks, she was listening to a friend, her face open and attentive, her eyes bright. I borrowed her warmth for the day, slipping it into my heart pocket. ⟲ I saw her again and again, often doing curb steps, up-down-up-down, stretching her ankles and working her thighs while she waited for her bus. Her positive energy swirled around her in wide arcs that caught me as I drove by. ⟲ One morning, three women dashed across the street from left to right, close enough to my oncoming car that they had to run. Two kept their heads down in concentration as they hurried across the pavement. One woman turned, smiled, and waved a quick thank you as I slowed enough to let them safely pass. It was my woman! ⟲ I didn't see her every day and soon I saw her only rarely. Catching sight of her as I turned the corner became a gift from the Universe for my day; one morning, midst a difficult week, seeing her on the curb felt like a benediction of blessing from God. ⟲ I haven't seen her for a long time; I don't know what changed for her. A different work schedule? Maybe she car pools now; maybe she moved or retired. Whatever the reason, she has moved on to another space and I no longer hope to see her. I don't need to see her; she remains in my mind's eye, in my heart, her energy lifting my own in a little jig of delight.

TINA BURKHOLDER

# OCTOBER 16

*"The great gifts are not got by analysis."*
RALPH WALDO EMERSON

## SILENCE AND SENSATION

I lose too much time

Holding on 'til life's better

Every breath is now.

Ocean Earth and Sky

Cellular recognition

My fingers tingle.

Slide out of my head

Heart and lungs and skin expand

Energy and rest.

TINA BURKHOLDER

*"And there were houses, he knew it, that breathed.*
*They carried in their wood and stone, their brick and mortar*
*a kind of ego that was nearly, very nearly, human."*

NORA ROBERTS

# BRIGHT FACES AND DIRTY BACKSIDES

I grab three hours to clean what I can get to in my house. I am on my hands and knees, scrubbing away dirt that has accumulated over a time longer than I can remember — must be years. I swab at smears of mud and unidentifiable blerps that must have come from our dog. I settle into the music, the rhythm of rag and muscle; my body recognizes this movement in this space. I croon to my little shabby house as I swipe and polish her walls and floors.

Stopping to get a drink of water, I swing my arms wide and sing to my house in gratitude for holding us for 30 years. This strong, crumbling, tired, beautiful house. I am aware of her breathing, of her delight in the — well, not even the clean floors — it is delight in my attention, my touch; arching up against my hand, like a cat who wants to be fed.

When my guests arrive for brunch today, my house won't be perfectly clean or fixed or decorated. The imperfections are our little secret. Maybe my love and gratitude to this space and her shining response will permeate the air and echo from the corners in the high ceilings. Maybe as my friends enter, they will feel a quick gasp as the cells in their bodies recognize the feeling of safety and welcome. Think of my house and me, holding hands, with bright faces and dirty backsides, our hearts expanded wide, wide, wide, knowing each other's soft spots and hard spots, content and calm, deeply satisfied.

TINA BURKHOLDER

*"Healing is not an act, it is a way of walking in the world."*

BECCA STEVENS

## BODY SLAM

I walked today,
leading with my hips.
Curvy, sensual,
feeling the earth on the
soles of my feet
creative and sultry.

I walked today,
leading with my heart.
Sliding open with
tenderness and strength
as I felt the echoes of other's
heartbeats in my chest.

I walked today,
leading with my navel.
Umbilicus out, connecting
me to the world
I walked as if I am beauty
and innocence.

I walked
as if I were meant to be.

TINA BURKHOLDER

*"The first problem for all of us, men and women,*
*is not to learn, but to unlearn."*

GLORIA STEINEM

# PEELING BANANAS

You grow up knowing how to peel a banana. Banana-peeling wisdom is passed down from grandmother to mother to child. You see it is the same in everyone's kitchens. ✎ And then one day, you see on Facebook there is a different way to expose that sweet succulence. You should start from the other end; it is how the monkeys do it. You are intrigued, you try it, and it works better! ✎ You show this new way to everyone who happens to be in banana-peeling reach and commit to yourself that you will forever engage in the easier, less intuitive way to peel. ✎ And then, months later you realize you are back to peeling bananas the way you were taught, the way your mother and grandmother were taught. ✎ It is habit; it is learned behavior; it is grabbing on to that extended bit of hard banana flesh because it appears easier than the soft end curving at the bottom. It is familiar. ✎ It is like believing all your life the negative messages you took in as truth when you were a child. It is a way of operating in the world that stems from familiar, comfortable (dysfunctional) belief patterns. It is assuming you know the truth when perhaps there is an entirely different perspective of what is true. ✎ Unlearning the old, and integrating the new takes commitment and persistence and creativity. ✎ The other day I saw a new way to cut a watermelon. Really.

TINA BURKHOLDER

*"We are cups, constantly and quietly being filled.*
*The trick is, knowing how to tip ourselves over and let the beautiful stuff out."*

RAY BRADBURY

## CHOOSING

Writing, for me, is like breathing: when I don't pay attention to it, stress takes over, my shoulders hunch up, my back hurts, and my brain doesn't get enough oxygen. I can't think clearly. ⟜ Therefore, my grand procrastinating methods of forestalling writing make no logical sense. Excited, I carve out an afternoon to write! And I find I need to make a cup of tea first, or check emails one more time, or sort through the old CDs that have been sitting on my table for two weeks. ⟜ Why is it that the very thing that gives me breath is what I studiously avoid? (Excuse me while I go water my hair — it is full of static.) ⟜ Not too long ago I grumbled my way out to my car after dark, in the cold, to drive to dance rehearsal. As I yearned for my comfy chair by the fire, my insight angel tapped me on the shoulder and asked a simple question: what is the alternative to not having dance rehearsal? To not dance? Is that what you want? ⟜ My resistance shifted to gratitude and appreciation for the opportunity to be with my dance comrades. Since that evening of dancing, asking myself *what is the alternative?* has been a clarifying process in understanding and embracing choice. I always have a choice; where will I put my energy? Into resisting and mumbling and procrastinating, or into embracing with full spirit what I agreed to do, what I chose to do, what I will do anyway, what I want to do? Do I sit by the familiar fire? Or do I dance?

⟜

TINA BURKHOLDER

*"To take that risk, to offer life and remain alive, open yourself like this and become whole."*

MARGARET ATWOOD

# GOTCHA*

If we are trapeze artists, the swing
on which I have been hanging
is tied with ropes of
loss, anger, and disappointment.
I am in isolation.
My knees are locked in position,
holding on with the surety of my truth.

Faith, then, is letting go on the upswing;
filling my lungs with buoyant oxygen
so I fly high,

releasing my legs and dropping my
arms stretched in a T, free fall into gravity
knowing in the abyss
is God,
strong and defiant in love,
waiting to catch me.

*Trapeze catchers say "Gotcha!" when they catch to signify they have
a good grip on the flyer and the flyer can let go of the fly bar.

TINA BURKHOLDER

*"The greatest thing in the world is to know how to belong to oneself."*

MICHEL DE MONTAIGNE

# ADOPT ME. PLEASE. I'M NO TROUBLE.

Summer of 2009 began as usual. I set about improving my teaching systems: lesson planning, data collection, social skill supports. But I call it the summer of my baptism: a simple morning run with Foreigner, Bare Naked Ladies, Andrea Bocelli, and a spontaneous baptism of fire. ⮌ Each year, teaching children with autism had grown richer. As the passion rippled through my marrow, I kept pouring it into my work. Trouble was, that included a quiet ascent to the slave driver in me. Rising at 4:00 a.m. to meet peripheral job expectations and help children learn became the norm. ⮌ The day before the jog, I found a photo of a sweet little four-year-old girl in a Mama-sewn plaid vest and pleated skirt, truly me. I remember fingering the shiny, flat buttons on that vest.

Asics hammer asphalt. MP3 declares: *I wanna know what love is! I want you to show me!*

Huff. Sweat. Puff. Stop.

Something in me whisper-screams: *Would you make this little girl get up*

*and work at four in the morning after just five hours of sleep?*

*Every day, Mir? Seriously?*

I weep, of course. I weep for the well-meaning abuser in me and for the one I have been exploiting just because she is easy to push around. I create a collage to remind me to love. Everyone. In word and deed. ⮌ Every. One. ⮌ In the church of my childhood, baptism was defined as an outer sign of an inner grace. Wikipedia calls it a sacrament of admission and adoption. ⮌ For me, meanings merge into a new and daily question, "Have I adopted me — all of me?"

⮌

MIRIAM EBERSOLE SHOWALTER

*"Inside every human being there are treasures to unlock."*

MIKE HUCKABEE

## AN EASTER CONFIRMATION

"Look how many I got!" Barbara is instantly beside me in response to Mrs. Warrick's whistle. Time's up on the second grade's 1968 Easter Egg Hunt. Contest rules: highest egg count wins. Stern admonitions: no pushing, no fighting. (Still, Elliot Baker has to be sent to Mr. Napshin's office.)  ✎  Competition, a daily rite in our primary school, is not my strong suit. I'm too dreamy. Cautious. Not one to part a sea of bodies vying for water fountains, not even to see pictures in precious Storytime books. So myriad opportunities pass as one egg after another is scooped up before my eager eyes. Then I spot it. The last unnoticed egg, low in a bush; plastic, not real; nearly matching the foliage. A quick scan: no one in range. Time is finally on my side! Proud warmth fills my shoulders as I nestle my discovery safely in Easter tinsel.  ✎  At the sight of Barbara's stash, shame returns. "I only got one egg." "But look!" Barbara reassures me, "It's bigger than mine. It might count for two!"  ✎  We are friends for a reason, Barbara and I. Eyes flash little-girl love. Hands clasped, flanked by Five & Dime baskets, we approach our peers. I'll be embarrassed, but it's okay.  ✎  "Oh, Miriam! You found it! You found the Prize Egg!" *Oh, my. Mrs. Warrick is ever so pleased with me. I won?*  ✎  Don't ask me what prize I got for securing that egg, but the feeling? That maybe I did have something to offer? Something uniquely mine? Even though I was a slow reader and an awkward runner? Even though I had to go to a class to learn how to skip? That's etched in granite.

MIRIAM EBERSOLE SHOWALTER

*"Learn the rules like a pro, so you can break them like an artist."*

PABLO PICASSO

# RULER OF RECONCILIATION

We caught each other's eyes as Mrs. Fischel made it clear that the class needed to straighten up. We were to line up at the sink, wash our hands, and get a drink. There was to be no talking in line. None. Or else. Side by side, we held our tongues for a full 2.7 minutes. Then Barbara told me her birthday party was coming up, and I whispered something back, and — oh! oh, we're not supposed to talk in line!  ᕱ   Back at my desk, I pondered my moral dilemma. Deliberated, really, complete with sweaty palms and a racing heart.  ᕱ   My hand crept up. "Yes, Miriam. Come on back." Solemnly, clearly, I confessed my iniquity. Eyebrows raised, with a helpless grin sneaking up on her, Mrs. Fischel assured me that rules are rules. "Well, Miriam. You know I have to spank you." I nod.  ᕱ   The ruler did actually touch my leg. I can still feel it, but barely.  ᕱ   The next time someone uses you as a confessional, consider resurrecting a Certified Fischel First Grade Edition Reconciling Ruler. Make 'em laugh. To the tune of gleeful grace and happy humanity.

ᕱ

MIRIAM EBERSOLE SHOWALTER

*"The thing is to free one's self: to let it find its dimensions, not be impeded."*

VIRGINIA WOOLF

## SNAKE IN THE GRASS AND HOLY ORDERS

I loved my mother's stories; her childhood or mine, didn't matter. But my favorite recounted the time I tumbled out of her arms, landing on terrazzo that literally took my breath away — until we arrived at the ER and I let loose a cry to rouse the dead. ⟡ In the Mennonite mindset of the 60s, God allowed such things to happen for the lessons they taught. Be sure that you do not spoil this child, and see, I have saved her for a purpose. So I suckled on the Similac of "I am special to God," and knew I was called to ministry, holy orders. ⟡ But by six, I didn't fit the little-girl-to-missionary-nurse template. I crouched beside ant nests for hours, dropping bread crumbs and observing their behaviors. I played with guinea pigs, not dolls; preferred conveyor belts to playing house. And once I tried to catch a snake. No idea how I conned my suspicious mother into letting me use the chicken wire behind the wringer washer. ⟡ Wait. Chicken wire? ⟡ Yes, my grand plan was to surround my prize with chicken wire. Let me tell you, it wasn't easy. Go ahead. Laugh. Heartily, please. ⟡ For that fugitive snake wove me a new narrative from which I've been peeling fragrant layers of meaning these 48 years hence. Sometimes, the big holes in the boundary are the holiest orders of all. Baby dolls can't climb through chicken wire, but snakes (friends, children, old mind sets) can slither out. ⟡ To where they need to be. ⟡ I'm not a cleric, but I keep finding sacred purposes for chicken wire boundaries, because letting go is the truth that sets me free.

MIRIAM EBERSOLE SHOWALTER

*"The wages of sin are death, but by the time taxes are taken out,*
*it's just sort of a tired feeling."*
PAULA POUNDSTONE

## ANOINTING THE SICK

Smiling, he examines my hot forehead and heavy eyes. Johnny Alison thinks I am such a good girl.  ⇝  The traveling preacher man who stays at our house when he's in town is on parole, bringing a special message to our little Mennonite congregation. It arrives with trumpets and angel shouts, for after Johnny murdered his wife, God saved him from hell and death row.  ⇝  Now he wants to pray for me, my mother waiting by the door. But first he provides an explanation: "Sometimes we do a bad thing. Maybe we steal or we disobey Mama … ."  ⇝  He tells me that if I confess my sin, God will take the sickness from me.  ⇝  My blistering throat begins to swell and I wonder if my mama can hear my heart pounding. I've sinned. Worse, I can't remember what I've done. If I make something up, will the lie be another sin that makes it worse? But already my head is pounding the pillow as Johnny shakes the holy hell out of it, praying for the demon to leave me.  ⇝  Mamas can only stand for so much. As soon as she ushers Johnny Alison out the door, she is by my side. "Dad and I don't believe God makes us sick because of what we do. We get sick because our bodies just get tired and need a rest. You didn't do anything wrong."  ⇝  I don't know what got into my mama but, whatever it is, I like it.  ⇝  And today, when I see an opportunity to usher a lie out the door, I try to follow her example, anointing the weary one — myself or someone else — with the oil of Not Your Fault.

MIRIAM EBERSOLE SHOWALTER

*"A bird took flight.*
*And a flower in a field whistled at me as I passed."*

ST. FRANCIS OF ASSISI

## EUCHARISTIC OPPORTUNITIES

One night last week I was working late when I got a text from our 30-year-old son. "Venus is pretty close to the moon right now." ✍ It could have been a text about schedules or plans or politics or "Have you seen the latest John Oliver?" He could have been injured or sick or even needed advice or a listening ear. Any of the above might have elicited my instinctual hallucination of the baby he once was: the sweet smell of his neck and the persistent pulse of his bubble giggles when he was eight months old. ✍ A gentle tear surprised my cheek. Stepping outside my classroom, I took in a marvelous waxing crescent next to a brilliant Venus and muted Mars. Remarkable. Hovering just above the pink outline of a Florida tree line at winter's dusk. A winking emoticon with a sideways smile. Or a baby climbing out of a cradle. ✍ My son, all grown up and still thinking of me. Aware of what I'm doing. Knowing which simple things I love. Nine words from a priestly celebrant on a cell phone. I wrapped things up and headed home. ✍ Holy communion in the heavens. The inclusive kind. Not one that makes you acceptable but one that declares your rightful place as a fully participating member of the human family. Never alone. Always treasured. Never forgotten. Always known. ✍ Forever. ✍ Loved. ✍ More deeply than we can take in, perhaps. ✍ The great feast is all around us. Every day. Waiting for us to drink it in. Or to administer the sacrament in nine words or less.

MIRIAM EBERSOLE SHOWALTER

*"We make out of the quarrel with others, rhetoric,*
*but of the quarrel with ourselves, poetry."*

WILLIAM BUTLER YEATS

# HOLY MATRIMONY

I have a dissociative disorder. There. I said it. Broadcasted it, in fact. People are alternately fascinated or frightened at this diagnosis I am advised to hide for job security and other practical purposes. But I wonder if those who do not share my condition are really so different from me:

Do we not all suffer arguments with self,
Some of them simple negotiations; others, raging battles born of fear:
I am but partially acceptable, piecemeal worthy?
Day by day, month by month, year after yearning year,
Do we not all seek to integrate
Diverse inner values, incompatible viewpoints, polarizing perspectives;
To designate no-combat zones within the fractured whole?
Marriage of selves calls for our best work. Listen!
Does your heart not hold
Raw pain, immobilizing fear, scorching, childish needs,
Opening eye and ear to a coexisting wonder?
Life's greatest work — Integrity — is won on Love's battlefield.
There. I said it.
Go ahead. Broadcast it. To your inner child.

MIRIAM EBERSOLE SHOWALTER

*"Charm was a scheme for making strangers like and trust a person immediately,*
*no matter what the charmer had in mind."*

KURT VONNEGUT

# FIRST IMPRESSIONS

I always try to smile — a big toothy smile — when I meet new people. It's a habit. My own personal strobe light that signals, "Hey, I'm nice." Still, when I was invited to be part of a group of snarky, sharp women called Bitchy Resting Face Wednesdays, I wasn't surprised. These were my people. On Wednesdays I don't have to pretend to smile. I can just be.  ᗖ  The "smile and smile big" directive came as most of my childhood memories did — with an amber, 70s backdrop under a haze of cigarette smoke. One evening as I was heading through the kitchen with girlfriends, ready to load into my 1978 Dodge Colt for a night of fun, my mother waved her burning Tareyton at me. "You. You have to be careful. You look like a bitch. You can't help it. That's the way your face is made." No one flinched. No one paused. This is the way my mother dispensed advice. Quick and dirty with a compliment buried in there. "Funny thing is, you're the nicest one I've got."  ᗖ  I retell that story today and people gasp. "Oh, my god, that's an awful thing to say." It's not. She was ahead of her time. She was right. I'm saddled with a face that says "country club, oyster-slurping snob" even though I hate clubs. I'm allergic to oysters. I prefer dive bars. So, I work hard on first impressions, except on Wednesdays.

ᗖ

DANA FOWLE

*"Grown-ups never understand anything by themselves, and it is tiresome for children to be always and forever explaining things to them."*

ANTOINE DE SAINT-EXUPÉRY

# MISUNDERSTANDINGS

I turned the corner and saw those eyes. The closer I got, the faster the wet streaks rolled down her round cheeks. My five-year-old was inconsolable. "I never get picked to be the farmer," she said burying her face into my side as my heart clenched.  ⮌  Tiger instincts positioned to jump, my mind raced. *Who is hurting my child?* But I hit pause. You see, my extrovert yin hasn't always fit so cozily into my daughter's introvert yang.  "Please, Mommy, don't say anything," she would say. But not today. Today she wanted me to know she was hurt.  ⮌  My daughter, small for her age, looked even tinier on the ground, putting on her blue canvas sneakers. I motioned for the teacher. This is not the first time my daughter has been upset about being passed over for the lead role in this daily game. I whispered, "Hey, Leo Rose says she never gets picked to be the farmer. Do you mind tossing her a bone next time?" With a face framed in gray, ropey dreadlocks, the teacher reached out to Leo Rose, "Didn't I call on you today and you said 'No'?" Tears rushed out of my little girl's big gray eyes again. "I'm sorry sweet girl, I thought I did. I'll make sure to get to her this week." The tears came faster. I crouched to meet her eyes. "You'll be picked this week." "Mommy, she asked if I had ever been picked and I said no, then she picked someone else."  ⮌  The teacher thought she'd said no. It was a simple misunderstanding. Except it's not when you're five and just learning to ask for what you want.  ⮌  And she might not have told me had I not learned to hush so that she could speak up.

DANA FOWLE

*"Sometimes I wonder if men and women really suit each other.*
*Perhaps they should live next door and just visit now and then."*
KATHERINE HEPBURN

## SPORTS, LIES, AND TELEVISION

I just bought my first TV. Ever. I'm almost 50 years old. We already had one TV in our home, but I was in a desperate situation; I had to get my own. You see, my husband lied to me. He told me when we met that he really only liked to watch football. That's it. Just football. ≈ I felt lucky. He would leave on Sundays, go to his local, smoky pub and stare at a big screen with a beer in one hand, a raised fist in the other with other people who cared about it, too. I had the house to myself. It was a great arrangement until the lie started. ≈ With the baby came baseball, watched from home instead of the bar. More time at home meant accommodating one more TV sport. Then the local basketball team actually got good. He was now up to three sports but still only one TV. ≈ In a huff that only a put-out wife can muster, I bought my first TV, our second one. A thin, lean beauty that looked much sleeker than the foot-deep, hand-me-down television pressed into a room corner. My husband truly was shocked. "What is that? We're not two-TV people. We brag about it. Now what are we going to say?" ≈ I knew where this was going. No. No. No. It is not my fault we now had TV number two. ≈ "You lied to me. You said it was football. That's it. Football. Year-round some sort of ball is flying across that screen. I want my own TV." Then he threw a hard ball. "I lied? Really? You said you were laid back and fun. I'd say we've both told our share."

≈

DANA FOWLE

# NOVEMBER

# NOVEMBER 1

*"Sometimes the questions are complicated*

*and the answers are simple."*

DR. SEUSS

# WISE WORDS

Standing there in her raggedy underpants, toothbrush hanging out of her mouth, a certain little four-year-old says, "Mom, you think too much. You should get out of your head and have some adventures." ⌒ Little does she know she's my greatest adventure yet.

⌒

DANA FOWLE

*"There were nights when I'd feel his stare and I'd wake up and he'd be sitting there.*
*And I'd reach out to stroke his hair. And sometimes I'd feel him sigh*
*and I think I know the reason why."*

JIMMY STEWART, from his dog Beau's obituary

# GETTING SAVED

It's not unusual as a reporter to look for people who are hard to find, to be blocked by disconnected phones and missing house numbers. But rounding a corner, armed only with a pen and paper, to face off a muscular pit bull snapping its shark jaws rattles you every time. I jumped back. It pulled forward. The chain strained. "Jesus! Why don't they just put that whole breed down?" I yelled, skirting the dog's perimeter. ✍ Then a fawn-colored pit moved in next door. I was terrified. My husband poked his arm through a hole in the chain link and scratched behind her ears. "See, I told you, she's harmless," he assured me. I didn't want Icy there, but I was surprised at how much I hated seeing her tied to a plastic igloo. Years passed. Then one hot, Southern day, I heard a whimper from the sidewalk. Sixty pounds of dog hung from a leash, two women struggling to lift her into a truck. Icy dangled inches from the ground. Her eyes showed panic. "What are you doing?" my voice cracked. "Getting rid of her," replied one girl. "Takin' her to The Bluff," said the other girl. The Bluff is a sad collection of brick apartments with screenless windows and doors hanging from hinges. It's a place where children disappear and no one notices. "David!" I yelled, "Do something." My husband lifted Icy into the truck. She forced her bowling ball-sized head under his arm. "She's shaking," he said. ✍ She still trembles when it thunders. But Daisy — that's her name now — does it from the couch with family. My family.

✍

DANA FOWLE

*"Once you sign on to be a mother, that's (24/7) the only shift they offer."*

JODI PICOULT

## RIGHT WHERE I'M SUPPOSED TO BE

I used to be fun. Truly, I was. I threw great parties. One, in fact, was legendary. People I didn't know drove in from out of state to pack into my attic apartment. And this was before the easy mass email alerted everyone to a must-see event; this message got out because people made it happen. The last person to leave was a 6'4" sweaty mess, his suit pants slung over his shoulder. He lost a shoe, and probably a little bit of dignity, that night. ⟿ Fast forward. "Didn't I say when I come back in this room I wanted you dressed?" That's me. The new me. The nag. "We are late. Move it. Move it. Move it." Nag. ⟿ "Did you pick up cat litter? No? It was on your list." Nag. ⟿ My husband and my daughter roll their eyes behind my back. I feel left out, but what makes me most sad is that this is how my daughter knows me. Not the person who hiked for days in the Andes, or the girl who liked a band so dropped everything and hit the road. I'm the nag. The reminder. The harpie. ⟿ No one ever calls me "fun" or "carefree." My husband snatches those up for himself when I'm busy begging everyone to try on the clothes I bought them on my lunch hour. ⟿ But ever so occasionally, my five-year-old sends a signal that reminds me that I am exactly who I need to be right now. "Mom, thanks for buying me those pants. I know you worry you're not any fun, but I know that moms are the workers and dads are for fun times. Dads are like nanas. Fun. But they're not exactly like nanas 'cause they're boys, and that means they're not that smart. And stuff."

DANA FOWLE

*"Anybody don't like this life is crazy."*

MANUEL MALOOF

# A BAR, A DRINK, AND THE PRESIDENT

For 60 years doctors have sat in well-worn barstools next to the neighborhood beat cop at Manuel's Tavern. It's the company it keeps that makes it an Atlanta institution. Its menu brags, "Here a doctor, a plumber ... or a construction worker can feel comfortable." This is also where I made out with President Jimmy Carter. Or at least, that's the story that goes around town.  So you can imagine I was part of the city-wide sigh when it was announced that Manuel's Tavern would be torn down and rebuilt as part of a fancy, four-story commercial complex.  What would happen to the rooftop chickens? What about the decades of memorabilia? A friend emailed, "Sorry to hear this. Isn't this where you and Jimmy C. had a moment?"  It was nearly 20 years ago. Like most young up-and-comers I worked hard, didn't eat, then met my friends at Manuel's. My seat was waiting and so was my vodka tonic with lemon. Bill, the bartender, said, "Hey, Fowle, Jimmy is here. I told him you'd like to meet him. Head over." I stood up and found out quickly that my drink went right to my head. Figuring I'd meet Mr. Carter there one day, I had my short speech ready. Instead an almost slurry, "I love you," came out. Yep, that's what I said to the former president. I was horrified. Then I slid a beer coaster over, "Can you sign this, please?" I couldn't stop the stupidity. But before I walked off, he kindly gave me a peck on a cheek now red hot with shame. Then I heard, "Hey!" When I turned around, Mr. Carter said with a wink, "Thanks for the kiss."

DANA FOWLE

*"There are more things in heaven and earth, Horatio,*

*than are dreamt of in our philosophy."*

WILLIAM SHAKESPEARE

# WORLD WITHOUT, WORLDS WITHIN

To gain the best view, should we not consider all perspectives? Let's go up, to the fish eagle's sky plains. And down, to a toad's earthy domain and whale's watery world. Let's trip in a bee's UV vision and owl's night sight. Entering creaturely kens, could we not gain new views, compound eyes? ❧ I try to see the world objectively, as it is. But can I trust my eyes? Going in, I probe subjective perception: how do I, bee, owl, take in the world? And now I spy a philosophic quarrel: Do I discover or invent my world? Or do I do both? Isn't a ruby intrinsically red, the sky blue, grass green? Strangely, only in my mind's eye do light wavelengths exist as color. As Cézanne said, "Color is the place where our brain and the universe meet." Sound, smell, taste are similar meeting places. ❧ Life evidently relies on practical fictions, or approximations of empirical reality, as inner view ever colors outer vista. Moreover, we're blind to other views. A black-eyed Susan has yellow petals, agreed? But a bee sees green-magenta petals that signal secret nectar sites. An owl hunts easily in woods that look dark to me. ❧ As creaturely worlds swirl within, we dream a colorful if dubious world twirling without. ❧ Absent life, what's left? Is it absurd to claim the cosmos vanishes with none to perceive it? In a sense it does. Sans eyes to see or ears to hear, the cosmos is eerily dark, dull, silent. ❧ Something exists apart from our perceptions, but what?

❧

ROBERT KING

# NOVEMBER 6

*"What is your life? For you are a mist*
*that appears for a little time and then vanishes."*

JAMES THE JUST

## WORLD, WIND & FIRE

"All is flux, nothing stays still," said Heraclitus. Entropy prevails and things fall apart. And in this fitful world coils a tension. To achieve anything of consequence, I must lose myself in the work, lean into life. Yet, to what end? What lasts? As the Ecclesiastes Teacher frets: "It's all pointless, like chasing the wind!" Whole civilizations unravel, like the Maya city state moldering in the jungle. Schools of thought lose luster and like poisoned schools of fish go belly up. Paleobiologists warn we're in the sixth great extinction, as species that take geologic eras to evolve bite the dust. To what end a hundred million years scratching to survive in a brutish world? This time the culprit is a wildly thriving creature: Homo sapiens, wise man. But like all life we too meet an end. Again, Heraclitus: "Man, like a light in the night is kindled and put out." ✎ So, what to do as a quicksilver world slips through my fingers? Pretend permanence, deny death? Shriek? Or relish and rue the fragile moment? ✎ Nestled in the now, the chef cooks a yummy dish that tingles the tongue then dissolves in tummy acid. The pianist perfects a score that sears the soul then vanishes. ✎ Tibetan Buddhist sand art illustrates a poignant, paradoxical response to impermanence. Monks precisely color a mandala circle, symbolizing cosmic perfection, eternity, and unity, only to sweep it into a vivid heap. In essence: lean in, let go. ✎ Like exuberant kids, we chase the wild wind. Will it, like the Greek pneuma, stir dust to life, kindle a fire in the belly? Or put out the light in the night?

ROBERT KING

*"Some like it hot, some like it cold. Some like it in the pot, nine days old."*

NURSERY RHYME

# A MATTER OF TASTE

Born in Cuba, my soul food is black beans and rice. But the Scot says, "Black pudding, please!" Why do I like this, you that? Why does my delicacy curdle your stomach?  Some of what we favor seems set by early experience. Young palates are primed to delight in local cuisine, while a chick can imprint in a critical period on either mother crane or ultralight plane and pilot. Other passions seem hardwired, like a monarch drawn to milkweed. This baby is captivated by color, that one by shape. My mother teased me that as a two-year-old I'd insist, "Straight, not crooked!" Why? Learned or innate, we seem no closer to parsing the spicy mystery. Yet how much of the human enterprise is a matter of taste? I love birds, butterflies and plead their cause, whereas you may prize industry over creatures. Naturally I cry, "So wrong!" Religious taste also seems cultured at family or tribal hearths. In our pot are fine fusions of food, music, and ideas, but bitter wars boil over whose God is most palatable, whose politics most pleasing. The same painting, song, or story character compels or repels, touching a tender spot in you, an irritable spot in me. Over time we acquire new tastes. A bland body of work grows piquant. Has the work changed? Rather, the bouquet ripens in us! These words you ingest? Just empty marks until digested as ideas, tasty or tasteless. Likewise, while tastant and odorant molecules evidently exist in the outside world, taste and smell do not. Only within is sodium chloride quickened, perceived, as salty. As such, in us the whole world simmers — salty or insipid, sweet or sour.

ROBERT KING

*"Popocatépetl smokes to show he's watching over Ixtaccíhuatl,*

*the sleeping beauty."*

NAHUATL LEGEND

## SAVORING THE DAY

I have tasted, my friends, of this lush life, this wondrous world. I have tasted the sweet mango, the acid lime, and sour green grape. I've soared with the bald eagle and hoped for the nestlings of the black and orange Baltimore orioles. I've sorrowed for the song sparrow crushed in the street, the light dying in its eyes. I've seen the moon wax full, flush red, and glow tawny yellow. I've looked too closely at the sun and shut my eyes. I've heard the cicada's siren call, the tree cricket's night clicking and the merry music of children playing. I have gone to the smoking mountain, to Popocatépetl, and touched its snow-covered flank and tarried in its tangy, green pines. I've been pierced by a nopal's defensive thorns and endured the brilliant pain of a Mexican caterpillar's toxic spines. I have felt the soft skin of a baby's cheek and the rough bark of the redbud. I've run for miles and in my mind's eye have traveled far in space and time. I could tell you tales of a Maya temple hidden in the Yucatán jungle, and of a nurse shark that lurks in a sunken ship at night off the coral coast of Bonaire. I have seen terrible things in the land of night dreams and lovely wonderful things that all fade in the light of day into flatter, plainer, more manageable dimensions. I've heard feral cats crying like lost and desperate children at night and I've seen dolphins dipping silently in the sea at dawn. I have savored all these sumptuous goods. *¿Y tú, amigo mío?*

ROBERT KING

*"The conclusion for Gödel is inescapable:*
*if [Einstein's] relativity theory is valid, intuitive time disappears."*

PALLE YOURGRAU

# THE DESERT SAGE

In a desolate corner of the Canyonlands where even scorpions, native Utes, and Gila monsters tread with care, there's rumored to live a hermit who seeks to crack the secret cosmic code. In the vein of Parmenides to Gödel, he's said to hold that the apparent passing of time is illusory; that there's but one eternal block of spacetime where past, present, and future coexist. Then like mercurial Hermes he pivots and attests to time's arrow: "Isn't it plain? Now is now, then was then!" But time flows or it doesn't, right? So he's cast as a nut: *Coco Loco.* ⟜ Some say this desert denizen is a writer's febrile fabrication, conjured to toy with time and temporal being. Others insist he's real and deny the writer exists. ⟜ Whatever the truth, stories persist, curling up around wisps of peyote and tobacco-sage smoke. The hermit is said to deliberate in dry arroyos with the ancients: sun-silvered Utah junipers, sandstone sentinels, Jurassic three-toed theropod tracks. "Can't you see," he says, "that we're but a moment's mirage shimmering between red rock and blue sky? That (after Borges) time is the fire in which we burn, the wash in which we flow? That there's an Infinity we can't know?" ⟜ Then like Kokopelli, the trickster wheels to play a flute of Mexican mesquite, and now seems to invoke a lyrical dreamtime, a time out of time. Exquisite unmetered notes drawn from a primordial well of loss and longing cool the fevered sand. But apart from a kiting raptor's keening cry the stoic audience is quiet, minding Wittgenstein: "Whereof one cannot speak, thereof one must be silent."

ROBERT KING

*"Come away ... To the waters and the wild ...*
*For the world's more full of weeping than you can understand."*

W.B. YEATS

# THE MEDICINE WOMAN

In a spring-cooled ravine in The Painted Desert, a medicine woman said variously to be Hopi, Diné, or Zuni-Spanish lives in an adobe casita by a twisted piñón where blue piñón jays and white-black magpies come to eat and argue. It seems this old woman is a healer schooled in the ancient ways and those who come to her leave restored. Some come with dread diseases and crippling ills, others with maladies that mystify their doctors. Some are in acute fear of death. Others fear life and seek a calming balm.  ✎   It's said the medicine woman has the gift of pure compassion, that she can look into your heart and though she might see fury, madness, pain, or panic, she makes no judgment but simply nods, a slight smile tugging at her leathery face, which like a millennia-old bristlecone pine shows uncounted years etched by sun and wind.  ✎   Strange tales surface. Once, gunmen — sure she'd been well paid by those grateful for her healing — rode up in the chill high-desert night, scheming to rob her blind. Instead they fled on rearing horses across the badlands shrub steppe, having met what they depicted as a monstrous gunman leveling a cannon-sized musket. This apparent shape-shifting troubled some. Was their healer's compassion so quickly quashed? Under attack had she resorted to defensive dark sorcery? But others averred that what so terrified the bandits — not naturally given to self-examination and insight — was the startling sight, on that fateful blue-moon night, of their own scarred souls mirrored in the clear and infinitely deep pools of the medicine woman's guileless eyes.

ROBERT KING

*"Was it in dreamtime that the seven sister universes cracked open,
like infinitely old dragon eggs?"*

THE DESERT SAGE

# I AM THE UNIVERSE

Let me tell you a tale of my thousand forms, my thousand and one lives. I am the lithe lizard who does push-ups off the burning Moab red rocks, the woodpecker who stores up scrub oak acorns for snows to come. I am the rapscallion raven, riding thermals that curl up the canyon rims of wind and water sculpted sky islands. I am the vanishing Mexican jaguar and cactus-crunching peccary, the irontree and paloverde. I am sandstone from long lost seas, curating fossils of a fierce past in ancient deserts of the sere southwest. I am each of these, and more! ✐ I am lightning, frightening and fiery, and thunder cracking open the darkling sky. I am the williwaw that howls across Tierra del Fuego, the katabatic Santa Ana winds that stoke chaparral fires. I am wild winter, sunny spring and sultry summer. I am irreversibly melting Antarctic ice and the lobster in a slow-boiling pot. I am the blue-throated hummingbird's tiny nest, and the colossal cities of the Anthro-pocene, the human era. ✐ I am carbon waking from deep sleep; matter morphing into mind to form these words, to tell of my thousand lives. I am every dream and dread that burns in sentient souls, every twitch of a trillion micro mites and water bears. ✐ I am the luminous Milky Way and hungry black hole round which it whirls. I am light bent by gravity, and moon gravity tugging at Earth's seven seas. I am quotidian clock time, recondite space-time, indigo dreamtime. I am orderly cosmos; disorderly chaos. ✐ I am the Universe, surely but one of many, ever unfolding. Am I not?

ROBERT KING

*"A daughter is one of the most beautiful gifts this world has to give."*
LAUREL ATHERTON

# A PERFECT MOMENT

She was two days old. We lay snuggled together at dawn listening to the nearby temple bells sounding. In that perfect moment, I experienced oneness with this new little being whose precious life had been entrusted to me as her mother. In that perfect moment, I also deeply and lovingly knew what I would later read in the works of the prophet Kahlil Gibran:

"Your children are not your children.
They are the sons and daughters of Life's longing for itself.
They come through you but not from you,
And though they are with you, yet they belong not to you.

You may give them your love but not your thoughts.
For they have their own thoughts.
You may house their bodies but not their souls,
For their souls dwell in the house of tomorrow, which you cannot visit,
not even in your dreams ..."

And now, 33 years later, looking into the eyes and soul of a beautiful, talented, intelligent, and dedicated young woman, I am filled with admiration and profound gratitude for who Rama is as her own person and as my daughter. Her smile creates a blessing. Her voice transports us to other worlds. She is generous and loving. Our world of todays and tomorrows is significantly sweeter with her in them.

NANCY J. DUNCAN

*"... We are listening. To the sun. To the stars. To the wind."*

MADELEINE L'ENGLE

# SIGNALS

So how are you informed?

How does God, Shakti, Spirit, Grace get your attention?

Is it an inner knowing?

Subtle first ripple

Stirring

Seeing

Horripilation

Intuition

In my heart I know

A soft breeze across the cheek

Words

A wave of nausea

Ticker tape message across your mental screen

Universal flirt

A pause in time

Whispers

Timings

Synchronicities and serendipities —

How are you signaled to your truth?

God is always speaking, are you listening?

NANCY J. DUNCAN

*"The winds have welcomed you with softness.*
*The sun has blessed you with his warm hands.*
*You have flown so high and so well that God has joined you in laughter*
*and set you gently back in the loving arms of Mother Earth."*

BALLOONIST BLESSING

## MY BIRTHDAY GIFT

"Really? You're testing the air currents with a red birthday balloon?" As I watched the happy little balloon play in the wind until it became a little dot in the blue ocean of sky, my excitement turned to terror. ✍ Our balloonist, Frank, was the only *aéronaute* sanctioned to fly the precious Navajo land of Arizona's Monument Valley. As flames shot up into the massive rainbow-colored balloon, we slowly ascended. Frank was eerily quiet, and all I could think was, *Jump now while you still can!* ✍ Oddly, the higher we rose, the calmer I felt. My terror dissolved into surrender, then trust, then a joyous freedom. I trusted Frank, the wind, my partner beside me, the benevolent spirits and the mesas. From our highest meta-view I saw the Three Sister Spires, King on His Throne Butte, Rain God Mesa, Bear and Rabbit, and my past, present, and future. Flying through the heavens, I knew that just as the flames keep the balloon moving through sky, the inner fire of yoga keeps my soul's journey alive. ✍ Our descent was gradual and gentle. We glided over the sacred lands with grace and ease carried now only by the wind and the balloon's fullness. What if this is how to be in life? What if we surrender, knowing that life's journey is a glide through sacred lands, replete with terror and excitement, surrender and trust? And what if the journey is perfect, just as it is?

✍

NANCY J. DUNCAN

*"My life is my message."*

MAHATMA GANDHI

# THE LONG GOODBYE

She was my friend, my teacher, a spiritual benefactor, and my grandmother. ᕭ Together we explored the seen and unseen worlds. She taught me how to make pierogis, and together we traveled to India to study meditation before it was fashionable. I always knew I would be near her as she left this world and embraced the next, and that the journey would be filled with sacred prayer and love. ᕭ As the moments and years passed, I would remind her of her age: 90, 91, 92, and finally 93 years old. She always seemed surprised at the number, we would laugh, I would give her a big kiss, and thank her for being my grandma. ᕭ Over time, she grew quiet and more indrawn, and it was an honor to just sit and be with her. Sometimes I offered prayer, sometimes family updates, sometimes tears. As I sat by her side, I sensed this: when her eyes closed, she touched divinity, and when her eyes opened, she touched the same. ᕭ This bond of love only sweetened as death approached. She spent her last hours listening to her favorite Sri Guru Gita chant, holding her prayer beads in one hand and my hand in the other. As I sat watching her breathe, watching her peace, she just left … as the room and my being filled with love.

ᕭ

NANCY J. DUNCAN

*"In all things of nature there is something of the marvelous."*

ARISTOTLE

# FOURTH FLOOR CAFÉ

We opened the avian café on the balcony of our fourth floor in support and appreciation of the neighborhood birds. The cold, windy city winters of Chicago are harsh, for all of us. Stocked with a wild bird seed mix, black oil sunflower seeds, suet baskets, a dryer vent, and big, warm Christmas light bulbs wrapped around the railings, we quickly became a refuge of shelter and sustenance. ≈ As our hearts warmed to our new friends, we began to name the regulars: the cardinal couple was Rhett and Scarlet; the red-headed woodpecker Mister Tux; the Blue Jays simply Jay; and the sparrows all shared the same name of Sweetie. ≈ One night, it must have been 2 or 3:00 a.m., Harold, our Shar Pei and self-appointed café security guard, woke us up with his crying at the balcony window. "Ugh, okay, okay, what is it, Harold?" I asked. A very large, confident raccoon sat quite happily, those four floors up, seemingly unfazed by his audience as he munched on a peanut suet cake. We named him Rocky.

≈

NANCY J. DUNCAN

*"If light is in your heart*
*You will find your way home."*

RUMI

# ONLY ONE QUESTION

As I stood before the master, he began to speak. In perfect detail he described the spiritual awakening I had experienced just an hour earlier during meditation — even though he had not been in the meditation hall at the time. The thunderous explosion had occurred in the depth of my soul releasing an energy that to this day, 40 years later, moves through my being. ✎ As I stood before the master, it became clear that only someone sitting in my heart could have known what had occurred. As tears streamed down my cheeks, I knew from a place without words that I had been waiting and longing for this moment for lifetimes. ✎ As I stood before the master, silenced by profound gratitude, the only question remaining was, *How may I serve?*

✎

NANCY J. DUNCAN

*"The heart is the hub of all sacred places.*
*Go there and roam."*
BHAGAWAN NITYANANDA

# MEDITATE

When I resist sitting for meditation, I pause and have a quick check-in with myself. *Hey, are you going to meditate or are you a fool? What is so important to keep you from approaching the blessedness within? What worldly cleverness is more delicious than inner stillness and silence?* That usually does it. This brief, honest, heart-to-heart stirs my soul's memory of the exquisite inner spiritual consciousness, so I sit, forget the world, and turn within to sacred peace.

NANCY J. DUNCAN

*"Bad weather always looks worse*
*through a window."*
TOM LEHRER

# THE SHOW

The rain flings itself
against the window.
Drops jostle and shove,
trip over each other
as they speed down the pane —
patrons in a theater
where someone has yelled
"Fire!"

ELLIE SCHOENFELD

*"My happiness grows in direct proportion to my acceptance,*

*and in inverse proportion to my expectations."*

MICHAEL J. FOX

# HOW IT IS RIGHT NOW

The monks move
under the trees —
red flowers
touched with gold.
The willows weep with joy
at the sight of them.

Small white flowers
in the carpet of grass
open themselves
to whatever falls into them —
insects, rain, sun, feet,
the ashes
from someone's cigarette
or burnt offering.

These flowers
accept it all.
These flowers
keep blooming.

**ELLIE SCHOENFELD**

*"While seeking revenge, dig two graves — one for yourself."*
DOUGLAS HORTON

# THE CURSE

One hundred years ago the monks of Moudras
placed a curse on this island village
because they blamed the villagers
for provoking an attack
which damaged the monastery.
Not the turn-the-other-cheek kind of monks,
they cursed them to nights
of little sleep
and bad dreams.

Now,
one hundred years later,
they are lifting the curse.

The news story does not say
what made them change their minds —
maybe someone had a dream
or they felt guilty
and couldn't sleep.

ELLIE SCHOENFELD

*"A poem begins as a lump in the throat,*
*a sense of wrong, a homesickness,*
*a lovesickness."*
ROBERT FROST

## SCENT

When he speaks

he reminds me

of the scent

of a new poem

rising up inside

the way the earth smells

after a certain sort of rain.

Even though I have

experienced it before

it always comes

as a surprise.

ELLIE SCHOENFELD

*"The universe is made of stories, not of atoms."*

MURIEL RUKEYSER

# THE STORY

Every word the storyteller uses

carries its own story

back and back and back

until we arrive

at the first story told

in a language made

from a speck of stardust

or a speck of something

whose name and whose tale

we do not remember

but which lives at the core

of each of our cells

and whispers over and over

the story we spend our lives

straining to hear.

ELLIE SCHOENFELD

*"The greater the obstacle,*
*the more glory in overcoming it."*

MOLIÈRE

# POTHOLES

I slide down the hill —
the stop sign has no power here.
Icy roads live
in the realm of luck, of fate.
Now I careen faster yet slowly
the way people describe
how time changes in some accidents.
Meanwhile the potholes filled with ice
become open mouths
full of loose teeth
howling the blues.

ELLIE SCHOENFELD

*"At home, I love reaching out into that absolute silence,*
*when you can hear the owl or the wind."*

AMANDA HARLECH

# OWL

Having coffee this morning with a boreal owl. It sits with Buddha stillness, only an occasional slow turning of the head to survey the circumference of its current world view, while I do a similar search with my newspaper. It gazes at me sometimes with its actual eyes, mostly watches me with the feathery ones on the back of its head, having somehow determined I am neither threat nor treat. It has the calmest bearing of any creature I have ever seen. Even while being dive-bombed by the giant ravens, it looks unperturbed, makes its eventual move from the deck rail to the apple tree a slow and elegant meander as though it had planned that all along. ⬳ I can see how the owl became equated with wisdom. This is accentuated by the newspaper filled, as usual, with humanity's lack of wisdom, and by the reflection the owl is inspiring which spotlights my own endless repetitive lapses. I like thinking that owl is seeing into the depths of my soul and I into the owl's and that the Buddhists are right about all of this being merely a dream, an illusion of separation between one person and the next, between the boreal owl and me. Meanwhile, an old friend has fallen into the next world, some vole is surely destined to fall into the owl's stomach soon and I sit at my kitchen table drinking a dark and slightly bitter, perfect cup of coffee.

ELLIE SCHOENFELD

*"Don't try to comprehend with your mind.*
*Your minds are very limited. Use your intuition."*

MADELEINE L'ENGLE

## UNUSUAL ADVICE

I have heard it said that, at the end of the day, what you give back to other people is all that matters. I don't think that's exactly true. Yes, because we are connected, what we pass on to future generations is critical, and that begins with how we interact with our fellow human beings. But I think it's just as important how we take care of ourselves. We have to learn how to stick up for ourselves, hold our ground, know what we think is right. How else will we know what to do?  ⤳  I call this source of wisdom my spirit guide (you might call it your higher self, common sense, or intuition), and have developed a visual representation of this voice inside. Surprisingly, it doesn't always speak in flowery rhyme. My spirit guide speaks just as often in the voice of warning. He wants to tell me what's wrong –– just as often as what's right –– in order to protect me from myself and from others.  ⤳  I'll never forget one time when I was in crisis and the voice inside my head told me: DON'T GET MAD, GET EVEN.  ⤳  *That's it? That's your advice?* I pressed the issue because: a) I wasn't used to being spoken to in this way, and b) I assumed from all of my well-meaning spiritual training that there must be more. *What are you saying?* I asked again. *What do you mean by that?*  ⤳  I have learned that when my spirit guide doesn't have anything left to say, he usually doesn't attempt to fill the void. In this case the voice spoke reluctantly once more: YOU CAN'T BULLSHIT A BULLSHITTER. That was the day my understanding of spirituality changed and became at once more unusual and more useful.

STUART HORWITZ

*"The truth is rarely pure and never simple."*

OSCAR WILDE

## AMERICAN SPIRITS

I was raised in one of the typical religions of the day. God was a fearsome judge. God was capable of transcendent miracles and rampant destruction. God was omniscient. But I wouldn't have predicted that God would use that power to whisper in my ear while I was at work, GO READ HER EMAIL.  My spirit guide was referring to my business partner who worked in the same office as I did. She and I had been experiencing some tension lately but I was comfortable in my daily routine and certainly wasn't predicting anything dire. GO READ HER EMAIL, the voice said again. "I'm not doing that," I said, whether out loud or to myself, it's kind of the same thing in these conversations. I turned my attention back to our recent sales numbers, which were excellent.  GO READ HER EMAIL! the voice thundered. *Okay, okay, no need to shout.* I went over to her computer, and her email was open. There was a thread with our boss that described how she had set me up earlier in the day to expect that one of us would get laid off (me). Come to think of it, we had just had the strangest conversation, considering we were the highest performing department in the whole organization. Why would they go down to one manager in a situation like that?  My world went black. I crawled to the corner store and bought a pack of cigarettes and smoked four or five, end to end, until the nicotine seemed to clear the fog of shock for a minute. I was going to have to find a new job. For no reason, out of nowhere, but there it was.  YOU'RE WELCOME, the voice said.

STUART HORWITZ

# NOVEMBER 28

*"Just because you don't understand it doesn't mean it isn't so."*

LEMONY SNICKET

## QUAILED (107 POINTS)

Over the years, I have become better at hearing my inner voice, but I can still push it off pretty well. Sometimes when my spirit guide is whispering to me, I'll chalk it up to having too much caffeine late in the day, or to my bedroom being too hot or too cold — *that's* why I can't sleep. One restless night I had the distinct feeling that not only was he speaking to me but that he was physically trying to get me out of bed. You might think I'm crazy, which I'm not going to confirm or deny. The point is, it worked, to the degree that I went downstairs to try to resume my sleep on the couch. ⤳ YOU HAVE TO LET HER GO. My spirit guide was referring to an employee of mine who was doing good work. Business wasn't great, and maybe she wasn't in her perfect position, and maybe her destiny did lie elsewhere, but we had pledged ourselves to each other and after some of my life experiences (previous page) I wasn't planning on being *that* boss. ⤳ YOU HAVE TO LET HER GO. Hearing something I was completely unprepared for was disquieting. I tried to tune it out by playing Scrabble on my smartphone. I was on the single player setting, playing against the computer, or so I thought; it turns out I was playing against my spirit guide. For each set of tiles I laid down, he formed another word relevant to the end of my employee's tenure, all the while scoring more points than me.

STUART HORWITZ

*"The most common form of despair
is not being who you are."*

SØREN KIERKEGAARD

## THAT'S WHAT I'M SAYING

Looking back on my life, I can see that my spirit guide has been with me since the beginning. Originally, it was hard to place, but somebody was whispering to me that I knew better. They called it your conscience at the time, but it didn't seem to belong to any particular morality system. It just wanted to remind me what I wasn't seeing at the moment. ☙ In college, when I joined the sailing team, I wasn't clear on my motivation. Sailing had been big in our family, so I was proficient in the sport and just sort of assumed that was how you made choices. ☙ I think there may also have been a cute girl on the team who was additional incentive. ☙ But when the coach started talking about the practice schedule, I got this really heavy, uncomfortable feeling. YOU DON'T ACTUALLY LIKE SAILING, the voice of my spirit guide reminded me. ☙ Wait, it's okay to say that? Okay, yes, then I feel much better! I quit.

☙

STUART HORWITZ

*"Your mind knows only some things.*
*Your inner voice, your instinct, knows everything."*
HENRY WINKLER

# DEAL ME OUT

When I was living with my ex-girlfriend, a recovering heroin addict with the ace of diamonds tattooed on her ass, I used to get really drunk and sleep out in the hallway. Not the best sign for how I felt about the relationship, but in all fairness I'm sure my antics weren't helping her recovery any either. ⌁ YOU DON'T ACTUALLY HAVE TO LIVE HERE ANY MORE, my spirit guide suggested. ⌁ For some reason, I had to go the traditional route and verify this with a real live human being, so I drove to Kinko's Copies at 3:00 in the morning and struck up a conversation with the security guard. ⌁ I'm not always as conscious as all this is making me sound, by the way. I thought I was going to do some printing and have something bound. But we ended up talking about that voice that people don't listen to. ⌁ "I got married eight years ago," he told me, "and there were some things I wasn't sure about, and it's the kiddies that kill ya." ⌁ *Wait, kiddies?* ⌁ I moved out that week.

⌁

STUART HORWITZ

# DECEMBER

*"These things I warmly wish for you:*
*Someone to love, some work to do, A bit o' sun, a bit o' cheer,*
*And a guardian angel always near."*

IRISH BLESSING

# 490 OLD EAGLE SCHOOL ROAD

My spirit guide — that voice within — does want me to know I am loved. His presence is a blessing, and if he has to shout sometimes that might be because I am a little hard of hearing. ᕗ The night I got married, we rented a giant bus that took a large percentage of the partygoers from the ceremony site and dinner reception to the after-hours party. It had a microphone system (unfortunately, I love the mic) and I entertained passengers all the way home with a running monologue while passing out potato chips randomly because that's what you do in that situation. ᕗ At the house where I lived with my now-wife, the driveway was pretty tight. I was helping the bus back out onto a busy street, where cars ignored the 45 mph speed limit and often whizzed by at over 60. Drunk and delighted that I had married the love of my life, I was paying no attention to the fact that I stood in the direct center of the road. ᕗ STEP BACK NOW! ᕗ I took one step back and a truck went whizzing past me in the dark going so fast I would have been killed instantly. There is no way the driver could ever have seen me. My spirit guide saved my life that night. When I tell people that, they often look at me like they don't believe me, which leaves us at an impasse because I'm not going to change my mind. There's no way I could.

STUART HORWITZ

*"The unexamined life is not worth living."*

SOCRATES

# DESOLATION ROW

When I was living in Prague in the early 90s, some of my expatriate circle and I had flung ourselves full force into the Bohemian lifestyle. You could find me many days quoting Bob Dylan lyrics on the main square, Vaclavski Namesti, with a hat out for tips. You know, like the one about not wanting to get letters unless they're mailed from Desolation Row. ✑ We stayed up all night drinking, writing, doing whatever drugs we could get our hands on, critiquing American society and hoping our money wouldn't run out too quickly. I would wait tables in the U.S. for eight months at a time and then come back to Prague where I could live for 13 months on my savings, and by selling stolen books back to a café for one well-timed meal of the day. ✑ One night, or early morning, I was crashed out against the side of a tavern with some of my buddies. PULL YOURSELF INTO THE LIGHT, my spirit guide said. ✑ I have always been so grateful that was the way it was phrased. I'm sure if the voice had said, RISE UP THIS INSTANT AND SAVE MY PEOPLE FROM SIN, I would have tried to do that and made a huge mess out of everything. ✑ Perhaps because of my stubborn nature, I had to hear it a few more times — PULL YOURSELF INTO THE LIGHT — before I dragged myself to the other side of the street where I squinted into drenching sunlight. Eventually I quit drinking altogether, but the voice wasn't setting its sights so high at that point. Just moving in the direction of sanity would work well enough for now.

✑

STUART HORWITZ

# DECEMBER 3

*"The great thing about getting older*
*is that you don't lose all the other ages you've been."*
MADELEINE L'ENGLE

## GOING BACK

I dreamt that I traveled back to my life as a 14-year-old girl. I carried a worn, brown leather suitcase stuffed with everything I know now. My luggage was heavy, but easy to carry as I entered my peach-colored bedroom and placed it on my teenage bed. ⬭ I took out the lessons I had carefully folded when packing, and put them away neatly in my closet: a fluffy pink sweater, worn blue jeans, a white halter top. This time around, when I wore the sweater, I was deaf to girls that teased me; their laughter evaporated and my soul did not shrink. In those soft jeans, I was flawed, but I felt no judgment. In the halter top, I sat in a circle with friends without feeling like I didn't belong. I was the same girl, except now I was impermeable. I did not shrivel against words and false thoughts. My clothing was like armor woven with the thread of light that came with maturity and insight. ⬭ When I woke from the dream, I knew the impossibility of wisdom without the gift of failure and the power of imperfection. It is only experience that can fill my luggage. Only the blemishes of life make reflection an epiphany. I am grateful for being excluded and whispered about. I thank the girls who clustered together and left me to stand exposed in my pilled red acrylic sweater. I needed the glitches of adolescence to weave new fabric. Insight is not born from endless joy.

⬭

MICHELLE COHEN

*"The best thing she was, was her children."*

TONI MORRISON

## BEAUTIFUL LIE

I lied to my mother on her deathbed.  I was 28, my children still babies. Her body was gray with cancer and disappeared into the sheet creases as her hand rested on mine. There was a tissue, wet, in my fist. The inevitable hovered above us, sticky and dripping, coating us and spoiling everything. The future where she would attend my children's dance recitals and graduations was gone. She would never again feel the joy that comes when new milestones swoosh by, blurred and precious. So I lied. I promised I would raise my children as she raised me.  It wasn't a lie, though, when I said it. All I was thinking about were the gifts of unconditional love that filled my childhood. All I was remembering was how she had been my envelope and I, her love letter. In that moment, I felt urgently pulled towards her and at the same time, some force pulled me away. It is impossible to repeat the footprint of our mothers, and, looking back, I wouldn't actually want to.  I discovered my own life when I was released from my mother's hugs. I took her words and composed my own dictionary, took her mistakes and mixed them with my own.  There is a blessing in the imperfection. I have felt the warmth of the light come through those broken places, cracked by her death. And no matter how deep the yearning to transfer what I have learned to my children, I know their deepest nourishment will come by finding their own route.

MICHELLE COHEN

*"Looking is a gift, but seeing is a power."*

JEFF BERNER

# THE GIFT

The first time I met my neighbor, the sun was setting behind him and the sky hadn't yet decided what color it wanted to be. His yellow lab tugged at its leash and I, with my own invisible leash, was pulled in. I had recently left my husband and moved into a small condo. My children were spending the weekend with their dad and I was feeling unnaturally torn from them. My neighbor and I started a conversation that led to a date that evolved into a relationship. ✑ A few months after we had been together, I was lying beside him in bed and we were close to sleep. He spooned me and I was wrapped in safe darkness. "I'm so happy for you when you're still," he whispered, his breath warm on my neck. ✑ My eyes were closed when he said it, but this opened them. In that instant I was seen for the first time. He had recognized my inability to be present, and offered me stillness. Until those words, I thought living in uneasiness was my path. He noticed what, for me, had been a blind spot. ✑ When he fell asleep, I picked my clothes up off the floor and tiptoed out and over the wet lawn to my condo across the street. That night my stillness was fleeting, but I was split open. That moment in the dark is what I reach for when life gets chaotic. He never knew the gift of deep peacefulness he gave me, but it is my stone, my talisman, that I rub between my thoughts. I carry it with me. I open it like a precious family album so I can remember where I came from.

MICHELLE COHEN

*"Wherever you go, go with all your heart."*

CONFUCIUS

# CHANGE IN WEATHER

Whenever I leave the heaps of dirty snow at the edges of Manhattan's sidewalks and return home to California, I feel stripped bare. I leave the wind that bit at my face and the ice that threatened my footing. I return to clear skies and palm trees backlit by the sun. ⇠ In New York, where I walk late at night, there is a throb. The crowds are leaving work, coming home, going out. Sometimes people have to turn sideways when they pass. Once in a while there is contact. I overhear a passing man's phone call to his girlfriend. Coffee shops are lit up and peppered with patrons. There is a crescendo of music as I pass a bar and then it fades like light on a dimmer switch. Pavement crevices are filled with the debris of life, crusted into corners like sleep in the eye of someone just waking up. Road construction forces me around pilasters. My weaving in and out, a confirmation that life is not a linear path. Orange cones remind me to stay the course. ⇠ I love Newport Beach: the open space, the salty air warm on my shoulders, but sometimes the space feels too vast. I am exposed here, unprotected. There are no coats and scarves to wrap myself in before I venture outside. And once outside, I am in my car, a different kind of cocoon. One that separates instead of integrates me. So I bring the vibrating city back with me and take it down to the beach. I lay it out like a towel on the sand. Then I sit on it, root myself to the earth, and watch the sunset.

MICHELLE COHEN

# DECEMBER 7

## VOYEUR

I sit outside on a third floor balcony on Oahu's North Shore, face to face with the top of a palm tree. A display of green strength peacocks itself as pride shoots from its tall, skinny trunk. From this height, I can see the palm closely. A branch shares itself with me. It wants me to see its brown tips. It wants me to know that the sprouted, majestic plumes that we see from afar are, in reality, frayed from weather and life. I can see the tiny uneven scissor-like rips along its edges.  The palmed branches are married to the wind. They are faithful to each other as they tickle the blue sky. I can feel the smile in all of it, the complete joy and synergy in their connection: the wind, the palm and their friend, the sky. In this moment it feels like a show, a spectacle they are putting on just for me, their audience of one. They are teaching me the magnitude of all the tiny processes that led to this exact tree in this very spot in this specific wind against this warm sky. From somewhere, invisible, a rooster crows.  I close my eyes and fold into myself. I search the empty fullness of my rational mind. I try to find the imprint for my own body in this symphony of nature. How do I extract the meaning for my life in their relationship? How do I carry this moment home with me? Then the wind rustles the palm and my hair brushes my cheek. This is their story. My purpose is simply being a witness.

MICHELLE COHEN

## DECEMBER 8

*"Forever is composed of nows."*

EMILY DICKENSON

# BE HERE NOW

"Notice how the air smells," said the Zen priest, breaking the morning silence. His voice was warm and round in the bracing Santa Fe air. We were walking a stone path on our way to practice morning zazen (seated meditation). I inhaled. This scent was new, other-worldly. Most of the trees were bare, but the smell was green, alive, almost edible, and then it blossomed yellow. Was there a nearby shrub whose leaves were pungent with the aroma of baking bread mixed with jasmine? I kept hearing myself ask what it was, but the words stuck like thick glue in my throat.  ⤚  I was at a writers' retreat at Upaya Zen Center. The 10 writers who walked with me that morning didn't comment either. We followed the priest, his body draped in reverence and knowledge, to the "hobbit house," as he called it. We lined up and ducked our heads to enter. It was a small square room with dark wood beams above, white stucco walls to serve as our chrysalis, and navy, square meditation pillows lining the room's edges. We bowed, sat, and arranged our bodies. I focused on the smooth knots in the blonde polished floors as my eyelids lowered. During meditation the earlier smell pricked at my consciousness, begging for a name, becoming an expanding ripple in my pond of zen.  ⤚  When it was time to exit, we rose, bowed, and lowered our heads again as we re-entered the big, pulpy, sensational world. I was ready for it; my awareness was sharpened now. I breathed in, waiting to taste the full bulbous scent. It was gone. All I could smell were the pumpkin pancakes that waited for us in the kitchen.

## MICHELLE COHEN

*"You must love in such a way that the person you love feels free."*

THICH NHAT HANH

# FROZEN MOMENT

There is a photograph I took with my phone almost three years ago. It was the night we left my son, Marc, in New York to begin his freshman year at NYU. I remember standing on the sidewalk watching him walk away and feeling my heart struggle to stay in my chest. ✎ I called after him, reaching for my phone in a panic that the moment would pass and he would be gone forever into that black night dotted with the neon letters and round lights of 7th Avenue. ✎ In the photograph, the stretch of pavement between us is long and bare. Marc in his blue button-down shirt and khakis is the center but he is far away, small and uneven. I can't see the details of his face. In the right foreground is a carousel of postcards that stands guard at a well-lit souvenir shop. Life seems to exist everywhere except in the space that separates us. ✎ I know he was teary-eyed too. I had felt it when our hug was complete. Finally, he heard me calling and turned, but kept his back foot touching the ground. It made an awkward twist at his ankle just as his foot had been at birth. When he was born I had thought it was a malformation, but within days it became a normal healthy foot. It had been forced to bend inside me. It needed space just like I knew this moment was the gift of space Marc needed. Here he was being released from me again. ✎ I am so grateful for this photograph and its ability to take me back to that night: an absolute intersection of ending and beginning.

MICHELLE COHEN

*"I wish there was a way to know you're in the good old days*
*before you've actually left them."*

ANDY BERNARD

# HERE AND NOW

I cried my eyes out when I watched the final episode of *The Office*, not only because it marked the end of one of my favorite shows of all time, but because Andy's sentiment about the good old days is so true. ✎ I have this habit of constantly looking back on pieces of my life and missing them only in retrospect, not having even realized how much they meant to me at the time. I don't think I'm alone in this. It's so easy to always look to the next big thing and then fail to fully experience or appreciate what's going on right now, wherever "right now" is. And understandably so — everywhere I look I see advertisements and photos and previews of what's coming next, or of someone else's "right now" that looks better than mine. ✎ What I'm encouraging myself and everyone to do is to stop right here, in your "right now" and appreciate just one thing (even if it is the most mundane of details, because those details are what make a place or a person or an experience what it is) about wherever you are, because that one thing might be something you look back on and miss a week, a month, or even a year from now.

KARI KING

*"In three words, I can sum up everything I know about life:*

*it goes on."*

ROBERT FROST

# VALE LE PENA

As part of my cross-cultural requirement for college, I spent three months living in and around Guatemala. One thing on the trip that amazed me was the ability of the human spirit to find itself in the shittiest of situations and somehow carry on. The first week, I met a woman who was deported seven times trying to return to her family in the U.S. When we asked her what's next, she said, "I'm going to try again." ➤ We visited a drug and alcohol rehabilitation community in Agua Prieta and met a heroine addict who cares for the 10 mentally ill patients in that community. He told us he lost his wife and children to the addiction, but now he has 10 new children to take care of. ➤ At an immigrant detention center in Arizona I was paired up with a 23-year-old named Deidy, who had been caught crossing the border and was waiting for her family to raise enough money for bail. When I asked her how she felt about *la migra* (the border patrol) and the people who run the detention center, she said, "I don't dislike them, because they're only trying to protect their land and their heritage. They take care of me here." ➤ I get pessimistic so easily, and something I'm learning is that looking on the bright side doesn't make a person ignorant or naive like I previously thought; it makes them strong. It takes an effort to take a terrible situation and pick out pieces of a life and put them back together, but we're all strong enough to do that.

KARI KING

*"The only gift that anyone has to give is the self.*
*I cannot imagine a more beautiful, beautiful presentation."*

EMMANUEL

# THE GIFT OF PRESENCE

"Thank you so much for coming. You're all very young. Not many people want to come here, because they're afraid, but we're glad you're here." ⤲ My classmates and I heard some variation of that greeting in every place we visited in our study term abroad, because people are surprised to find a group of 22 young adults willingly and eagerly trekking through violence and poverty in Central America. ⤲ At first I felt completely inadequate every time we were faced with a new conflict or a new example of the same conflicts: violence, poverty, corruption, immigration issues, addiction, racism. Each time we visited a new place and saw suffering, it evoked a new chorus of the same questions: "Now what? What am I supposed to do? How can I do anything?" But in one of our debriefings, a girl in my group suggested that maybe being present and willing to learn and listen like a child is all we're supposed to be doing right now. Presence, listening, and willingness to engage are precious gifts that often go unrecognized, but they are crucial building blocks toward understanding and peace. We're trained and sometimes even encouraged to feel that if we aren't actively *doing* something, we're wrong. But I think the first steps to doing something real might be stopping to listen and simply giving the gift of presence.

KARI KING

*"Out beyond the fields of wrongdoing and rightdoing,*
*there is a field. I'll meet you there."*

RUMI

## INCLUSIVE LOVE

"Made in the image of God and loved by God" was a mantra that my classmates and I heard many, many times during our week at the U.S./Mexico border. ✒ I could easily see the migrants' point of view, because in a place where there is very little money or safety, they're driven by need. The border patrol is doing what they feel — or what they've been told — is right. The drug mules and the "coyotes" are doing what they can to make money and support themselves, as disreputable as those jobs are. The drug cartel leaders are harder for me to justify; they have massive amounts of money that one can see just by looking at their homes, yet they still want more. But I don't know how they chose this life. Maybe it was a product of their upbringing. Maybe their father or mother wasn't around, or was also involved in drug trafficking, or was killed and that same drug-based survival was the now-cartel-leader's only choice until it became a way of life. ✒ So that catch phrase "made in the image of God and loved by God," stuck with us, because even the members of the cartels belong to Him, along with the migrants and the border patrol and the coyotes, and that means they deserve to be loved simply for their value as human beings, no matter what way of life they've been caught up in.

✒

KARI KING

*"In the space between yes and no, there is a lifetime."*

JODI PICOULT

# JUST SAY YES

I have an unfortunate habit of saying no more often than yes, because it's so easy to say no and avoid whatever is being offered that would require extra energy, patience, or time. Being an anxious person makes me naturally inclined to avoid fun in order to preserve my safety and ensure my well-being. ⮞ But within in the first month and a half of my Central American study term, I learned to say yes. I held a tarantula, went skinny-dipping in a crocodile-inhabited lake at night, went kayaking in a rainstorm, split an entire box of ice cream sandwiches with Lamar on the way home from class, and allowed myself to be awakened at 5:00 a.m. to watch a sunrise. Stories and memories come from saying yes, even if the yes is to something as small as trying a new food or agreeing to hold hands and jump into a freezing lake with someone. ⮞ A life with a lot of yes is a life worth living and sharing.

⮞

KARI KING

*"For a list of all the ways technology has failed to improve the quality of life,*
*please press three."*

ALICE KAHN

# DISCONNECTING TO CONNECT

For the first few weeks of my study semester in Central America, I tried to loosen my grip and let go of my connection to technology, and I couldn't quite do it — as much as I wanted to just be where I was and nowhere else. I would be reading my phone and hear laughter and wish I was a part of it, and then realize I was the only one tethering myself to this technological anchor I didn't even want. ∽ One morning, when I finally put down my smartphone and walked away from it, I felt a tangible weight lift from me. There's a strange discomfort at first with trying to detach, but I find much more value in real people and real conversations and real experiences. And looking down at the screen, even for just a second, too often means missing a moment or a joke or a comment, and then it's gone. Be with the people you're with and not always the ones in the screen.

∽

KARI KING

*"Home is where they want you to stay longer."*
STEPHEN KING

# IS THIS HOME?

Before January 7th of this year, I had never been on my own away from my home for more than a week at a time. ≈ I quickly discovered that a valuable life skill is to learn to make home into a fluid concept rather than a physical place. It might take the shape of a house, or a climate, or a person, which means a person can go through life with a hundred homes or just one. ≈ I learned quickly that if I limit the idea of home to one place, I'm going to spend a lot of my life homeless; however, once home becomes a fluid concept, it can be found or made anywhere. I left behind one home in Harrisonburg, Virginia, but I made a second home in Agua Prieta, a third in Guatemala City, and a fourth in Tikal. And actually what felt the most like home during my travels were the 23 beautiful people who came with me. ≈ It seems that as long as friends are near, and as long as I have people all over the world loving me from a distance, any place can be a home.

≈

KARI KING

*"Oh, bird of my soul, fly away now,*
*for I possess a hundred fortified towers."*

RUMI

# NEST

On my porch step this morning, I sip dark coffee, listening to the morning's soft sounds as it listens to mine. It hears the sorrow, fear, and frustration that have dogged me this weekend; invites me to send them out into the crisp dawn air and watch them float away. As I do, there comes a faint, muffled, bird sound, from where I cannot determine, but it makes me smile, sounds cozy for some reason, as though it is snuggled in a warm nest and just making happy sounds, though I don't suppose that could be. I open my heart and I hear everything.

AMY KALMON

*"Quit this world. Quit the next world. Quit quitting."*

RAM DASS

# TANGLE

On my porch step this morning, settled in with dark coffee, dark chocolate and a dark tinge of heart, I listen to the birds, chat up the tiny snowman on the railing, breathe deeply and sit with my wonderings. There is bird song, there are tears, the chocolate runs out and the coffee cools. Down my block, the triplets — tall, elegant trees — toss their beautiful tangle of branches to me and I catch, getting lost in their tracings of branch upon sky — a dark charcoal sky ceding slowly to dawn. I often see only two steps or one, sometimes none, when looking ahead on my own tangled path. Difficult that is, for this vulnerable heart, but the trees give me solace, bring clarity today and I know, truly now, I'm on the right course and need only continue in faith. I may misstep or fall, may go backward at times, but on my porch step, I trust. I am found.

AMY KALMON

# DECEMBER 19

## SPARROW

On my porch step this morning,

I was so still that a sparrow came

and sat on the step with me and stayed a bit,

in all its tiny perfectness.

AMY KALMON

*"Behold, my friends, the spring is come;*
*the earth has gladly received the embraces of the sun,*
*and we shall soon see the results of their love!"*
SITTING BULL

# NEAR SPRING

On my porch step this morning,

the coffee is dark and super hot,

the chocolate just mediocre,

the birds have their spring-sing-thing on full, beautiful blast,

church bells chime softly,

and I listen to the little scritchy sounds of snow

giving way, bit by bit, to spring.

At almost dawn, there is a louder scritchy sound, very near,

and I look, just in time to witness

a forsythia branch being released

from the snowbank's icy grip.

AMY KALMON

*"Spring has returned.*
*The Earth is like a child that knows poems."*
RAINER MARIA RILKE

## ORANGES

On my porch step this morning, I'm smiling at yesterday, remembering the big bag of oranges bottoming out just as I reached the edge of our winter-bound street. Oranges plunged, then they bobbed in a great slushy puddle that snuggled the curb, a dozen bright little suns in the gray of that day. Nearby, a stranger, lone witness, grinned along with me and we bent to fill our arms with sunshine.

AMY KALMON

*"The day breaks not, it is my heart."*

JOHN DONNE

# DAWN

On my porch step this morning,

dark coffee, no chocolate, pondering me,

a lot of quiet, a solitary crow,

the gentle snapsnapsnap of a flag in the breeze

and the ping of its cord on the pole.

A vibrant flush of rose rising through the dark skeleton trees.

AMY KALMON

*"I work from awkwardness. By that I mean I don't like to arrange things.*
*If I stand in front of something, instead of arranging it,*
*I arrange myself."*
DIANE ARBUS

# STANDING

The lake is my porch step this morning, soft gray.

I wade deep in her murmuring waters ... stand strong,

sipping hot coffee ... surprise tears on my cheek.

Part of my heart, my spirit, all days,

this lake gives me counsel ... I take it as prayer.

Smile. Laugh. Keep an open heart, a kind heart.

Be honest. Be trusting. Be vulnerable.

I will.

Heron grace glides over waves, through my tears

touching the pastel dawn of this day,

and the lake brings a splash, makes me laugh

with surprise as it urges me onward, chin up, once more.

AMY KALMON

*"God speaks to each of us as he makes us,*
*then walks with us silently out of the night."*

RAINER MARIA RILKE

# I DON'T KNOW

I wrote a book of prompts, suggestions, nudges, statements (declarations, even) of ways to think, live, love, and be. 365 of them, to be exact.  ✺  But somehow between then and now, I've decided that I don't know.  ✺  I don't know what's the right prompt because I don't know if you need to grow or rest or fall back or move ahead.  ✺  I don't know if I should be adding to the continuous stream of voices vying for your attention — and mine.  ✺  I don't know if writing is my savior or my demon.  ✺  I don't know what matters most, what I should value least, or what loves deserve my undying, unfaltering devotion.  ✺  I don't know what to do, what not to do, what to be, or what not to be.  ✺  I don't know why. Or when. Or how.  ✺  But I know this: I know right now. I know this moment, now this one, now this one, and in each moment I am fine. I am whole. I am.  ✺  And that's all I need to know.

STARLA J. KING

*"Creativity takes courage."*

HENRI MATISSE

## OF MOMENTS AND MUFFINS

I don't have time, I tell myself, to stop.
I don't have time to putter around
tending my garden
my heart
my house
my soul.

I don't have time to wander today
through the pages
ideas
muffins
and flea markets.

I don't have time, I insist
even as I know full well
I have the time
just not the courage.

STARLA J. KING

# DECEMBER 26

*"We have to dare to be ourselves,*
*however frightening or strange that self may prove to be."*

MAY SARTON

## CHAMELEON

Chameleon change

I'll take on your color mood.

No. Choose plain lizard.

STARLA J. KING

# DECEMBER 27

*"Loyal companions are an unequaled grace,*
*stanching fear before it bleeds you numb, a reliable antidote for creeping despair."*

DEAN KOONTZ

## COMPANIONS

Music dancing through the room

Cat rumbling peace beside me

Wife working a city away

Tree keeping watch outside my window

Workmen hammering our shared wall

Books resting on their shelves, coffee table, my desk, my night stand

Water bottle offering health at my side

Ceiling fan breezing above me

Sunlight whispering joy in each ray

Wedding rings promising their love on my finger (and hers)

Birdsong calling from the bushes, trees, wires

Pen and notebook showing me ... well ... me

Teachers, mentors, guides smiling from this life and before

And above all, this breath, and the next, and the next.

All of these, dear little hellos on the shipwrecked island of me.

STARLA J. KING

*"Don't be afraid to make a mistake, your readers might like it."*
WILLIAM RANDOLPH HEARST

## AUTO CORRECT

My troubles fade into *te able*

Ego doubts itself as *who*

Testing is easy as a *testufn*

And Uh oh loses its edge as a mere *Uh ih*.

A shift of the moment

one letter

or an extra space

and the lie turns to *life*.

STARLA J. KING

*"My longing for truth was a single prayer."*

EDITH STEIN

# THE GREATEST BOOK

Thirsty for myself

I close my journal

and read instead

my heart in the sky.

STARLA J. KING

*"In the sweetness of friendship let there be laughter,*
*and sharing of pleasures. For in the dew of little things*
*the heart finds its morning and is refreshed."*

KHALIL GIBRAN

# AMY

A friend of a friend, I knew her first only from photographs on Facebook — snapshot views, most often of nature. Yes, they were visually pleasing, but what really drew me in was the quiet in each photo, offered it seemed, to share a moment of peace, of beauty, of pause. In the loud stream of social media, she offered me a quiet room of connection and ... what was it? Hope. ☙    Then I knew her from her porch step mornings, the before-dawn blanket of words telling us how her heart was beating, the air felt, the kind of chocolate she was savoring with that rich cup of coffee in her unhurried morning rituals. In the raw start of morning, I sat beside her words and breathed, smiled, even loved. ☙    Then cancer. Hair loss progression and friend-insisted Benefit for Amy photos joined the glimpses of nature, toes in water, and warm bakery lights whispering a welcome to the cold, dark mornings. ☙    Porch step morning musings spread into chemo, surgery, recovery, and remission notes. She didn't play it up, she didn't play it down. She simply played it as it was, a thing of life: this beautiful life, a gift no matter the exact circumstance. ☙    I thought I was too small to change the world. Amy shows me I'm not.

☙

STARLA J. KING

*"How many weeks are there in a light year?"*

GEORGE CARLIN

# JUST BETWEEN EDITORS

Toward the end of the *Wide Awake. Every Week.* project, the editors discovered they were living a lie. ⮐ They had assumed that each year had 52 weeks, with seven days per week, for a grand total of 365 days per year. ⮐ Until, that is, the day they actually did the math and found that 52 x 7 = 364. ⮐ Stunned, they asked each other, "How can this be? How can an entire day be missing from the year? Did too much editing compromise our grasp on reality?" ⮐ After some research, they discovered they weren't crazy, just *wrong*. Apparently 52 weeks is an estimate, not an exact figure. Turns out there are 52.1775 weeks in a year. ⮐ Time as they had known it was irrevocably changed. ⮐ *How had we not known this? Did everyone else know this?* They could theorize, but more important was the very convenient December 31st aha moment it provided. ⮐ "May you notice and appreciate your aha moments, however they show up and no matter how many days are in your year." – *Starla* ⮐ "I want a refund from my grade school teachers." – *Roslyn*

⮐

STARLA J. KING & ROSLYN A. NELSON

# ABOUT THE AUTHORS

 **BRIDGETTE BOUDREAU** is a Master Life Coach and CEO of Martha Beck, Inc. "I started this spiritual journey looking for something outside of myself that would make me feel better. That didn't work. Instead, I just had to get comfy with being me. Now, I help others do the same." Bridgette is writing a book entitled either *Enlightenment Tastes Like Salt* or *I Didn't See That Coming: Confessions of a Lesbian Life Coach.* bridgetteboudreau.com.

 **TINA BURKHOLDER** believes that writing provides an avenue for healing ourselves, and by extension, healing to the world. She is inspired by nature, city streets, and the transformative power of love. Tina welcomes contact at tinaburkholder@verizon.net or YourWriteOfWay.org.

 **MICHELLE COHEN** is a truth writer who believes life's challenges are gifts that enrich our lives if we are awake to their messages. She is a certified coach in Holistic Health and the Psychology of Eating, and has a B.A. in English from the University of Southern California. Michelle is a blessed mom, inspiration junkie, bliss seeker and style lover. You can find her at MichelleLisaCohen.com.

 **REBECCA P. COHEN** believes time outside transforms our lives for the better. Rebecca is author of the new children's book series: *PJ's Backyard Adventures,* as well as author of *15 Minutes Outside: 365 Ways to Get Out of the House and Connect with Your Kids*, and creator of *Rebecca Plants Curiosity Cards*. She is also host of the video series, *Get Out of the House,* which shows fun ideas for time outside in every season. For Rebecca's inspiring blog and free downloads, visit BeOutsideAndGrow.com.

 **WARNER COHEN** is 10 and lives in Vail, CO with his mom, dad, older brother, and his black lab Sampson. He enjoys soccer, reading, sometimes writing, and arts and crafts. His favorite books include the *Fable Haven* and *Beyonders* series by Brandon Mull, *Eragon* by Christopher Paolini, and *Harry Potter* by JK Rowling. Reading inspires him in many ways. He will continue to write and publish.

 **DEBORAH COOPER** authored five collections of poems, including *Under the Influence of Lilacs* (Clover Valley Press). In 2013, the anthology *Bound Together: Like the Grasses,* a poetry collection by her writing group of many years, won the Northeastern MN Book Award for Poetry. Deborah co-edits three poetry anthologies published by Holy Cow! Press of Duluth and was 2012-14 Duluth Poet Laureate.

 **MARY DOUGHERTY** moved to Bayfield, WI in 2007 with husband Ted, five children and three dogs. She has owned a restaurant, taught cooking, volunteers, and is deeply committed to the region. Mary enjoys exploring the Apostle Islands, photography, and cooking. She believes that advocacy and stories that evolve from imagining strong, vital communities are keys to creating lasting, positive change. Find her at wordsforwater.com.

Nationally recognized as an expert in the field of fitness, particularly pre and postnatal, mompreneur **LISA DRUXMAN** is the creator of FIT4MOM®. She is a mom on a mission to raise healthy moms so that they can raise healthy kids in a healthy world. She is the author of *Lean Mommy*, creator of the *Mama Wants Her Body Back* DVDs, and host of the *Motivating Mom* podcast.

**NANCY J. DUNCAN** is a professional certified life coach, business coach, and fitness consultant who supports others in cultivating and expressing their deepest inner potential. She delights in the richness of life through the beauty of nature, yoga, meditation, and the appreciation of people and their inherent greatness. She can be reached through her website at nancyjduncan.com.

**JEN FANUCCI** is a traveler, writer, tour leader, event organizer, and specialist in travel to India. She believes in the big picture of life and the important piece we each contribute to its mysterious, beautiful puzzle. Founder and creator of Big Picture Travel and India Travel Coach, Jen believes strongly that travel can help us connect with ourselves and each other in positive, life-changing ways. Find her at bigpictravel.com or indiatravelcoach.com.

**TOM FITZ** is Associate Professor of Geoscience at Northland College, Ashland, WI (B.S., St. Lawrence University; M.S., University of MN; Ph.D., University of DE). He enjoys researching the Mellen Gabbro local bedrock. "The setting in the beautiful Lake Superior region is also valuable. I was attracted to my field of study by the amazing stories recorded in rocks and Earth's history. I enjoy bicycling, canoeing, and cross-country skiing."

When **DANA FOWLE** first led her elementary school in the Pledge of Allegiance, it was clear she was destined to use a microphone. Dana is an award-winning TV journalist currently working for Atlanta's Fox 5 I-Team. Her investigations helped shut down shady businesses and con men. Her Emmy Award-winning probe exposed failures in Georgia's child welfare system and helped change state laws. She lives in Atlanta with her husband and daughter. danafowlebiz@outlook.com.

**DARLENE FRANK** is a writing and creativity coach who helps people navigate their writing journey and produce powerful work. She enjoys working with people who have undergone a radical life transformation and want to create art from that experience. A professional writer and editor for over 25 years (training materials and books), her creative nonfiction (mostly memoir) appears in *Times They Were A-Changing: Women Remember the '60s & '70s* and in *Fault Zone* anthologies. DarleneFrankWriting.com.

**ROB GANSON** is a poet/activist from the shore of Lake Superior and has been published in various journals, magazines, and anthologies, as well as having published four volumes of poetry. He considers himself a citizen of forests, streams, his garden, and tends to write on themes of nature, place, the human condition, and the vanishing wilderness. Rob is 70% water.

**LESLIE HAMP** holds a master's degree in mass communication, authored *Create the Life You Crave*, co-authored *Guerrilla Marketing on the Frontlines* and *Love Stories of the Bay*, offers journaling workshops, and received a Bronze Award for feature article writing from the National Council of Marketing & Public Relations. She journals and blogs from the road in her tiny teardrop camper (having created the "life she craved!") and is working on a second book.

**RAGE HEZEKIAH** is a former farmer, baker, and doula, who earned her MFA Degree from Emerson College. She was a finalist in the Hurston-Wright College Writers Contest and a Showcase Poet in the Fall 2014 issue of *The Aurorean*. Her poems have appeared in *Fifth Wednesday, Mom Egg Review, Really System*, and *Riding Light*, as well as other journals. Her work has also been anthologized in *Other Tongues: Mixed Race Women Speak Out*.

**STUART HORWITZ** is founder of Book Architecture, a firm of independent editors based in Providence (BookArchitecture.com). Book Architecture's clients have reached the best-seller list in fiction and non-fiction. His first book *Blueprint Your Bestseller* (Penguin/Perigee), was named a 2013 best book about writing by *The Writer* magazine. His second book, *Book Architecture: How to Plot and Outline Without Using a Formula*, was released in 2015.

**KAYCE STEVENS HUGHLETT** is an artist of being alive. Her passions include (but are not limited to) writing, speaking, lifestyle coaching, and SoulStrolling™ around the world. Her 2012 non-fiction book, *As I Lay Pondering: daily*

*invitations to live a transformed life*, is a lyrical, lucid treasure inviting readers to new awakenings throughout the year. Look for her debut novel, *Blue*, in Fall 2015. Learn about Kayce and her offerings at kaycehughlett.com.

**BOB JAUCH** retired in 2014 following a 32-year career serving in the Wisconsin Legislature. Throughout his service in the Assembly and State Senate he focused on children, education, natural resources, and health. He loves the outdoors and is an amateur photographer. He lives with his wife, a former teacher in Poplar, WI, 20 miles from Lake Superior.

**AMY KALMON** has called northern WI home since kindergarten. She considers Lake Superior a great blessing and guiding force in her life. Amy creates primarily with photography, jewelry, and photographically-based mixed media, but more and more often, words are finding their way into her work. Contact her at tumbleheartstudio@gmail.com.

**MAGGIE KAZEL** works with Rural AIDS Action Network in Duluth, MN. Juggling art, activism, and motherhood, she lives by the words of writer Grace Paley: "Art is too long, and life is too short!" Some of her works are published in *Thunderbird Review, Sinister Wisdom*, Holy Cow! Press, and in the Sibling Rivalry Press anthology entitled, *This Assignment Is So Gay*.

**EILEEN M. KENNEDY** is a writer who lives in the Chicago area with her husband and daughter and has two stepchildren in college. She finds inspiration in the challenges and blessings of daily life and is currently writing a novel.

**BETH KEPHART** is the award-winning author of nineteen books, including *Handling the Truth: On the Writing of Memoir*. She teaches creative nonfiction at Penn, writes a monthly column on the intersection of memory and place for the *Philadelphia Inquirer*, and reviews regularly for *Chicago Tribune*. Follow her blog at beth-kephart.blogspot.com.

**SALLY KESSLER** has lived near Cornucopia, WI for over 40 years. She co-founded Lake Superior Big Top Chautauqua and spent 25 summers as a performer and director. She continues to pursue her theatrical proclivity at StageNorth in Washburn, WI. Her daughter is a teacher and artist in Portland, OR and her son is a musician in Mpls., MN. Recently retired from the WI Department of Public Instruction, she maintains sanity with three cats, a dog, and long beach walks.

**HEIDI C. KING** likes to help make the invisible visible — both people and ideas. In administrative work in the Mennonite Church, she suggested that support staff and pastors are equally important. She is currently pondering the art of listening and works as a freelance editor. She lives in Wakarusa, IN, where the jellybeans are as big as the town, in an intentional community with cats, children, and adults. HeidiSeeKing@gmail.com.

**KARI KING** was born in Harrisonburg, VA, into a family with which she shares a profound and insatiable interest in the world of writing and introspection. She is completing a degree in Spanish at Eastern Mennonite University, with minors in Psychology and English. She experiences writing as a window to the soul and avenue to the ultimate discovery of what makes a person who they are.

Along with the allure of natural science, literature, religious texts, mythology, and philosophy, **ROBERT KING** admits to being under the curious spell of magical realism, and his writing may reflect an inchoate wish to revisit the charmed, hushed, and a bit musty reading rooms of a dimly-remembered British library somewhere in the wildly beating heart of Mexico City, where sweet childhood hours passed in timeless jaunts to exotic lands & fantastic haunts. bluemotmot@verizon.net.

**STARLA J. KING**, author of *Wide Awake. Every Day. Daily Inspiration for Conscious Living*, is a writing coach through her company, OutWrite Living. Written words are her primary creative medium, with photographs a close second — both of which she uses to advocate for compassionate living through a practice of seeing the usual and mundane as exquisite and miraculous. Starla lives in Philadelphia with her delightful wife and feline troublemakers. Co-editor of *Wide Awake. Every Week*. OutWriteLiving.com.

**JAN LEE** has worked as a professional singer, actor, director, and playwright for 30 years. Originally from the Twin Cities (MN), Jan taught acting at Northland College (WI) from 2000-05 and was a director and featured performer at Big Top Chautauqua since 1987. As founder and co-owner of StageNorth from 2000-10, Jan was named an official "Wisconsin Treasure" by Governor McCallum for her work as its artistic director. Currently, she's a vocalist for the Alone Together Jazz Trio.

**ELIZABETH MADSEN-GENSZLER** lives in Ashland, WI and works in the library at Northland College. She is a reader who longs to be a writer and is working on that process.

**MAUREEN MATUSEWIC** feels strongest in nature — especially in the Penokee Hills of WI near Lake Superior — and weakest when trying to figure out individual disasters and abuses and politics that harm people, the land, and water. People who know Maureen best think of her as a storyteller and poet who happened to teach for a long stretch. "My family is beautiful and my friends are great. The WAEW pieces are about these things."

**EMILY MCMASON** loves her children and her work, as well as a cocktail with her husband on date nights. Emily has a master's degree in education from Harvard, holds a graduate certificate in Parent Coaching from the PCI at Seattle Pacific University, and completed a postgraduate program entirely dedicated to childhood sleep. As a personal and parent coach, Emily has worked with parents all over the globe. Visit emilymcmason.com.

Ever since she was a kid hand printing a neighborhood newspaper, **ANNE RUD MILLER** dreamed of being a writer. An avid reader and retired high school English teacher, she resides in northern WI near her three daughters. Her first novel, *Mashkiki Rapids*, is set in the aftermath of the Korean War and combines history, small town life, romance, and the questioning of social mores. She is at work on her second book.

**LIZ MINETTE** received a 2014 Career Opportunity Grant from Arrowhead Regional Arts Council, and with the funds published a 24-page poetry chapbook titled *November* (http://lminette.wix.com/november---poems). She's been writing for 20 years. Publication credits include *Golden Walkman Magazine, Calyx - A Journal of Art & Literature By Women, Nerve Cowboy* as well as the recent anthology *Pressure Press Presents*. She lives, works, writes near Duluth, MN.

**BETH ANDRIX MONAGHAN** believes that words can change the world and mend its tears. An advocate for women's equality, she has been featured on NPR, NBC News, *Forbes*, and *The Boston Globe*, and in 2014, Governor Deval Patrick appointed her to the MA Women in the Workplace Task Force. Beth is co-founder of InkHouse, a fast-growing PR and content firm. She also supports Boston's GrubStreet creative writing center where she is a member of the Director's Circle. Twitter and Medium: @bamonaghan.

**RACHEL MOORE-BEITLER** is honored to be a part of this creative project, to sync up with other sojourners also "living the questions." She recently

received her Masters in Five-Element Acupuncture (rachel5element.com), and enjoys watching the change of seasons with her sweetheart at their home on a pear orchard in Hood River, OR.

**LAURA NEFF** has been in private practice as a Life Leadership Coach since 2006, where she gets to do her most favorite thing: bring people home to the unshakeable, unwavering anchor that is their core selves. She's been described as a sprightly, wise, funny, nurturing, butt-kicking lover of people and life, and she is often bowled over with gratitude. Laura lives with her husband, dogs, cats, and chickens near Charlotte, NC. LifeLeadershipCentral.com.

**ROSLYN NELSON**, author of *Snow on Fire* and *Raving About Summer - Fussing Abut Winter* lives near Lake Superior in a very small Wisconsin town where she is renovating a 100+ year-old storefront for her graphic design and book design activities and for life-in-general. Co-editor of *Wide Awake. Every Week.* littlebigbay.com and glacialdrift.com.

**LAURIE OTIS** raised four daughters, earned a B.A. with an English major and did advanced work in Library Science. She worked for over 30 years as a librarian for a WI technical college, and later as a communications instructor and PR representative. She has had major roles in several plays: Last Lists of My Mad Mother; Old Ladies Guide to Survival; Song of Survival; A Christmas Memory, and Moon Over Buffalo. Author of *The Amarantha Stories* and *The Cloud Factory*.

A retired anthropologist, **HOWARD PAAP** and his wife of over 50 years reside in Bayfield, WI where he sees Lake Superior and Madeline Island from his office windows. When not writing, he walks family dogs and fills in behind the counter at What Goes 'Round Quality Used Books.

**USHI PATEL** is an award-winning poet, designer, and entrepreneur. She is the author of *Brave the Unknown* (Skywriter Books), her debut collection of poetry, and winner of the Benjamin Franklin Award. She is also co-founder and the Brand Architect at BoominGroup, a company that is reinventing the way people do business, so they can make a livelihood through expressing and offering their unique gifts to the world.Ushi@ BravetheUnknown.com or BoominGroup.com.

**LORI SCHNEIDER** is an international speaker, mountaineer, adventurer, author, teacher, and global advocate for those living with neurological disorders and disabilities. Lori is the first person with multiple sclerosis to summit Mt. Everest and complete the "Seven Summits" — scaling the highest peak on each continent. Her organization, Empowerment Through Adventure, inspires others to take their own leap of faith and climb beyond their own preconceived limitations. LoriSchneider.net.

**ELLIE SCHOENFELD**, a poet from Duluth, MN, enjoys working on projects with artists of various genres and has collaborated with musicians to produce poetry/music CDs. She co-founded Poetry Harbor, served on the board of Spirit Lake Poetry Series, and remains grateful to the

Arrowhead Regional Arts Council for past fellowship support. She has one collection of poems in print, *The Dark Honey: New & Used Poems*, (Clover Valley Press) and her work is a part of *Bound Together: Like the Grasses* (Clover Valley Press), an anthology with the four other women in her writing group.

 Currently in career transition, **MIRIAM EBERSOLE SHOWALTER** has taught, learned from, and advocated for children with ASD (autism spectrum disorder) for the past 13 years. She's all about a Sunday afternoon piano and fiddle jam session with her dream husband of 35 years, and she loves a thoughtful trek on Sarasota's beaches, bridges, or rainforest canopy walk, especially when their sons are visiting. Writing is her spiritual oxygen.

 **PHILIP SORENSEN**, Ashland, WI, taste tests mayonnaise when not studying aeronautics. Hobbies include measuring the front and back rises on his jeans. Currently, he writes five-star ratings for Amazon.com products. He remains concerned his obituary will state no more than his enjoyment of the Packers, playing crazy eights, and he always told you what he thought even if it was not what you wanted to hear. Contact Mr. Sorensen in the Bay City Creek Ravine by shouting, "Hey! You down there?"

 **DEBORAH THOMAS** spends her days in an office looking for the humor and stories to be told, while dreaming of the day she can call herself a writer. She is grateful for the opportunity to participate in this project. Deborah lives in Northern, NJ with the love of her life, Jeffery.

 **NICK VANDER PUY** has guided fishing parties for 30 years, produced a major documentary about wild rice and the Anishinaabe, written extensively and ran for office, opp- osing plans for a mine upstream from the Bad River band of Lake Superior Chippewa. "I'm finally beginning to understand Walter 'Makoonse' Bresette's advice to love this land as deeply as the Anishinaabe do and be willing to defend it with my life." Nick lives in Mellen, WI.

 **TERESA J. WAGNER** is an avid cook, reader, writer, traveler, and knitter. She acquired her no-nonsense editing skills as an Executive Editor of the William Mitchell Law Review. She is currently at work on a novel and a series of travel essays. When she is not on the road, she lives in Washburn, WI.

 **STEVEN WIEBE-KING** was born in Cuba to Mennonite missionaries. Most of his childhood was in Mexico City. Trips to the Aztec pyramids through burning fields, and to the endless flower gardens of Cuernavaca past pulque-drunks staggering down dusty dirt lanes were his lifeline to a world of mystery and wonder. He does his best to distill and crystallize beauty, which in his wanderings leaves a faint trail as it trickles through holes in his pockets.

 **MIKE WIGGINS JR.** is Chairman of the Bad River Band of Lake Superior Chippewa in northern WI. Raised on the Bad River Reservation, Mike learned how hunting, fishing, and harvesting were essential to the Tribe's cultural and spiritual traditions and why the Tribe's ceded territory rights were important to protect for this generation and the next.

**BARBARA WITH** is a peace activist, author/publisher, psychic channel, composer, performer, and speaker. She has authored: *Guerrilla Publishing*, a candid look into building a small publishing company; *Imagining Einstein: Essays on M-Theory, World Peace & The Science of Compassion*, winner of two 2007 national book awards; and *Party of Twelve: The Afterlife Interviews*, winner of the 2008 Beach Book Awards for Spirituality. barbarawith.com.

**LIZ WOODWORTH** has been a teacher of English for over 25 years. She is also a director, writer, and performer at StageNorth (Washburn, WI) and Lake Superior Big Top Chautauqua (Bayfield, WI) and has written for and performed in the MN Fringe Festival. She and her husband enjoy playing music, winter, and raising their pert-near perfect daughter Emily.

# THE WIDE AWAKE SERIES
## BOOKS AVAILABLE AT ONLINE BOOKSELLERS

BOOK 1 OF THE WIDE AWAKE SERIES

## WIDE AWAKE. EVERY DAY.

*Daily Inspiration for Conscious Living.*

**Wide Awake. Every Day.** offers 365 readings to turn awareness into a loyal and creative friend, every day of the year. Each page serves up a delectable vignette from the author's keen and loving observations. Gentle, do-able action steps bring the day's inspiration into enlightening focus. Summary quotes are at hand with on-the-go food for thought. King's insights, informed by secular and spiritual practices, make her ideas resonate with readers from all walks of life. Religious? No. Spiritual? Yes. You'll find yourself here in — a whole new way.

**WideAwakeEveryDay.com**

BOOK 2 OF THE WIDE AWAKE SERIES

## WIDE AWAKE. EVERY WEEK.

*52 Voices ~ 365 Aha! Moments*

**Wide Awake. Every Week.** is a dazzling collection of 365 Aha! Moments offered by 52 people from all walks of life. Eye-opening essays, poetry, humor, reflection, and insight fill these pages for a full year of inspiration: from poet to politician, tribal chair to operations manager, mountaineer to mother, and more. Experience a fresh point of view every week as authors give voice to pivotal moments that allowed them to see life in a new way. **Wide Awake. Every Week.** provides a spark that will unleash Aha! Moments for readers.

**WideAwakeEveryWeek.com**

LOOK FOR **BOOK 3** IN THE NEAR FUTURE!

## WIDEAWAKEWORDS.COM

Roslyn A. Nelson: littlebigbay.com & Starla J. King: outwriteliving.com

CPSIA information can be obtained at www.ICGtesting.com
Printed in the USA
LVOW03s1329210815

451055LV00010B/332/P